PRAISE FOR

THE LAND
OF
ENTERPRISE

"Teachers trying to meet the growing demand for sweeping surveys on American business history have long lamented the lack of a readable overview on the subject. Benjamin Waterhouse's book more than fits the bill. This fast-paced, lively, and concise narrative is the perfect place to begin for anyone interested in the history of capitalism in the United States."

—Stephen Mihm, author of *Crisis Economics* and
A Nation of Counterfeiters

"Waterhouse's new history is my go-to book for understanding the long sweep of American business. Want to understand how we got from the Massachusetts Bay Company to Wal-Mart? This is your book."

—Louis Hyman, author of *Debtor Nation* and
American Capitalism

"An invaluable overview of the central role business has played in American history, from conquest and enslavement to the financial crisis of 2008. Waterhouse adroitly synthesizes the most significant scholarship in business history into a brisk, engaging narrative. He's an admirably clear guide both to the shifting organization of American enterprise and to the legal, financial, and managerial ecologies that have enabled it."

—Bethany E. Moreton, author of *To Serve God* and
Wal-Mart: The Making of Christian Free Enterprise

ALSO BY BENJAMIN C. WATERHOUSE

*Lobbying America: The Politics of Business
from Nixon to NAFTA*

BENJAMIN C. WATERHOUSE

THE
OF
ENTERPRISE

A BUSINESS HISTORY
OF THE UNITED STATES

SIMON & SCHUSTER PAPERBACKS

NEW YORK LONDON TORONTO SYDNEY NEW DELHI

Simon & Schuster Paperbacks
An Imprint of Simon & Schuster, Inc.
1230 Avenue of the Americas
New York, NY 10020

First Simon & Schuster trade paperback edition April 2018

SIMON & SCHUSTER PAPERBACKS and colophon are registered
trademarks of Simon & Schuster, Inc.

For information about special discounts for bulk purchases, please contact
Simon & Schuster Special Sales at 1-866-506-1949 or
business@simonandschuster.com.

The Simon & Schuster Speakers Bureau can bring authors to your live
event. For more information, or to book an event, contact the Simon &
Schuster Speakers Bureau at 1-866-248-3049 or visit our website at
www.simonspeakers.com.

Interior design by Ellen Sasahara

Manufactured in the United States of America

10 9 8 7 6 5 4 3 2 1

Library of Congress Cataloging-in-Publication Data is available.

ISBN 978-1-4767-6664-5
ISBN 978-1-4767-6665-2 (pbk)
ISBN 978-1-4767-6667-6 (ebook)

For Luna and Gabriel

CONTENTS

CONTENTS

INTRODUCTION

HOW BUSINESS EXPLAINS AMERICA

Americans love to think that their country has been inherently entrepreneurial throughout its history, and that this nation's path to greatness and global power was laid by its exceptionally capitalist value system. We hail the mighty railroads that crisscrossed a continent and the technological marvels that defined the ages, from steam engines to automobiles to smartphones. Yet when we tell our national story, we tend to focus on disembodied questions of ideology, cultural identity, and politics. Too often, we relegate business to the margins of the tale, as though merchants, manufacturers, workers, and bankers existed on a separate plane, independent of the major currents of our history.

This book offers the opposite. It argues that when traditional approaches to the history of the United States fail to integrate the history of business itself, they overlook a key aspect of our national story that helps explain how the United States developed into the land it is today. President Calvin Coolidge famously remarked in

1925 that "the chief business of the American people is business," by which he meant that Americans were notably oriented toward "producing, buying, selling, investing, and prospering in the world." This book takes Coolidge's aphorism and expands it: The chief business of American *history* is business. The story of the nation is the story of business history.

Sometimes it takes moments of disaster for us to see the links between business and the broader arc of national experience, and the financial meltdown of 2007 and 2008 provided just such a crisis. As the American housing market tanked, giant banks collapsed, and a global economic catastrophe threatened to plunge the world into a new Great Depression, people called out for explanations. Scholars rushed in, promoting research on such dry subjects as the history of debt, regulation, banking, and monetary policy. Thick academic books like *This Time Is Different: Eight Centuries of Financial Folly* by economists Carmen Reinhart and Kenneth Rogoff and Thomas Piketty's *Capital in the Twenty-First Century* gained widespread readership during and after the Great Recession.[1] Op-ed pieces, graduate seminar papers, and book proposals flowed from the keyboards of historians, economists, and others who hoped to capture that rare academic gem—relevance!—by linking their research to the crisis.

It's a shame that such a world-historic cataclysm had to erupt to draw attention to the vital lessons that history has to offer about the modern world of business. Today's college students graduate into a world of work fundamentally different from the one their parents and grandparents entered. The top performers are most likely to find jobs as consultants or bankers who work within the global financial services juggernaut, whereas few will work for manufacturing firms. Others may secure less remunerative employment in a variety of service fields, from retail and hospitality to business-services and IT, but almost none will join labor unions. Just as important, only young people in the highest percentiles will earn salaries much above what they would have forty years ago. Finally, young graduates encounter a political culture that is deeply divided over the role that government should play in business and economics—how (and where, and whether) to "bring the jobs back," whom to tax and how much, and which problems to leave to the private sector. By linking the pivotal events of business history to our national story, we can gain a better understanding of some of today's most pressing public debates.

The origins of today's fights over global commerce, local industries, and jobs, for example, go back to the country's birth. No sooner had the ink dried on the Constitution in the 1790s than a fierce fight emerged between entrenched factions over the balance between trade and the protection of domestic manufacturing. What role should the young government play? Should the United States actively support the growth of industry through tariffs, subsidies, and a centralized banking system? Or should power devolve to the local level to empower individual small-scale producers—yeoman farmers—preserving a free society? That foundational debate dominated politics in the early national period and carried over into more than two centuries of disputes over business practices.

Other problems of business history likewise resonate today. Late-19th-century monopolies such as John D. Rockefeller's Standard Oil provoked a fierce public blowback against undemocratic privilege and the concentration of economic power. The story of those giant corporations and the trustbusters who challenged them provides important lessons for today's arguments over massive financial institutions—those banks that are "too big to fail."

The history of business does more than provide the backstory to today's issues, however. It also gives us a critical vocabulary with which to assess our current moment by highlighting how the nature, character, and even definition of such vital concepts as "firm" and "corporation" have changed over time. Early businesses were small and locally controlled, but the rise of industrial capitalism in the

late 19th century brought about impersonal and hierarchical corporations. By the middle of the 20th century, these large, integrated,
and bureaucratic corporations reigned over the American economy.
Proponents hailed corporate structure as a boon to efficiency and
productivity, yet critics saw only social conformity and worried that
corporate bloat would stifle innovation. Whatever one thought of
"Big Business," however, that model grew less common by the turn
of the new millennium. Today's corporations, even the largest and
wealthiest, are structurally leaner and more inclined to outsource
business functions around the country and around the world. To
understand how the modern business environment took shape—from
global financial titans to local shops—we must put these developments in historical perspective. The story that emerges helps explain
how corporations both shaped and were shaped by global trade, competition, and the consumption patterns of people around the world.

From debates over trade to questions of labor policy, from notions of individual rights to concerns about growth and technological innovation, the story of business is deeply intertwined with the
development of America's political institutions and national values.
Exploring those links shows how much business needs history, and
how much history needs business.

The twelve chapters in this book chart the major developments
in the history of American business and argue for their indispensable
importance to vital issues in our national history, from slavery and
immigration to foreign affairs and modern political debates. Naturally, I am not able to cover every monumental innovation, successful entrepreneur, or groundbreaking policy. What I have tried to
do, though, is highlight the most important historical developments,
especially changes in business practices, the evolution of different
industries and sectors, and the complex relationship between business
and national politics.

Although business historians have traditionally focused on firms and the men and women (usually men, until recently) who run them, this book tries to a take a broader approach. Using business to tell the story of the United States allows us to incorporate the unnamed millions who shaped history by trading their labor (sometimes by choice, often not) or deciding what products to consume (sometimes by informed choice, often not). This story encompasses those who fought against what they saw as an oppressive system of exploitation as well as those who defended free markets from any outside intervention. From executives and bankers to farmers and sailors, from union leaders to politicians to slaves, business history *is* American history.

1

CONQUEST, COLONIES, AND CAPITALISM

We don't know who the first person born in Europe to set foot in North or South America was, and it is clear that no European could ever "discover" a gigantic plot of land where millions of people lived. But we do know that, beginning in the 1490s, European monarchs began to claim a right to lands in the "New World" of the Western Hemisphere. Within a few decades, those rulers sent thousands of soldiers, miners, farmers, and others to bring back precious metals, furs, timber, human slaves, and other goods.

We also know that, between 1500 and 1750, the center of economic power in Europe shifted from the southern parts of the continent—Italy, Spain, and Portugal—to a small island in the North Atlantic comprising England, Scotland, and Wales. The kingdom known as Great Britain after 1707 emerged in that early modern period as a dominant sea power, an imperial colonizer, a global trader, and the leader in factory-based manufacturing. And then in 1776, a major part of Britain's colonial empire seceded, fought a long global war, and achieved political independence.

The economic relationship that Anglo-Americans cultivated with Britain during the colonial period proved pivotal. As part of the British empire, white colonial Americans participated in a vibrant, trade-oriented economic system rooted in the exploitation of natural resources and the creation of increasingly sophisticated business forms. After independence, the future of that economic landscape appeared uncertain, and vital debates unfolded about what type of economy the new country should pursue—one devoted to export-based agriculture, or one that built on the new manufacturing technologies that Britain had pioneered in the second half of the 18th century? As American politicians sat down to write the Constitution in 1787, these questions created powerful rifts as competing factions argued—with far-reaching consequences—over the future of business and the legacy of the colonial economy.

The World Economy, c. 1500

To grasp the economic challenges that the first generation of Americans faced when the United States achieved political independence, it is helpful to take the long view of business practices during the period of European colonization. As the major powers of Europe spread their navies and peoples across Africa and the Americas in the late 15th and early 16th centuries, economic life came increasingly to revolve around transatlantic trade.

By 1500, intercontinental land-based commerce had flourished across the Eurasian landmass for several hundred years. The expansion of the Arab empire across the Middle East and North Africa, as well as the Moghul Empire in the Indian subcontinent, connected China, India, North Africa, and Eastern Europe. Powerful rulers across that vast geography secured trade routes and reaped significant wealth from the labor of agrarian people. Fabrics—silk from the East;

wool from colder climates—as well as spices, wood, and precious metals all traveled tremendous distances.[1]

Further south, traders from the Arab and Ottoman empires did a brisk overland business with their counterparts in West African kingdoms across the Sahara. In the mid-15th century, seafaring Europeans, particularly from Portugal, began to arrive regularly by ship along the West African coast to trade textiles for goods such as ivory, sugar, and gold. And by the end of that century, such trade regularly included slaves. Portuguese and later Spanish and other European traders purchased captured Africans to work first on sugar plantations they established on the Canary Islands and later, by the first decades of the 16th century, in the Caribbean and South and North America.[2]

Before the 1500s, people in the Americas lay outside these trade networks. The indigenous population of the American continents included vast empires such as the Aztec in present-day Mexico, major city-states such as Cahokia near present-day St. Louis, Missouri, and smaller societies of more mobile and less agriculturally rooted people, particularly near the Atlantic and Pacific coasts of North and South America. Trade was extensive within and between the Americas before 1500, but the continents were cut off from the rest of the world. As most students of history know, that situation changed with the advent of European transatlantic voyages in the 1490s, with devastating consequences. In the next three hundred years, a combination of disease, war, and genocide at the hands of European conquerors decimated the native populations of the Caribbean, destroyed empires such as the Incas in Peru, and dramatically affected the number of indigenous people of the eastern woodlands of North America, pushing many inland away from the coast. By the late 16th century, entrepreneurial English businesspeople looked to those "abandoned" wooded areas along the Atlantic as promising sites for colonies.[3]

The most significant change to the world economy, therefore, was the ascent of European seafaring merchants whose newfound prowess in shipbuilding and navigation allowed them to reach parts of Africa, Asia, and the Americas in greater numbers, and to profit immensely in the process. These new trade ventures changed the distribution and settlement patterns of people around the world. But just as important for the development of business and modern capitalism, the "Age of Exploration" (as the textbooks somewhat cheerfully call this period) also marked a monumental reorganization of the European economy.

Historians have traditionally tried to capture the changes in European social, political, and economic life that developed around 1500 in response to increased global trade by suggesting a transition between the earlier "medieval" period and the subsequent "modern" (or "early modern," to be more precise) period.[4] Essentially, what happened was a change from a *feudal* model of economic organization to a *mercantilist* model, the forerunner to a *capitalist* system.

As with everything in history, this shift was far more complicated than such a simple claim would suggest. Many people quibble over these terms, since the period of so-called feudalism included such diverse experiences over time and space. Ditto for *mercantilism*, *modern*, and, for that matter, *capitalism*. After all, history is a long-running, continuous process, and human beings never jump from one way of living to a different one overnight. So suggesting a clean break from a "feudal" past to a "capitalist" present does injustice to truth. However, if we're taking a long view and accept these concepts as generalities, not rigidly defined systems, this division provides a helpful way of characterizing important changes.

When historians use the term *feudalism*, they are attempting to describe an economic system in which power relations among people formed the building blocks of society. In a classically feudal model (not to be confused with reality), most people worked as farmers (the peasants), giving over their agricultural product to a local ruler (the lord) in exchange for military security. Political power flowed from the strength of these personal connections. The concepts of *private property* and *individual rights* did not factor into these arrangements, and most people's socioeconomic status was fixed at birth. Wealth was tied up in the control over land and agricultural production. Trade existed, but not on a massive scale, and most of the agricultural yield was consumed locally.

Even within an archetypal feudal society, not everyone lived this way. Off the feudal manors, artisanal craftspeople populated small towns and produced tools, equipment, and clothing for the agricultural system. Artisans typically conducted such manufacturing out of the home and adhered to a strict labor hierarchy: Masters taught their skills to apprentices, who hoped to one day move up to the master level. Guilds—organizations of skilled craftspeople—regulated the number of up-and-coming apprentices to keep competition low and prices stable.

Another key group in medieval towns was the merchants, who exchanged the surplus production from both the farmers and the craftspeople for foreign-made goods. In places such as Italy, traders accumulated significant wealth and many turned into bankers, making their living by guarding other people's money and lending it out, at a price.

These town-dwellers—manufacturers, shopkeepers, bankers, and traders—constituted an important minority in feudal society. Known as "burghers," from the Latin word for a fortified dwelling, they constituted a social class distinct from either the landless peasants or the land-owning feudal rulers. When Europe's dominant economic paradigm shifted toward capitalism, they became the core of the *bourgeoisie*, the property-owning middle class.

Europe transitioned away from feudalism in the 15th and 16th centuries. Monarchs in Spain, France, and England grew wealthier through trade, which spread from the Mediterranean to coastal West

Africa, and then to the Americas. In the process, they consolidated military power at the expense of local lords. A new economic philosophy that historians call *mercantilism* gradually took hold, reflecting the conviction that economic activity should bolster the wealth and power of nations. Western European monarchs in particular found new ways to expand, promote, and protect trade, reaping both profits and the political power that came with it. This decidedly unfeudal attitude toward external trade led European powers to business opportunities emerging in the New World.[5]

The Business of Conquest

The renowned historian Carl Degler famously wrote about America that "capitalism came in the first ships."[6] His point was that the European conquest of the New World coincided historically with the profound economic changes that produced a recognizably new system that we call capitalism, but the story was quite a bit more complicated, of course. Capitalism did not emerge as a coherent system. It has never achieved that status. As a system of economic organization, capitalism has taken on many forms across time, and exists in a variety of manifestations even today. But even though "capitalism" defies a simple definition, Degler's notion still stands that major changes in economic organization and business opportunities accompanied the European colonization of the Americas, beginning around the year 1500.

Europeans' exploration, exploitation, and ultimate inhabitation of the New World was at heart a financial undertaking, enacted in the mercantilist spirit of profit-making for the realm. Just as important as its causes were its consequences: The act of setting up colonies—with all the bloodshed, atrocity, and hardship it entailed for native people—had long-range consequences for the way European and colonial economies operated. From gold and silver mines in New

the new world post 1492 was a race for resources.

Spain to fur trapping by the French in present-day Canada to massive sugar, indigo, tobacco, and eventually cotton plantations, European colonizers used the Americas to create new wealth, new types of business, and new ways of thinking about property, profit, and enterprise.

For students of American history, it's an old story: ships funded by the Spanish and Portuguese governments began to journey regularly to the Caribbean and South America starting in the 1490s in search of material riches. And, in general, they found them. During the 16th century, Iberian soldiers and merchants traded and stole untold quantities of precious metals, kidnapped natives for sale into slavery in Europe, and established permanent settlements—frequently after waging genocidal war on local inhabitants—to facilitate this exploitation.[7]

Those initial conquests followed a traditional economic model: Generate wealth by accumulating valuable stuff. At the same time, these mercantilist exploits brought a major economic downside. The huge amounts of silver shipped back to Spain flooded the currency market, sparking a bout of inflation that lasted a century and crippled the Spanish economy. In spite of its large land-holdings in the Americas, Spain would never recover the economic power it wielded in the early 16th century.[8]

By the mid-1500s, a second wave of European voyages to the New World brought merchants from France and England who had motives and strategies similar to those of their Iberian counterparts. With the powerful Spanish and Portuguese empires laying physical claim to lands to the south, early French and English explorers headed north. Given France's superior military and economic position, the French crown began to fund fur-trading outposts along the St. Lawrence River in present-day Quebec.[9]

England, poorer than the major continental kingdoms, showed less interest in establishing Atlantic trading routes until later in the 16th century, by which time political and economic power had shifted away from Spain and Portugal. In the 1570s and 1580s, Queen Elizabeth authorized and underwrote imperial operations first in Ireland and then across the North Atlantic in Nova Scotia, urging explorers to claim lands for the crown and search for precious metals.[10] While the quest for riches proved disappointing, these ventures led to permanent colonial establishments. Over the course of the next hundred years, several hundred thousand English people migrated to the New World. Most of those early migrants lived along the Atlantic coast in former Indian towns that had been abandoned during the plague epidemic that forced survivors inland from the coast in the late 16th century.[11]

From the outset, the English colonization of North America was driven by economic imperatives. Although Americans often remember the religious motivations behind that process—stressing the story of the Puritans in Massachusetts, for example—business opportunities and economic institutions played just as important a role. Just as explorers sailing for Queen Elizabeth had scouted the continent for hidden riches, so, too, did English colonists create more durable communities in the 17th century as part of a larger, transatlantic business venture. In fact, the first two successful English colonies in what would become the United States—Virginia (1607) and Massachusetts Bay (1620)—were themselves private companies.[12] More specifically, each was chartered in the style of a *joint-stock company*, an early-modern legal entity that grew increasingly important to the global economy during the height of Europe's colonial expansion.

Joint-stock companies, the forerunners of today's publicly owned corporations, pooled private sources of capital under the official protection of the crown, funding ventures that were too expensive or risky for an individual person. Drawing on a system of legal contracts developed in Italy centuries earlier, 16th-century English monarchs pioneered the practice of issuing corporate charters that granted an exclusive right to trade in a certain area to a particular group of subjects. In addition to creating a helpful monopoly, these charters created legal entities whose ownership was spread among several investors. These people purchased shares, or stock, to make up the whole company, which they owned *jointly*. Hence, "joint-stock company."

Under the legal and military protection of the crown, English merchants gained tremendous advantages. Large sums of capital came together to form the Muscovy Company (chartered in 1555 to trade with Russia) and the East India Company (1600). Building on the English model, the kingdom of the Netherlands chartered the Dutch East India Company in 1602.[13]

In 1606, English joint-stock investors expanded from trade to colonization. That year, King James I issued a charter to the Virginia Company to establish a settlement in the part of the Atlantic coast near the Chesapeake Bay that, about thirty years earlier, English people had renamed "Virginia" in honor of Elizabeth (the never-married "virgin" queen).

According to the charter decree, James specifically bestowed on a group of investors, whom he cited by name, a "licence to make habitacion, plantacion and to deduce a colonie of sondrie of our people into that parte of America commonly called Virginia." Those investors could choose "anie place upon the saide coaste of Virginia or America where they shall thincke fitte and conveniente" between specific lines of latitude. Most crucially, the king continued, "noe other of our subjectes shalbe permitted or suffered to plante or inhabit behind or on the backside of them . . . without the expresse licence or consente of the Counsell of that Colonie."[14]

The florid language of the charter, in other words, gave the Virginia Company's investors exclusive trading and exploitation rights and the explicit promise of military backing from the crown. James intended the Virginia Company's colony to send back products such as timber, fur, and, the investors hoped, precious metals from the vast woodlands of the mid-Atlantic. He also hoped the colony could grow sugar and citrus, whose appeal was growing in England but that had

the first idea of private property

to be imported. (Turns out those crops couldn't be grown in Virginia, a fact that only worsened early Virginia's fortunes.) In addition, the king hoped English settlers would locate the mythical "Northwest Passage," a water route through North America to the Pacific, which England could then claim. (No such waterway existed.) Finally, James had geopolitical motives: A permanent agricultural community, he wagered, would provide a buffer against French and Spanish expansion and help solidify his land claims.

In 1607, employees hired by the company established a camp at a site called Jamestown and began working the land, building forts, searching for gold, and trading with Indians. The project turned disastrous. The company's workers found no precious minerals and failed to cultivate exotic produce—or really enough food to live on—and the colony fought a series of wars with the Powhatan confederacy, on whose land the Jamestown settlement sat. Approximately 80 percent of the English migrants to Virginia between 1607 and 1624, or close to five thousand, were dead by 1625. Hemorrhaging money and unable to attract new investors, the Virginia Company failed in 1624, when the English government declared Jamestown a royal colony.[15]

Running the Virginia Colony as a private business failed, but the joint-stock model of colonization persisted. English private investors, buoyed by royal support, established permanent English habitations in places such as Newfoundland (for fish) and Bermuda (for tobacco). In 1617, a small group of religious dissenters known as Separatists, fleeing persecution from the Church of England, purchased special permission called a patent from the (not yet dead) Virginia Company to create a settlement near Jamestown. Three years later, approximately one hundred people—a combination of the Separatists who had bought the patent and others who purchased their own passage directly—landed by accident far to the north of Jamestown in a former Massasoit Indian town, which they renamed Plymouth. In 1629, a group of English Puritans—other religious dissenters from the Church of England—secured a royal charter to establish the Massachusetts Bay Company, which founded a colony just north of Plymouth the next year.

But Massachusetts Bay proved to be the last North American colony founded on the joint-stock model. England thereafter established many colonial settlements along the Atlantic coast and in the Caribbean, but used a different model based on direct land grants to individual proprietors (notwithstanding competing claims of ownership by people already living there) and direct political rule from London. And in the 1680s, infighting among Massachusetts colonists led the crown to nullify the corporate charter and disband the unprofitable company, just as it had in Virginia.

The use of joint-stock companies as instruments of colonization left a profound legacy for the development of British North America. Like their joint-stock forebears, the businesspeople who managed early English colonies had a clear mandate to exploit natural resources, expand farming and artisanal production, and export surpluses for profit back to England. As those colonies increasingly identified themselves as distinct—and increasingly as "American" as the 18th century wore on—they retained the focus on commerce, profit, and independent business activity that had marked their founding.[16]

In 1748, the Philadelphia printer Benjamin Franklin—then in his early forties—summoned the business-oriented attitude of the colonies in a letter of advice to a younger friend. "Remember, that *time is money* . . . that *credit* is money . . . that money is of the prolific, generating nature," he wrote. "In short, the way to wealth, if you desire it . . . depends chiefly on two words, *industry* and *frugality*."[17]

British North America on the Eve of the Revolution

The colonial settlements in the parts of North America claimed by Great Britain were economically vibrant in the mid-18th century. (We start to refer to "Britain" instead of "England" after the Acts of Union in 1706 and 1707 by the English and Scottish Parliaments unified those two countries into the United Kingdom of Great Britain.) An active consumer culture emerged among white colonists as their communities and cities became more permanent. "The quick importation of fashions from the mother country is really astonishing," one British visitor to Maryland wrote. "I am almost inclined to believe that a new fashion is adopted earlier by the polished and affluent American than by many opulent persons in the great metropolis [of London]."[18]

Most colonial Americans lived close to the ocean and made their living growing and exporting raw agricultural products. Mid-Atlantic colonies like Pennsylvania grew wheat, while the hot and humid climate of the Carolinas and Georgia supported the cultivation of rice and indigo. In New England, where rocky soil and cold winters made large-scale commercial agriculture difficult, colonists supplemented meager crops with an elaborate fishing industry. The most profitable crop of the colonial period, tobacco, flourished in the Chesapeake region of Virginia and Maryland. Cheap and easy to grow, tobacco remained the mainstay of the colonial export economy until the American Revolution, when the total value of tobacco exports nearly equaled that of all food grains combined.[19]

Yet while farming occupied most people's energies, seaports in the North—especially Boston, New York, and Philadelphia—also developed a thriving merchant class rooted in the transatlantic trade. Colonial merchants acted as wholesalers who financed trading voyages but did not undertake significant travel themselves. Rather, they managed the money, owned the trading ships, and invested in the cargo—the wheat, tobacco, timber, indigo, whale oil, human beings, and other products that crisscrossed the ocean. They operated by collecting a return on profitable voyages to offset losses from piracy or shipwrecks.

As they accumulated wealth, many merchants branched into related activities, setting up shipyards and selling ships themselves or establishing retail outlets for items such as books, equipment, and clothing imported from Britain. Still others parlayed trading successes into finance, operating as local colonial bankers.[20]

Business opportunities were generally more varied in the North than in the South. With fewer major ports and a climate conducive to cash crops such as tobacco, rice, and indigo, the southern colonies remained nearly entirely agricultural throughout the colonial period. (Charleston, South Carolina, which boasted a bustling merchant and artisan class, supported by both free and slave labor, was a notable outlier.) Large plantations tended to specialize in exporting cash crops, and they relied on smaller local farms for much of their food and other supplies. Small-scale colonial farmers had less surplus than their plantation neighbors, but they moved what extra goods they had to market, using any profits to expand their landholdings. Those small farmers helped inaugurate what would become a classic theme in the history of business and modern capitalism: small operators aiming to become big.[21]

Slavery, in addition to land, represented a major marker of wealth in colonial America. The practice of racialized slavery expanded in the British colonies as early settlements became increasingly stable and market demand for mass-produced crops, starting with tobacco, exploded in Europe. The American slave population became self-sustaining in the early 18th century, so even as the international trade declined, the population of enslaved people grew. By the 1770s, nearly seven hundred thousand people, or 15 percent of the total non-Indian population of the United States, were enslaved. Although slavery remained legal throughout the British empire, it was increasingly rare north of Pennsylvania. Almost 95 percent of all enslaved people in the United States at the time of the Founding lived in Delaware, Maryland, Virginia, the Carolinas, and Georgia. One-third of the population of those southern colonies was enslaved, and approximately one-third of all southern households owned slaves.[22]

slavery enabled capitalism. cheap/free labor allowing expansion an lower prices

British North America included far more than the thirteen colonies that declared independence in July 1776, and economic conditions played a critical role in determining which seceded and which did not. Compared to their counterparts in Quebec and the Caribbean, white colonists who lived between New Hampshire and Georgia enjoyed a more diverse economy and relatively greater security. By the 1770s, only about one hundred thousand Indians lived in those thirteen colonies, along with more than 2 million white Europeans and half a million Africans and descendants of Africans, the majority of them slaves. The push for national independence grew strongest in the parts of the British empire that could envision their economies operating without the British army present.

On the other hand, Europeans on the periphery of the British empire depended greatly on the mother country. In present-day Canada, which Britain acquired from France after the Seven Years War in 1763, ongoing conflicts between the substantial native population and far-flung European fur traders and fishers meant that colonists depended greatly on British military support. In the slave societies of the West Indies, native inhabitants had been almost entirely annihilated, and small numbers of English colonists owned massive sugar plantations farmed by African slaves, whose numbers eclipsed those of their white owners by as much as ten to one in 1780. Landowners relied on brutal violence, sanctioned and backed by British law, and the strength of the British military, further cementing their ties to the crown.[23]

the british supported to get the cash crop imported back

Writing the Constitution: The Place of Business in a Young Nation

In the summer of 1787, fifty-five delegates from thirteen American states convened in Philadelphia first to reconsider, and then to replace, the governing structure known as the Articles of Confederation, which had organized the states since their independence from the British empire the decade before. When I poll my college students about the reasons behind the Constitutional Convention, they all demonstrate a clear sense of the common story: The Articles of Confederation devolved too much power to state governments at the expense of the national government; internal conflicts, such as Shays's Rebellion, abounded over unpaid veterans' benefits; and the weak central Congress couldn't raise national taxes to pay foreign war debts. All this left the country weak and vulnerable to attack.

That story is largely accurate, but the standard telling of the Constitutional Convention often misses the intense debate over fundamental economic questions that propelled the convention. Questions about the separation of powers and the distribution of rights among the people, the states, and the federal government were not merely philosophical abstractions. Rather, they reflected material issues that pitted different business interests against each other, and their resolution had real consequences for the development of business in the United States.

More than one hundred years ago, the historian Charles Beard published *An Economic Interpretation of the Constitution of the United States*, in which he argued that the Founders created a particular structure of government to serve their immediate financial interests.[24] Beard claimed that the wealthy merchants and bankers who had loaned money to the war effort could only hope to be repaid if a strong national government compelled the individual states to repay them. Subsequent historians threw considerable cold water on parts of this thesis, demonstrating that many of the Constitution's opponents, called the Antifederalists, *also* had significant financial interests at stake. Ideological concerns about republicanism and self-government, they showed, were at least as important to the Founders as economic gain. Clearly the story is more complicated than Beard suggested.

But even if Beard overreached in his particular condemnation of the Founders as wholly profit-driven and self-interested, he was right that promoting a healthy national business climate was a paramount issue for them. "The prosperity of commerce is now perceived and acknowledged by all enlightened statesmen to be the most useful as well as the most productive source of national wealth," boasted Alexander Hamilton in one of his essays defending the federal Constitution. Union, the Founders insisted, would only create greater economic opportunity and, as a result, political security.[25]

The Constitution, drafted in 1787 and ratified the next year, affirmed the central place of business in early American politics. The first three sections of the document laid out the roles and responsibilities of the three branches of the federal government: the Congress, the presidency, and the judiciary, in that order. Section 8 of Article 1—the longest section of the entire document—provides a substantial list of Congress's powers. Here is an abridged list of what that section says:

Article I, Section 8: The Congress shall have Power:

To lay and collect Taxes;

To borrow Money;

To regulate Commerce with foreign Nations, and among the several States, and with the Indian Tribes;

To coin Money;

To provide for the Punishment of counterfeiting;

To establish Post Offices and post Roads;

To promote the Progress of Science and useful Arts, by securing for limited Times to Authors and Inventors the exclusive Right to their respective Writings and Discoveries;

To define and punish Piracies and Felonies committed on the high Seas, and Offences against the Law of Nations.

Section 10 then lists things that states *cannot* do:

> No state shall . . . pass any . . . Law impairing the Obligation of Contracts.

Through this list of enumerated powers, the Founders made clear that the federal government was responsible for creating a stable, profitable environment for private enterprise. Some of these points may appear obvious: The power to borrow money and collect taxes meant that people who loaned money to the public purse, particularly wealthy merchants and southern planters, could be confident that they would be reimbursed. In addition, the power to coin money and punish counterfeiters allowed the federal government to stabilize the national economy—people in New York could conduct business with people in South Carolina using a verifiable, trustworthy currency. And the oft-cited "Commerce Clause" guaranteed that the federal government should monitor and regulate business transactions that crossed state lines or involved foreign countries. That clause made the land from New Hampshire to Georgia a giant free trade zone, where products and people could move free of tariffs or other barriers.

In addition to enumerating specific rights, this part of the Constitution illustrates the Founders' business-oriented *values*. By retaining the right to define and punish piracy on the high seas, they declared that protecting private property—that which pirates were most likely to abscond with—was in the *national* interest. By establishing post offices and roads, Congress would create a vital infrastructure for transporting goods and facilitating communication across state lines. And finally, by enshrining the principles of patent protection—the "exclusive Right to their respective Writings and Discoveries"—the Constitution protected intellectual property at the highest level. For businesspeople, this clause promised that the federal government would protect them from dishonest competitors and promote new ideas and innovations.

Finally, and perhaps most important, the Founders enshrined the paramount importance of *contracts* by barring states from contravening legal agreements. The Contracts Clause represented an overt exercise of federal authority—remarkable in a document committed to the separation of powers—that reaffirmed the critical role of the government in economic transactions from tobacco wholesaling to whaling to slaving.

Most public discussions of the U.S. Constitution today tend to stress the document's contribution to political philosophy, including questions about individual liberty and the limitations of governmental authority. Reading the document from an economic perspective, however, reveals the vibrant, enterprise-oriented legal system its authors envisioned. By the 1780s, business practices in the United States had grown more diversified than they had been earlier in the colonial period. As industrialization spread across the Atlantic from Britain, American businesspeople would benefit tremendously from the economic order created by those who wrote and ratified the Constitution.

2

⚈

THE BUSINESS OF BONDAGE

In the early spring of 1841, a farmer and part-time violinist named Solomon Northup traveled from his home in Saratoga, New York, to Washington, D.C., for what he believed was a temporary job playing music for three dollars a night, plus a dollar a day for travel time. He arrived in the nation's capital amid the public commemorations of the funeral of President William Harrison, the first U.S. president to die in office. Shortly after his arrival, Northup was drugged, kidnapped, and sold for $650 to a slave trader. Since kidnapping and selling a free citizen violated the law, that merchant, whom Northup later called a "speculator in human flesh," beat and tortured his new acquisition to force his silence about his true status. Within weeks, Northup arrived in a slave pen in New Orleans, where would-be buyers inspected his body. The slave pen's keeper, a business partner of the original slave trader/kidnapper in Washington, hoped Northup would fetch $1,500, but settled on $900. (The decreased selling price may have reflected Northup's exposure to smallpox during the trip south; to negotiate even that price, the pen keeper had to lie about Northup's age, claiming the thirty-two-year-old was twenty-three.) Twelve years later, when Northup regained his freedom and returned to New York, his market value as a slave may have approached $2,000.

The abject horror of Solomon Northup's ordeal became known, particularly in the North, when he published a memoir called *Twelve Years a Slave* in 1853.[1] Along with countless other slave narratives, Northup's book became a powerful weapon rallying public sentiment against the barbarity of slavery. At the same time, it provided a vivid picture of the cold, calculated financial considerations that underlay the hell he had endured. Chattel slavery was a complex business deeply intertwined with the country's economic growth and industrial development, in the South as well as the North. As integral parts of the expanding American economy, slaves were more than unpaid workers. They were also stores of capital value, both as hired-out day laborers and as tradable commodities. Traders such as Northup's kidnappers were speculative investors, buying low-priced human cargo in bulk and selling it at inflated prices.

Slavery devastated millions of lives and left an unending and ugly moral legacy for the United States. It was also integral to national economic development from the colonial period until 1865. The story of the business of slavery winds through the physical expansion of European- and African-descended Americans into the interior of the North American continent. That continental movement not only solidified the country's geopolitical power, but also created a vast domestic market for American-produced goods. As plantation-based slavery in the South became the "big business" of the antebellum era, it created a new class system that defined American politics until the Civil War. And most important, the wealth produced by enslaved hands in the South created the engine for industrialization in the North and abroad. Far from a peripheral part of the story of business and capitalism, slavery was central to the economic development of the United States.

Trading in Flesh

The business of modern slavery began long before the existence of the United States. It predates the permanent settlement of non-indigenous people in the Americas by several generations. Beginning in the early 15th century, merchants from kingdoms and city-states along the west coast of Africa established commercial relationships with Portuguese merchants, trading gold and spices for European metals and textiles. From the beginning, African-European commerce included the trade in human beings. At first, most human trafficking was internal, as Portuguese merchants would purchase slaves at one point along the coast and resell them at another to African merchants who needed laborers to transport bulky European goods inland. Yet within a few decades, the outflow of African slaves to Europe and Atlantic sugar islands (especially Cape Verde and the Azores) outpaced the circular coastal trade. Between 1450 and 1520, Portuguese ships exported 150,000 human captives away from Africa. Over the next century, as early conquering expeditions in the New World gave way to permanent European settlements, demand for slave labor grew and the trade expanded to include other European powers, particularly the Spanish, French, Dutch, and English.[2]

The first African slaves to live in what would become the United States arrived in Spanish-claimed territory in what is now Georgia and Florida in the early to mid-16th century. In August 1619, a Dutch sea captain set anchor in the struggling colony of Jamestown and sold approximately twenty Africans whom he had pirated from a Portuguese slave ship. Virginia tobacco farmer John Rolfe (famous for being the widower of Pocahontas, the teenaged daughter of the leader of the Powhatan confederacy) reported that the colony's leaders bought the human cargo "for victualle" (food) and paid "the best and easyest rate they could."[3]

The slave trade, controlled by Dutch and Portuguese companies, remained mostly focused on the Caribbean and South America during the early years of the English colonial presence in the New World, and mainland English colonists purchased a relatively small number of African slaves. By 1675, scholars estimate, only four thousand Africans had arrived in the mainland British colonies, while more than two hundred thousand were sold to the far more agriculturally sophisticated (and profit-making) sugar colonies of Jamaica and Barbados. Most of the grueling and exploitative agricultural work in the English colonies—the type performed by enslaved people elsewhere in the New World—was instead done by European indentured servants. Those workers, while less than fully free, labored for a fixed period of time, generally in exchange for their passage to the colonies.

That arrangement changed by the end of the 17th century. After the tumultuous civil war of the 1640s, England's economy stabilized and its sea power expanded, creating major growth opportunities for all its colonies. By breaking the Dutch and Portuguese oligopoly on the Atlantic slave trade, English merchants reduced the costs of slaving. At the same time, prosperity reduced the supply of indentured servants, as members of the English lower classes found more attractive opportunities at home. As demand for labor in the North American fields and the cost of European workers rose, English colonists increasingly turned to African slaves. Slave importation grew dramatically: 11,000 people arrived between 1675 and 1700; 39,000 between 1700 and 1725; 107,000 between 1725 and 1750; and 119,000 between 1750 and 1775. By the turn of the 19th century, a total of 388,747 people had disembarked as slaves in the land that, after 1776, became the United States.[4]

Such statistics blur two important facts. First, some 84,000 *additional* people left Africa on slave ships destined for British North America but perished during the journey. Second, the slave population of the British North American colonies became self-sustaining by the early decades of the 18th century. American slaves, despite their horrendous living conditions, survived long enough to have children, and a sufficient number of those children reached adulthood to increase the native-born population of African Americans who inherited the legal status of their parents. (In much of South America and the Caribbean, by contrast, slave-owners more frequently worked people to death and continually imported slaves from Africa to maintain their workforces.) By the 1780s, the African American population of the United States reached approximately 750,000 people, the vast majority of whom had been born in the New World.

As Britain's North American colonies grew during the 17th and 18th centuries, the trade in human beings developed into a massive business. When Americans today think about the economics of slavery, most people tend to think about the value of the labor slaves performed for their owners. Just as important to the developing business of slavery, however, were the profits reaped from the *exchange* itself. The act of buying, transporting, and reselling slaves created tremendous business opportunities and contributed to the growing wealth of the colonies.

Over the course of four hundred years, European, American, and African businesspeople kidnapped and transported approximately 10.7 million African people to the New World (and another 2 million were sold out of Africa but died during the voyage). From 1450 until the early 19th century, many more Africans crossed the Atlantic Ocean than Europeans. Most of that trade was organized through state-sponsored joint-stock companies that engaged in a "triangular trade": African merchants supplied slaves to the Americas, where land-owning colonists sent raw goods to Europe, which manufactured finished products. As colonial cultivation of staples such as tobacco, indigo, cotton, and particularly sugar expanded, European investors in those trading ventures earned rich dividends, and their rulers reaped revenues through taxes and import duties. As the prominent historian of slavery Walter Johnson has put it: "People were traded along the bottom of the triangle; profits would stick at the top."[5]

The transatlantic slave trade slowed considerably in the late 18th century, around the time of American independence. In 1807, both the British Parliament and the U.S. Congress outlawed the international trade of slaves. (The Constitution of 1787, in an effort to forge a compromise between slave-owning interests and antislavery advocates, had included a clause prohibiting any move to ban the trade for twenty years.) By 1820, all other major European powers had as well.

Nonetheless, the internal slave trade remained a vibrant and vital part of the economy of the United States until the Thirteenth Amendment abolished slavery after the Civil War. As the country expanded its territorial boundaries to the south and west, slaves moved with them. In the antebellum period, approximately one million people were forcibly relocated within the United States, mostly from the Upper South states of Virginia and Maryland to the Deep South, where indigo, sugar, and increasingly cotton production created an ever-rising demand for slave labor and an increasingly profitable business for "speculators in human flesh."

Varieties of American Slavery

By the end of the colonial period, the legal structure of American slavery had grown rigid and racially defined. Generally speaking, African and African-descended enslaved people were defined as chattel property in perpetuity—they remained slaves until they died or (in rare circumstances) their owners freed them, and status passed from mother to child, regardless of paternity. Enslaved people generally could not legally own property, vote, participate in the legal system, or enter contracts such as marriage. And they had no legal recourse when an owner chose to sell them, an injustice that resulted in unquantifiable suffering and the destruction of generations of families.

American slavery by the 19th century was largely confined to the South, but despite that regional limitation, the nature of slave work varied in important ways. Many Americans have an image of slavery along the lines projected by Hollywood movies such as *Gone with the Wind*: expansive cotton or sugar plantations, where landlords owned hundreds of slaves. Reality, however, was more complicated.

Large plantations certainly wielded disproportionate economic power, but most southern whites were not slave-owners. Historians estimate that, by the time of the Civil War, about 385,000 out of a total of 1.5 million white households in the South owned slaves. (African Americans and Native Americans did not own slaves in significant numbers, and were usually legally barred from doing so.) About half of these slave-owning households owned between one and five slaves; another 38 percent owned between six and twenty. Although they held a vastly disproportionate level of wealth, the remaining 12 percent of slave-owners (those who had twenty-plus slaves) represented only 3 percent of all white households.[6]

About half of enslaved people labored on small and midsized farms, which produced a variety of agricultural goods. Whether they employed slave labor or not, such farms grew grain and vegetables and raised livestock. Among their biggest buyers were large plantations that dedicated most of their resources to cash crops such as cotton and sugar and needed to supplement their daily provisions with local products. In addition, small and midsized farms supplied urban areas in ports such as Charleston and New Orleans. The daily toil of enslaved people on such farms included a variety of tasks, from field tending to carpentry to artisanal work.

Other slaves participated in industrial production. We don't typically associate the antebellum South with manufacturing, and with good reason—the vast majority of such production took place in the North. Even so, some enterprising whites in the Upper South managed to construct textile mills modeled after New England's factories and even iron-works facilities. And, although the experience was not typical, some southern industrialists used slave labor. In fact, by the mid-19th century, approximately two hundred thousand slaves worked in industrial settings. At the outbreak of the Civil War, more than sixty worked for, and were owned by, William Weaver, a native Philadelphian who moved to Virginia in 1814 to establish an iron forge with two charcoal blast furnaces in the Shenandoah Valley.

The dynamics of industrial slavery differed critically from slavery on farms, as the historian Charles Dew has recounted. Violent coercion and discipline often proved ineffective, since beatings could leave a slave physically unable to perform factory work. Moreover, resentment from a beating could inspire industrial slaves to commit expensive sabotage, such as breaking a valuable piece of equipment. To compel obedience, Weaver deployed a reward system, granting "overwork credit" with which slaves could purchase commodities on their own. Yet many industrial slavers, such as the Virginian James Davis, compared "the negro to the dog": To maintain authority, "you must whip him occasionally & be sparing of favors." Whatever their use of physical violence, industrial slave-owners also found that the threat of selling slaves away and breaking up families was a highly effective tool.[7]

A significant number of enslaved people lived in urban areas such as Charleston and Baltimore. There, some slaves labored for, and often alongside, their owners in workshops, but many were owned by urban professionals—doctors, bankers, and lawyers who kept slaves as investment property. Some performed domestic duties, but more often they were hired out to work for private companies or to perform public works projects, such as digging canals or dredging harbors. Slave-owners received hourly pay for their slaves' labor, and in many cases the enslaved people themselves brought home those wages in cash. In both cases, urban slaves often labored alongside free workers, both black and white.[8]

Through the variety of their experiences, enslaved people contributed to many different aspects of the American business system. While most slaves toiled in agriculture, others performed skilled and unskilled industrial labor, specialized in artisanal craftwork, or provided domestic services. Critically, though, their economic importance came not only from their daily labor, but also from their market price. On average, slaves were worth $200 each in the early 19th century, and some were worth far more—Solomon Northup recounted a negotiation over an attractive young girl for whom a white man offered $5,000. By the eve of the Civil War, historians estimate that the total cash value of the 4 million slaves in the American South was $3.5 billion in 1860 money. At more than 80 percent of the country's total economic output, that figure would be roughly $13.8 *trillion* today. Understood in that way, enslaved people were *capital assets* worth more than the country's entire productive capacity from manufacturing, trade, and railroads combined.[9]

Slavery and the Rise of the Cotton Kingdom

In 1776, when Thomas Jefferson declared the "self-evident" truth that "all men are created equal," nearly 15 percent of the 4 million non-Indian inhabitants of the United States were enslaved. Although slavery remained legal in all states, almost 95 percent of enslaved people lived south of Pennsylvania, and the highest concentration was in Virginia. Beginning in the 1770s, however, legislatures in northern states began to pass first gradual emancipation laws and ultimately complete bans on slavery. By 1804, every state north of Delaware had legally abolished the practice, and new midwestern states and territories that joined the nation in the decades to come likewise prohibited it.[10]

Meanwhile, the enslaved population in the South exploded in the first half of the 19th century. From fewer than 700,000 in 1790, the number of slaves grew to 1,191,000 in 1810—two years after the importation of slaves from abroad was outlawed. It ultimately reached 4 million by the eve of the Civil War. As the territorial boundaries of the United States extended south and westward, so too did slavery. By 1860, the enslavement of black Americans defined social and economic life from Maryland to Florida, and westward to Missouri and Texas.

Why did slavery disappear in the North yet expand in the South in the fifty years after independence? The answers lie in the severe economic, social, and political dislocations that rocked the young country and erupted in the bloody Civil War.

Slavery in the North died out because of the organizational power of antislavery activists combined with the lack of large-scale commercial agriculture in the region. Farms in the North never achieved the scale and specialization of southern plantations, and never came to rely on slave labor. In addition, the growth of industrial manufacturing and urban living militated against slave labor. Abolitionist messaging, rooted in religious appeals to human freedom as well as overtly racist warnings about racial mixing, shaped public discussion and the votes of state legislators. Evidence suggests that many, if not most, white northerners had no moral problem with slavery, but few powerful interests had much to gain by defending it.

The story of slavery in the South is more complex and more hotly debated. As the rate of importation of African slaves declined after the mid-18th century, the future profitability of cash crops such as tobacco and sugar came into doubt. No one can say for sure what *might* have happened (and woe to the historian who tries!), but many prominent white southerners in the 1770s and 1780s believed slavery would soon die out on its own. Early in his public career, the slave-owner Thomas Jefferson believed that slave labor represented an inefficient and unenlightened method of organizing work. Moreover, his racist dismissal of blacks as inferior led him to predict that whites and blacks could not long live together, even if one were master of the other. By the early 1800s, however, Jefferson changed his view, telling a correspondent: "I have long since given up the expectation of any early provision for the extinguishment of slavery among us."[11]

What had changed? Why did a system that seemed to be declining make such a comeback in the few short decades between the 1780s and 1800s? The answer is cotton. Cotton changed everything.

The rising demand for raw cotton first came from England in the 1780s, where textile factories in places such as Manchester fed a growing global market for cheaply produced cloth. These British manufacturers wielded a technical monopoly over the textile industry and offered high prices to cotton farmers who could best meet their needs. Most important, after experimenting with various types of cotton grown around the globe, these industrialists came to prefer a particular type—a variety of the genus *Gossypium*—that grew well in the Deep South of the now independent United States.[12]

In the years immediately following the Revolution, American farmers searched for more marketable crops. Separating from the British empire had meant an end to price subsidies for tobacco, rice, and indigo, and profits from those crops declined. Cotton offered a new and promising source of revenue.

A timely technological innovation helped further drive the growing profitability of southern-grown cotton. In 1794, a twenty-eight-year-old Yale-educated New Englander named Eli Whitney, engaged as a tutor for the children of a plantation owner in South Carolina, patented a machine that mechanically separated cotton fibers from cotton seed. According to the traditional story, Whitney invented this "cotton gin" (gin was short for "engine") after observing enslaved people slowly and painfully removing seeds from cotton balls. It is clear that Whitney patented his design the next year and went into business to manufacture and sell his product, but historians debate the degree to which he "invented" it. It is probably more accurate to say that Whitney found a mechanical way to improve on a technique that slaves on many plantations already employed, at times, to scrape the seeds from the fibers with metal rollers.[13]

Yet to argue about whether Whitney "invented" the cotton gin misses the larger point. The process of mechanically separating seeds from fiber, whether through one of Whitney's patented machines or one of the many imitators that followed, revolutionized the process of cotton production in the American South. Mechanization decreased the processing time necessary to render raw cotton salable, so plantation managers could direct their enslaved workforce to spend more time in the fields, harvesting the crop itself. The amount of cotton an individual enslaved person could prepare for export rose as use of the mechanical devices spread. By some estimates, the per-slave cotton yield increased 700 percent.

Business history is full of stories of entrepreneurial and innovative people such as Whitney. As students of the past, however, it is important for us to understand that technological breakthroughs can only drive change when the social and economic context is right. (Just ask Leonardo da Vinci, who came up with ideas like the helicopter four centuries before human beings mastered air flight.) Did innovation drive the market, or did the market drive innovation? In most cases, including this one, the more complete answer is that the two mutually reinforced each other.

Before long, domestic textile producers joined English factories in propelling this cotton boom. American textiles underwent a technological revolution at the turn of the 19th century, and mill owners in the North began to compete with more established British cloth manufacturers. International conflict led to a trade embargo between America and Europe in 1807. While that hurt international merchants, it benefited American textile producers by making their cloth more competitive. And fueling this massive increase in textile production was the critical raw material—southern cotton, grown on large plantations and harvested by the unfree hands of African American slaves.

The results for the cotton industry were astounding. Southern planters produced around 3,000 bales of cotton per year in the early 1790s. By 1820—by which time domestic textile manufacturing had spread considerably—that number approached 450,000. By the eve of the Civil War in 1860, the South grew and exported (either domestically or abroad) nearly 5.5 *million* bales of cotton per year.[14]

This explosion in cotton production redefined the economic landscape of the American South. Large plantations came to specialize in a single crop, cotton, to a far greater degree than they had during the colonial period. With more resources dedicated to reaping high profits from cotton, southern planters relied more than ever before on manufactured goods brought in from the North and overseas, as well as on small and midsized southern farms for supplementary food crops. More important, their reliance on slaves—the hands that picked the cotton—grew ever stronger. Earlier notions that slavery would peter out vanished before the might of the global cotton trade.

The new economics of cotton also produced fierce competition for land and resources among white southern landowners. Looking for more fertile soil, many migrated south and west into what is now the Deep South. And where cotton and cotton planters went, so, too, did slavery. The enslaved population of the Mississippi Territory increased by 400 percent in the first ten years of the 19th century alone, from approximately 3,500 to 16,700.

By the turn of the 19th century, those migrating white Americans and their burgeoning cotton business gratefully received tremendous assistance from the federal government. Conflicts with the various Indian nations, as well as the remnants of Spanish settlements, were common, and the cotton frontier was only secured through territorial treaties backed up by the strength of the American military. After President Jefferson negotiated the purchase of the Louisiana Territory in 1803 from Napoleon (whose right to sell it, even by European standards, was shaky), government officials sent soldiers to secure the area, surveyors to chart and subdivide the territory into farmable plots, and agents to organize the sale to private ventures.[15]

Because most cotton was grown on large plantations that employed more than twenty slaves—and in some cases in the Mississippi Valley up to a hundred or more—the wealth from the cotton boom became increasingly concentrated in fewer hands. As the cotton economy expanded, the people at the helm of this industry—both the landowning planters and the merchants who moved the product through a series of ports to its final destination in the mills—coalesced into a powerful ruling class. Wealthy southerners had long held sway over American politics. Even in the 1780s, when many people thought slavery would die out, Constitutional Convention delegates from states such as South Carolina had insisted that the nation's founding document protect the interests of slave-owners from abolitionists. Yet with the cotton boom, the power of plantation owners—which contemporaries often dubbed the Slave Power, or the Plantocracy—reached new heights.

A South Carolina senator named James Henry Hammond put a rhetorical point on the issue in 1858. During a congressional debate over whether Kansas should become a state and allow slavery, Hammond—who had ridden his success as a plantation owner to a political career—rose to defend the slave-based economy of the cotton South. The South, he declared, was no mere feeder-system to the industrializing North. Downplaying the importance of industrial manufacturing, Hammond claimed that the South's ability to produce vital agricultural staples made it *more* powerful than the North, whose livelihood depended on southern cotton. Without southern cotton, he asserted, "England would topple headlong and carry the whole civilized world with her, save the South." None would "dare make war on cotton," Hammond chided the North: "Cotton is king."[16]

The cotton "kingdom" fueled business development in the early United States. Tremendous wealth flowing to plantation owners and merchants created a political class of men such as Hammond, whose fervent defense of slavery would lead to disunion in 1860 and 1861. The cotton they produced fed an increasingly industrial society in Europe and in the North, propelling changes in business operations and changing the social context in which Americans worked and consumed. And most critically, the expansion of the cotton economy cemented and promoted the practice of slavery. By the beginning of the Civil War, slavery had expanded to record levels across the South. The 4 million women, men, and children confined to chains were, for "speculators in human flesh," tremendous financial assets, as well as the labor power that fueled the southern economic juggernaut.

Slavery and Capitalism

Traditionally, scholars considered slavery and capitalism to be separate, even contradictory historical phenomena. Nineteenth-century economic thinkers often framed capitalist economic relations in terms of freedom: freedom to make contracts; freedom to own property; freedom to generate profits from one's activity. Perhaps most important was the freedom to negotiate a price for labor. Karl Marx, who was simultaneously capitalism's fiercest critic and its most trenchant analyst, viewed slavery and capitalism as incompatible. Without the freedom to contract for labor, society could not have the essential features of capitalism—a class that owned the means of production (factories, for instance) and a class that sold its labor in the form of wages. Slavery, for Marx, represented a different stage in economic development that served as a necessary precursor to capitalism (just as capitalism, for Marx, was a necessary precursor to socialism).[17]

And Marx was not alone. Even people who otherwise had no interest in Marxist theories agreed that unfree labor was, by *definition*, inimical to capitalism. Throughout the 20th century, many historians buttressed that claim with evidence that slavery was an economically inefficient and costly way to organize labor. Slaves certainly did not live well, but they had to eat, and providing basic necessities constituted a business expense for their owners (which was not the case with wage workers), as did the costs of imposing coercive violence. Economists argued that agricultural production was inherently linear and could not experience the exponential returns on investment that capitalistic enterprises achieved. A farmer who doubled his land-holdings could potentially double his yield, while factory owners and industrial investors could improve productivity many times over and achieve much higher rates of return.

More recently, however, historians have begun to challenge the notion that capitalism and slavery existed in separate spheres. Recent histories paint southern cotton producers as efficient, modern businesspeople, very similar to their capitalist neighbors to the North. Farmers in the antebellum South managed to generate ever-growing stocks of cotton not only by bringing more land under cultivation, but also by adopting more productive business practices. Plantation records show that they developed increasingly efficient accounting systems, surveying tools, and plans for maximizing crop yields.[18] Slave-owners also increased cotton production through brutal work-force management, adopting labor policies that resembled those of industrial factories. Whistles and horns regulated the workday, labor was divided, and overseers, acting like factory foremen, supervised individual workers. And as historian Edward Baptist has shown, slave-owners used violence not merely as a tool of social control, but deliberately as a strategy to increase productivity. Beatings and torture pushed slaves to work harder and faster, increasing the yield of the cotton kingdom.[19]

Slavery and capitalism were also deeply linked through the dual nature of slaves themselves—as not just a source of labor, but also a store of capital value. Southern slave-owners used their chattel human property as collateral for mortgages to expand their landholdings. Planters like James Henry Hammond made capital investments outside their own industries, purchasing stocks in railroad corporations. And urban slave-owners renting out their slaves' labor monitored the market to consider when to buy and when to sell. The spirit of capitalism was far from uncommon in slave society.

The history of slavery was deeply intertwined with the history of capitalist development in the sixty years after American independence. The northern and southern economies both developed rapidly and in tandem, and businesspeople in both the slave South and the free North relied on the federal government to advance their economic interests. Southerners used the military to secure new territory, the police to enforce slave codes and prevent rebellion, and the taxing authority of the federal government to promote the export of cotton. Northerners relied on state investments in infrastructure and the protection of domestic manufacturing. From wealthy slave-owning planters to northern merchants and bankers, as well as the manufacturers who grew rich producing textiles from slave-grown cotton, the business of bondage shaped all aspects of the early American economy.

3

FACTORIES COME TO AMERICA

I n January 1790, the first U.S. Congress commissioned a special report by the secretary of the treasury, Alexander Hamilton. Facing profound internal disputes about what the economic future of the young country should look like, Congress charged Hamilton, a West Indian immigrant and veteran of the American Revolution, with assessing the place of "manufactures," the common term for finished products, from textiles to iron to shoes. In a land overwhelmingly populated by farmers, what role should manufacturers play? And what steps should the national government take to keep the United States "independent [from] foreign nations, for military and other essential supplies"?

Nearly two years later, Hamilton delivered his Report on Manufactures, the last of three major reports he prepared on national economic planning. (The first two dealt with public finances and led Congress to consolidate the country's war debts into a single national debt and create a national bank.) In his report, Hamilton made a principled case that, while the United States should not abandon its tradition of self-sufficiency and commercial agriculture, Congress should take steps to develop the manufacturing sector as well. "[T]he establishment and diffusion of manufactures," he argued, would make "the total mass of useful and productive labor, in a community, greater than it would otherwise be."

Government policy, Hamilton insisted, should encourage Americans to build mechanized mills, expand factories, and devote resources to creating better machines and equipment. In addition, Hamilton promoted levying selective import taxes, or "protecting duties," and stricter inspections on imported products to raise the cost of imported goods and provide a boost to domestic ones. Furthermore, he urged, the national legislature should make inland trade easier by putting money into national roads and highways, and should provide financing options for small American manufacturers.[1]

Hamilton's Report on Manufactures was controversial and exposed the political and economic schisms in the United States in the early national period. In the 1790s, most of the country engaged in agriculture or other endeavors that exploited natural resources. Even though Hamilton argued for a mixed economy of *both* farming *and* industry, many of his critics believed that his defense of manufacturing amounted to a veiled attack on agriculture. His trade policies, they charged, would disproportionately benefit wealthy northern elites (like Hamilton himself) at the expense of farmers. That conflict formed the core of a political debate that would define American business history throughout the 19th century.

Congress took no immediate action on Hamilton's industrial policy recommendations, but the rapid rise of industrial manufacturing in the following decades would make the issues he raised unavoidable. Hamilton himself died in 1804, shot in a duel by the sitting vice president, but his early advocacy for manufacturing proved prescient.

In the half-century after independence, the production of finished goods moved from small shops and households into increasingly large-scale factories and mills. Fueled by a booming international trade and growing global demand, as well as technological advances in transportation and communication, American craftspeople and artisans—almost entirely in the North—created larger business operations than had ever existed in the past. Important innovations, including early forms of assembly-line production, the separation of ownership from labor, and the rise of the corporate legal form, propelled this new economy forward.

Just as slavery drove the southern economy, manufacturing became increasingly important to the economies of the Northeast and, by the middle of the 19th century, the Midwest. And just as slavery's social and economic reach extended far beyond the South, so, too, did industrialization exert a powerful influence on all Americans. Economic growth spurred population growth, infrastructure, and new methods of production, communication, and transportation. Just as important, the production and trade of manufactured goods gave rise to a new model of social organization that historians often call the "Market Revolution."[2] From simple day-to-day purchases to long-distance shipments of cotton, iron, wheat, and slaves, Americans became more connected to one another through the market economy. And the growth of the factory model altered traditional working arrangements. As labor moved outside the home and off the farm, new categories of wage-earning workers developed and urban populations boomed. By the late 19th century, industrial manufacturing, as Hamilton had predicted, came to dominate American economic and social life.

Business Becomes Specialized after Independence

When Alexander Hamilton wrote his defense of manufacturers in the early 1790s, business enterprise in the United States looked much as it had during the last hundred years of the colonial period. Most Americans worked on farms, and most farms—even large southern plantations—were controlled by individual households. Industrial activities such as mining and smelting were organized around family units, and the production of textiles, metals, and farm equipment took place either in homes or in small artisanal shops. Atop that economy sat general merchants, who ruled over domestic and international trade in port cities, supervising and profiting from the flow of a variety of products.

This situation began to change at the end of the 18th century. Businesses began to specialize and general merchants were replaced by a network of enterprises devoted to specific business activities—from canal building to money lending, from wholesaling to textile production.

What prompted this shift from a personalized business world to a more formalized structure based on specialized firms? Among the most important factors were new opportunities to trade that opened up after the American Revolution. No longer bound by their place within the British empire, American merchants could seek markets in continental Europe, the Middle East, and China. In addition, independence and expansion into Indian land in the West, as well as immigration from Europe, brought about rapid population growth, creating a vast domestic market that manufacturers back East could serve.

But the most significant force behind specialization was the advent of industrialization itself—not in the United States, but in Britain. In the last half of the 18th century, Britain emerged as a world leader in the increasingly mechanized production of cotton textiles, and it owed its competitive advantage to a series of technological innovations. The spinning jenny increased the speed of spinning cotton fibers into thread, helping make cotton a viable alternative to traditional materials like wool, which was heavy and scratchy. And British weavers harnessed the power of steam to propel the looms that wove thread into cloth. These innovations increased output and lowered costs. Britain's geopolitical dominance helped its textile merchants corner the global trade in textiles, undercutting competitors from India and China.[3]

Most important for business in the United States, Britain's textile revolution created a tremendous demand for cotton. A specialized chain of middlemen emerged to facilitate the movement of ever-greater volumes of slave-grown cotton from farms in the South to relay centers and port cities, and onto ships bound for Manchester and Liverpool. At the same time, the young United States became a key market for finished textiles produced in British factories. Growing volumes of trade propelled merchants to specialize in importing those goods, which they handed off to wholesalers and retailers, and finally to shopkeepers.[4]

Textile Mills: The First Factories

Techniques for mechanically producing textiles crossed the ocean from Britain to the New World in 1789, when an English mechanic named Samuel Slater immigrated to the United States. Born in Derbyshire, Slater began working in cotton mills as a child and developed a deep understanding of the machinery he worked with. To circumvent British laws prohibiting the exportation of industrial designs, Slater committed much of the process to memory and, at age twenty-one, sailed to Rhode Island. After teaming up with a candle manufacturer who fronted the advance money, he created a water-powered mechanized textile mill in the early 1790s and amassed a fortune.

At the turn of the 19th century, others imitated Slater's successes. Most notable was a Boston-born merchant named Francis Cabot Lowell. In 1813, Lowell used his connections with the New England trading community to form a partnership called the Boston Manufacturing Company, based in Waltham, Massachusetts. That group, which soon changed its name to the Boston Associates, established an integrated production facility that united the processes for spinning, weaving, and finishing textiles. Slater, by contrast, had followed a more traditional model and performed each of these activities in a separate location, frequently sending packets of work out to farming households to be performed after hours or in the winter. Capitalizing on a more efficient production method, Lowell's company grew. The partners reinvested their profits, founding a new mill on the Merrimack River northwest of Boston in 1822. That development grew into one of America's first "factory towns"—the city of Lowell.

The scion of a well-connected family, Francis Cabot Lowell benefited from a much higher social position than Slater, and so had access to considerably more start-up capital. Historians estimate that Lowell's original mill in Waltham started with twice the funding that Slater had, which partly explains his greater success. Lowell's foray into factory production came at an auspicious moment. In 1807, U.S. president Thomas Jefferson enacted an embargo on goods imported from Britain and France in response to aggression against American ships by the two warring European powers. Five years later, the United States entered the War of 1812 with Britain. The war curtailed imports of manufactured goods, most significantly cotton textiles. In this vacuum, well-financed and technologically sophisticated factories created by the Boston Associates achieved great success.[5]

The water-powered, machine-intensive textile factories of Lowell required a significant labor force. For the first several decades of their operation, the Lowell factories found a promising source of workers among the young women of the local farming communities. The Boston Associates engaged so-called "mill girls" to perform the difficult and monotonous work of textile production. Primarily the daughters of white Protestant farmers, these workers encountered a paternalistic social system at the mills, designed to "protect" their feminine virtue and convince their parents to allow them the social

[handwritten: → creating own spaces so the can always]

independence to live away from home. Lowell provided dormitories for workers as well as churches, libraries, and stores.

[handwritten: work]

Work in the textile mills was monotonous, dreary, and strictly supervised—workers' lives were not their own. Yet some claimed that their compensation, economic stability, and relative freedom during the down hours made up for the drudgery. "The time we *do* have is our own," reported Josephine Baker, a "Lowell girl" who contributed to a pro-industry magazine called *The Lowell Offering* in 1845. "The money we earn comes promptly; more so than in any other situation; and our work, though laborious is the same from day to day; we know what it is, and when finished we feel perfectly free, till it is time to commence it again."[6]

The experiment with "mill girls" only lasted until the 1840s, when the Lowell mills increasingly turned to poor, immigrant labor. Throughout the Northeast and Midwest, industrial factories that employed hundreds of workers upset traditional social structures by shifting the site of work away from the home. In the process, a new class—a working class—started to take shape. These factory workers, whether young women from local farms or, increasingly, European immigrants (both women and men, and frequently children), developed a different relationship to their labor than home-bound spinners and weavers had. They worked for hourly wages, put in long hours on dangerous machinery, and faced harsh discipline from owners and overseers. Machinists on cotton mills typically worked twelve or fourteen hours a day in large, noisy rooms, and faced the constant threat of debilitating or deadly accidents. The growth of industrialization pulled many Americans away from farms and toward factories, where they joined with European immigrants to boost the population of America's cities. In 1790, only 5 percent of Americans lived in urban settings; by 1860, 20 percent did.[7]

[handwritten: + community + ... ersion is ... dignity that ...respect purpose gone]

Revolutions in Transportation and Communication

In the first half of the 19th century, Americans performed business transactions across ever-greater distances and, more and more, with people they had never even met. Some traded their own labor, while some dealt in the labor of others. Some focused on production, but many also specialized in moving finished products from factories to warehouses, from wholesalers to retailers. The result was a market-oriented economy that only worked because of the changes in how people and information moved across the vast and growing country. And vitally, these innovations depended on a combination of factors—state and federal governments, municipal authorities, and private firms—all of which contributed to the infrastructure to make long-distance trade and industrial production possible.

In the early 19th century, nearly all commercial goods traveled from their place of origin to their final destination by water. Inland roads were poorly maintained and dangerous, and their usefulness was limited by the speed and strength of horses. Beginning shortly after independence, private companies in New England and the mid-Atlantic states built and maintained roads, known as turnpikes, and charged tolls to travelers to recoup their expenses and turn a profit. Despite a boom in road construction, most of those businesses struggled to make money. Over the next several decades, state governments stepped in, promoting and financing road development. Even with this additional investment, however, road travel remained expensive and perilous, and not at all suitable to an expanding industrial economy.[8]

Unlike roads, waterways allowed merchants to move large quantities of textiles, iron, slaves, and foodstuffs over significant distances. According to one estimate, the amount of money it took to ship a ton of goods from Europe to an American port city would only get the same cargo about thirty miles inland pulled by a wagon.[9]

The rising levels of international trade in the early 1800s propelled a revolution in transportation technology. At the heart of these developments was steam power, captured by pouring water over heated coals and using the rising steam to turn turbines. That essential technology had developed generations earlier in Britain, where early steam engines, while inefficient, competed with animals, wind, and water as the preferred power source for the growing textile industry. In 1807, two Americans—inventor Robert Fulton and financier Robert Livingston—applied steam technology to power riverboats. By the 1820s, steam routes crisscrossed the country.[10]

This new ability to move goods swiftly from the interior to the ports encouraged westward expansion by both farmers and entrepreneurial industrialists. Coal-powered iron mills developed in the mineral-rich lands of western Pennsylvania, and the small town of Pittsburgh grew into an important manufacturing center. Towns along major interior waterways prospered, specializing in the increasingly mechanized processing of agricultural products such as meat and grain.

Steam power enabled ships to move goods and people more easily along existing waterways, but they were obviously restricted to where the rivers flowed. Man-made canals presented a promising workaround and marked a second critical development in the transportation revolution. These trenches—a few feet deep, a few dozen feet across, but sometimes hundreds of miles long—represented a tremendous engineering challenge. They were designed so that draft animals could walk parallel to the water, dragging nonmotorized barges laden with goods. As a result, the canals had to rise and fall with the landscape. The most famous, New York's Erie Canal, employed eighty-three locks to adjust for changes in elevation and eighteen aqueducts to bypass other rivers and streams as it cut a 360-mile swath from Albany on the Hudson to Buffalo on Lake Erie. Completed in 1825, the Erie Canal brought vast quantities of wheat and timber from the Great Lakes region to New York City, and then up and down the Atlantic seaboard. Towns sprang up along the canal route as private businesspeople established distilleries, flour mills, and other processing outfits.[11]

At a cost of some $7 million (perhaps $2 billion in today's money), the Erie Canal exceeded the scale or scope of earlier canal-building operations. It also signified a new era of publicly financed infrastructure. Before 1820, the few built canals had relied on privately raised capital. Starting with the Erie, however, canal building depended on money from state governments and municipalities. Large canals entailed tremendous up-front costs years before any tolls could be collected, so builders found that private financiers were loath to invest. Only local and state governments commanded sufficient public trust to sell bonds and invest in large sums of corporate stock, and thus raise money for the ventures. In most cases, municipal governments saw a positive return on their investments, not only in direct payments but also through the tremendous economic growth generated by the new system of canals—three thousand miles' worth by the 1840s, linking the Atlantic seaboard with midwestern cities such as Terre Haute, Indiana, and Cincinnati, Ohio.[12]

In spite of historians' tendency to label these changes in transportation a "revolution," they didn't take place all at once. The expansion of inland roads, steam power, and canals reshaped economic life in early America and contributed to both the rise of industrial manufacturing and the movement of white Americans into the interior. However, this "transportation revolution" was constrained by technical and economic limits for many decades. Even by the 1840s, steamboats were not technologically sophisticated enough to replace wind-powered ships on open sea, either crossing the ocean to Europe or sailing between eastern port cities. And while canals increased the ease with which large quantities of goods could be moved from the interior to the seaboard, ultimately those goods moved only as quickly as the oxen dragging the barges.

But these innovations in transportation created new incentives for accelerating overland travel. The rise in trade and production, facilitated by canals and steamships, generated great profits. And by the mid-19th century, that newfound wealth laid the foundation for the development of a new type of overland vehicle—one that would *really* revolutionize transportation: the steam-powered railroad.

Like many aspects of America's industrial revolution, railroads originated in England. By the 1820s, British engineers had found ways to use the steam engine to power land-based mechanized locomotives, and early rail lines emerged to connect coal deposits to processing centers. The American foray into rail began in 1828, when the state of Maryland chartered the Baltimore and Ohio Railroad company, which laid tracks to the west to create an alternative to canal traffic. The first steam-powered locomotive to travel those rails moved slower than a horse, but within two decades, the technology improved. The railroad boom took off in the late 1840s, and the number of miles of tracks multiplied. Americans laid more than twenty-one thousand miles of railroad track in the 1850s. By the eve of the Civil War, a New Yorker could reach Chicago in two days, a trip that would have taken three weeks in 1830.[13]

These phenomenal changes in the speed and efficiency of transportation also led to major developments in the speed of communication, with tremendous effects for business. Faster transport—whether on turnpike roads, canals, steamships, or railcars—increased the volume and speed of mail delivery between the 1810s and the 1840s. The U.S. Post Office, which was granted a special license and responsibility by the Constitution to deliver the country's mail, expanded from seventy-five branches in 1790 to more than eighteen thousand by 1850. Just as important, private companies began to profit by delivering larger packages. In the 1840s, a group of investors formed a rapid-delivery service that charged customers high fees to move parcels by stagecoach westward from the East Coast. Within ten years, that original partnership broke up into several specialized companies, including Wells Fargo and American Express.[14]

But even more important than overland mail and package delivery · was the advent of electronic telecommunications: the telegraph (from the Greek for "writing at a distance"). The first telegraph was created by the French government in the 1790s to allow communication from Paris to twenty-nine cities up to five hundred miles away. But those original telegraph networks were *optical*, not electronic. To make them work, trained operators staffed towers spaced ten to twenty miles apart, from which they sent coded signals by shifting the positions of specialized panels. Although nothing in the United States matched the complexity of the French system, smaller networks of optical telegraphs emerged along the Atlantic Coast in the first decade of the 1800s, and others connected New York and Boston to their outlying farming communities in the 1810s.

Optical telegraphs created complex networks of nodes organized through a hub-and-spoke system. That infrastructure proved vital when technicians created ways to send signals electronically. In 1837, an American portrait artist named Samuel Morse became the first American to patent such a machine. Morse's telegraph machine sent electromagnetic pulses through a cable and registered those pulses by clicking a mechanical device at the other end of the line. Morse took credit as the "inventor" of the telegraph, although controversy emerged over its true provenance. Nonetheless, Morse's patent guaranteed him the right to develop and profit from the invention, and within a few years, he and some partners developed a code to convert the clicks into letters and numbers, based on their pattern and duration—the famous Morse Code. In 1844, they completed a forty-mile demonstration line between Baltimore and Washington, funded with a $30,000 grant from the U.S. Congress, a profound demonstration of the power of this new technology.

Morse and his partners struggled to plan or launch a large-scale network. Rather than pay the up-front costs of laying cable over tremendous distances, they opted to license the machine to private businesses. As a result, the nation's telegraph network expanded a piece at a time, rather than as an integrated, planned system. Over time, those private actors created a continental telegraph network. By the 1850s, tens of thousands of miles of telegraph cable had been laid. And by the start of the Civil War in 1861, those cables stretched as far as California, enabling intercontinental communication at nearly light speed.

Although telecommunications would revolutionize interpersonal communication among citizens (as it continues to do today), in its early years, commercial businesses and governments were the telegraph's primary users. Newspaper publishers, for example, quickly realized the value of rapid information. When the United States invaded Mexico in 1846, media outlets established a sophisticated network that employed horseback, steamship, railroads, and the fledgling telegraph system to bring reports back home at record speeds—only a few days.[15]

But the telegraph's most significant influence on business was in the burgeoning railroad industry. Electronic communications allowed railroad managers to coordinate schedules, adjust prices to changing circumstances, and, critically, decrease collisions. That relationship between railroads and telegraphs was mutually reinforcing. To create their networks, telegraph operators had to string cables across vast, sparsely populated areas. By erecting poles alongside railroad tracks, telegraph companies made all parts of their network accessible, so they could perform maintenance and protect against the elements and sabotage. Thus, as railroads spread across the continent in the mid-19th century, the electronic telegraph went with them.[16]

Corporations Arise

Industrialization and new forms of transportation and communication changed the environment for doing business in the United States in the years leading up to the Civil War. In response, businesspeople began to adopt new ways of organizing their operations. The most important development was the rise of general incorporation laws and the consequent spread of the *corporate legal form*.

Before the 1850s, most American companies organized either as sole-proprietorships or as partnerships among a small number of people. Under the traditional system, those owners took on all the risks associated with the company and were accountable for all debts if the venture failed. They also shared in all the company's successes. This system encouraged a conservative approach and provided few incentives for businesspeople to assume large risks.

These traditional partnerships were by far the most common way of organizing a business enterprise, but they were not the only one. Joint-stock companies had developed hundreds of years earlier, based on the model of *incorporation*. The key to incorporation was the charter, the document by which the government (originally the king or queen, later an elected legislature) recognized that a group of people constituted a distinct entity that had its own legal existence. In fact, the word "incorporate" has its root in the Latin word for "body," reflecting the notion that a corporate charter created a body—or a legal person—where none had existed before. Unlike a traditional partnership, which dissolved upon the death of one partner, a corporation had a life independent from its owners.

Yet before 1800, corporate charters were far from common, and almost no business enterprises were incorporated. Because charters had to be granted by the sovereign—the king or Parliament in colonial times; the state or federal legislature after independence—the few corporations extant were almost exclusively public operations, such as turnpikes, bridges, churches, and cities, including New York. During the entire 18th century, charters were issued to only 335 businesses—and much more than half of those were issued in the last four years of the century.

During the first half of the 19th century, however, more private businesses organized through legal incorporation. As they expanded into increasingly capital-intensive operations—first in textile factories and iron mills, and later into the expensive railroad industry and the banks that financed it—American business owners recognized that their ability to grow depended on their ability to attract investors. Becoming a corporation provided a number of advantages.

One advantage to incorporation was having an independent legal existence. Unlike today, when incorporation is granted in perpetuity, most antebellum corporate charters were limited in time, set to expire after a fixed period of ten, twenty, or thirty years. Nonetheless, having a distinct legal existence separate from their owners made corporations appear more stable and predictable, and made them more attractive to investors.

Another legal innovation that helped attract investment was borrowed from the joint-stock company model: establishing ownership through stock certificates. Investors purchased shares—actual pieces of paper, the distant ancestors of today's electronic portfolios—which entitled them to an ownership stake in the corporation. If a shareholder died, stock certificates transferred along with other property to the heirs. Just as important, the value of that stock fluctuated with the fortunes of the company, and shareholders could buy or sell stocks on exchanges.

In addition, the increased use of *limited liability* clauses in corporate charters made the concept more appealing to 19th-century business owners. Under a traditional arrangement, a group of partners might borrow money to finance a business venture, but if they suffered a catastrophic loss—such as the sinking of a merchant vessel—they were all individually responsible for the debts their partnership had created. A limited liability clause in a corporate charter changed that dynamic by guaranteeing that no individual investors could be held responsible for debts that exceeded the amount of their original investment. By the 1830s, limited liability had become a dominant feature of corporate charters.

Thus, as industrial manufacturing spread and the revolutions in communication and transportation created a far more interconnected national market for manufactured goods, state legislatures faced growing numbers of requests for special charters. Many members of the political class saw corporate charters as the key to promoting domestic industry by enabling risk taking and pooling capital. Yet the process was cumbersome, since charters had to be considered individually and granted by specific acts of legislatures. The paperwork alone was overwhelming. Slowly, states turned to a new model known as *general incorporation*, granting corporate charters administratively, rather than legislatively.

In 1811, New York became the first state to enact such a law for manufacturing firms. In 1837, Connecticut became the first state to allow general incorporation for *any* kind of business. And by 1870, every state had some type of general incorporation law on the books. Just as important, the privileges of incorporation that we know today—including permanent life and limited liability—had become dominant features of the law. As the nation recovered from the Civil War, it inherited a system of corporate law that positioned the business community to embark on a period of massive and permanent growth.[17]

A Market Revolution

Within the space of only a few generations, industrial manufacturing wrought unimaginable changes on American economic, social, and political life. A nation of farmers increasingly became a country of locomotives, telegraphs, and factories. Traditional forms of business organization and labor relations persisted, but a new industrial age had dawned. More and more Americans lived in cities, particularly in the North, and many now worked for wages. Everyday life—from the clothes on one's back to newspaper accounts of far-off battles—had grown more interconnected. Businesses had become more specialized, farms more profitable, and slavery more entrenched. By the time that toxic practice cleaved the nation in two in 1860, new opportunities for American businesspeople abounded.

Yet the "Market Revolution" that transformed how Americans interacted with each other, how they labored, and how they organized entrepreneurial activities presented no easy path. Ever larger and more socially intrusive business ventures—from textile factories to railroads to banks—faced deep resistance and long-standing fears about the tyrannical tendencies of concentrated power.

4

THE POLITICS OF BUSINESS IN THE EARLY REPUBLIC

Thomas Jefferson wrote his own epitaph. As he intended, the words on his tombstone declare three accomplishments that he believed defined his worldly contributions: author of the Declaration of Independence, author of the statute of Virginia for religious freedom, and founder of the University of Virginia. Historians have long noted the false modesty that precluded Jefferson from including any mention of his presidency (the nation's third), his vice presidency (the nation's second), or his term as secretary of state (the nation's first). His grave at his Monticello plantation is also silent on his role in negotiating the Louisiana Purchase, which doubled the geographical expanse of the United States, as well as on any of his contributions to science, or his conflicted defense of slavery.

From the perspective of business history, the most glaring oversight in that simplified list is Jefferson's political and economic vision for the nation, which historians call "agrarian democracy." As early as the 1780s, Jefferson argued that self-sufficient farmers represented a bulwark against tyranny and warned that a society that moved away from agriculture and toward industry risked corruption. Although many of his specific stances shifted throughout his long life, his general suspicion of banks, manufacturing, and concentrated economic power became central to the political philosophy that would come to bear his name: "Jeffersonian Republicanism." As the American economy expanded in the half-century preceding the Civil War, conflicts between Jefferson's supporters and opponents became pivotal.

During the presidency of George Washington in the 1790s, debates over industrial progress, trade, and economic policy—which would rage until the Civil War—began to crystallize. On one side stood Alexander Hamilton, who, from his position at the Treasury Department, pushed for a strong central banking system and protective tariffs to bolster domestic manufacturing. As he earnestly argued to Congress in 1791, "It is in the interest of nations to diversify the industrious pursuits of the individuals who compose them." Although the Washington administration was officially nonpartisan (and the president wished to give the impression of remaining above the fray of party politics), Hamilton emerged as a powerful spokesman for a faction that came to be known as the Federalist Party.[1]

While Hamilton argued that the federal government should play a vigorous and active role promoting business, Jefferson—also a member of Washington's cabinet—stressed the country's natural resources and agricultural output. A landowning Virginian, Jefferson believed that self-reliant and small-scale family farms, not impersonal factories (or, ironically, large slave-labor plantations like his), provided a bulwark against tyranny and ensured the future of self-governance. In Jefferson's mind, the drudgery of manufacturing work and dependence on daily wages stripped away personal independence. In his characteristically exaggerated way, Jefferson opined: "While we have land to labour then, let us never wish to see our citizens occupied at a work-bench."[2] Such faith in a virtuous nation of independent free farmers clashed both with the slave system that Jefferson (ironically) profited from, as well as the mixed industrial economy that Hamilton envisioned.

To be sure, this "Hamilton-Jefferson Debate" was far more complicated than quick sound bites would suggest. Jefferson, in truth, was no more "antiworkshop" than Hamilton was "antifarmer." Nonetheless, their different points of emphasis and divergent conceptions of the type of economy the United States should pursue characterized the tumultuous politics of business in the first half of the 19th century. Between the 1780s and the 1810s, that schism helped define the first system of political parties, in which Hamilton's Federalists, including President John Adams (1797–1801), distinguished themselves ideologically from Jeffersonian Republicans. (Also called Democratic-Republicans, this party is not related to today's Republican Party, which was formed in the 1850s.) In 1800, the center of gravity of national politics began to shift when Jefferson defeated Adams for the presidency. In the years to come, the Jeffersonian Republicans completed the rout of the Federalists at nearly all levels—by the War of 1812, the Federalist Party barely clung on in remote and far-flung corners of state and local politics, but had largely disappeared as a national force.[3]

Yet the central division between Jeffersonian Republicans and Hamiltonian Federalists persisted until the Civil War, particularly over protecting domestic industry with high tariffs versus promoting agricultural exports through free trade. And in a larger sense, the fundamental disagreement lasted much longer, even to the present. How should government promote enterprise, and how should it choose among different sectors? Does the government serve the public best by protecting American businesses, or by leaving them on their own? Variations on these themes have been central to American politics throughout the nation's history.

Jeffersonianism in Practice

Thomas Jefferson and his political supporters interpreted their over-whelming electoral victories in 1800 as a revolution in national poli-tics. After twelve years of Federalist rule, the party that represented "the people" appeared to have triumphed. However, in many ways, the partisan split was more evident in ideology and rhetoric than in practical policy.

Once in power, Jeffersonians came to recognize some of the advan-tages that a robust federal government could provide. Under Jefferson himself and his successor James Madison (also a Virginian slave- and landowner), the federal government directed vital resources into in-ternal infrastructure, particularly roads and canals. That commitment came from pressure by a Swiss immigrant named Albert Gallatin, who served as secretary of the Treasury under both presidents between 1801 and 1814 (the longest tenure of anyone in that position). In 1808, the final year of Jefferson's term in office, Secretary Gallatin delivered a grandiose *Report on Roads, Canals, Harbors, and Rivers* to the U.S. Senate, proposing a ten-year, $20 million federal project to expand infrastructure. (For comparison, the entire federal budget for 1808 was $10 million; Gallatin wanted to spend a fifth of that on internal improvements.) A spectacular outlay of public funds, he claimed, was crucial to create a national economy. Although Gallatin failed to secure all of the funding he sought, his report set a prece-dent—particularly among Jeffersonian Republicans—for using the federal government to promote commercial expansion.[4]

The push to improve conditions for transporting goods within the country took on a new urgency when the physical size of the country doubled with the Louisiana Purchase of 1803. That year, President Jefferson negotiated the sale of more than 800,000 square miles in the middle of the North American continent from Napoleon Bonaparte of France (whose authority to sell it came from an earlier treaty with

Spain, with little regard to the hundreds of thousands of Indians who lived there). Jefferson was primarily motivated by national security concerns, particularly access to the port of New Orleans; even so, continental expansion would have profound effects on business. The federal government devoted vital resources to removing Indians and fighting off Spanish settlers in the territory, as well as sending surveyors to divide the land into parcels that could be sold off to white American farmers.[5]

The War of 1812 with Britain provided further incentive for the ruling Jeffersonian Republicans to reconsider their stance on promoting economic development, particularly manufacturing. Led by Madison and Republicans in Congress, the United States declared war to protect American trade with continental Europe from interference by the British navy, which was battling Napoleon's French empire. Republicans in the West and South favored war, both because they wanted to promote exports to Europe and because they hoped to reduce British support for Indians in the interior of the country, who were warring against invasive American farmers. Shipping interests in New England opposed the war, reflecting the old Hamiltonian logic that commercial ties with industrial Britain were essential to America's economic vitality.[6]

Despite a few victories in the two-year war, the United States also suffered important losses, particularly an ill-fated effort to invade lower Canada and the British sack of Washington, D.C., in 1814. The peace treaty that ended the fighting changed little in terms of territorial boundaries between the two nations, but the experience convinced many Republicans that America's general lack of manufacturing capacity was a major disadvantage. When the war (and the embargo that preceded it) hampered transatlantic trade, wealthy merchants, such as Francis Cabot Lowell and others among the Boston Associates, had redirected their business ventures toward domestic textile production. Now, as trade resumed, those young manufacturers faced renewed threats from larger and more sophisticated British factories. In response, Republicans in 1816 at last adopted Alexander Hamilton's suggestion from 1791 to promote nascent domestic manufacturing through a protective tariff. That tariff raised the prices American consumers paid for foreign-made goods in comparison to their American-made competitors, without returning any additional profit to the British manufacturers. In addition to protecting budding northern factories, the tariff also raised revenue that the federal government could spend on internal improvements of the type Treasury Secretary Gallatin promoted.[7]

After the War of 1812, many Jeffersonian Republicans came to embrace aspects of the old Hamiltonian position. With the demise of the Federalist Party as a political force, a newly nationalistic Democratic-Republican Party consolidated support. Northern elites, many of whom were transitioning from shipping toward manufacturing, increasingly backed protective tariffs and the party of Jefferson and Madison. At the same time, the party retained its traditional base among southern agrarians, both large-scale slave-owners and independent farmers. This system of economic alliances sparked a ten-year period of consensus and muted partisan feuding, known as the "Era of Good Feelings."

During that decade, from 1815 to 1824, economic debates centered on a policy proposal known as the "American System," most forcefully pushed by Kentucky senator Henry Clay. While running for president in 1824, Clay channeled Alexander Hamilton (dead since 1804) by declaring that what the country needed most was "a market for the sale and exchange of the surplus of [its] produce." To create and foster that market, he continued, required robust policies by the federal government. In addition to protective tariffs, Clay pushed the government to charge private investors high prices for land in the new western territories, raising funds to pay for better national roads and canals. He also called for a robust and active banking system. These three pillars—tariffs, internal improvements, and a national bank—formed the essence of the American System.

But the brief "Era of Good Feelings" did not survive the bitter four-way presidential election of 1824, after which national politics grew divided. Tennessee war hero Andrew Jackson won the most electoral votes, but no one claimed a majority, and the House of Representatives—prodded in part by Henry Clay, who saw his dreams of high office squashed—voted for John Quincy Adams, son of the former Federalist president. In the wake of that election, a political realignment known as the Second Party System emerged, splitting Jeffersonian Republicans into two factions that clung to different economic visions. Chief among their differences were the divisive issues of the tariff and the national banking system.[8]

The Bank War

During the first half of the 19th century, rapid economic growth sparked a dramatic clash among competing interests in the political arena. In the 1820s and 1830s, the question of national monetary policy—how to regulate currency and the supply of credit, and what role financial institutions should play in those processes—aroused fierce passions. The resolution of that debate, albeit a temporary and imperfect one, came with the defeat of Hamilton's dream for a national bank in 1832. In the process, the showdown over the bank spawned the formation of an entrenched two-party system, the descendant of which still dominates American politics today.

The story of the "Bank Wars," which loomed over the presidency of Andrew Jackson between 1829 and 1837, began way back in 1791. That year, in response to Hamilton's advice in his *Report on Public Finance*, Congress granted a federal charter to the Bank of the United States.

The Bank, in a grand marble edifice located in Philadelphia, was a semiprivate corporation that derived its legal existence from a specific grant of authority from the federal government. Its charter prescribed the details of its operations, such as the number of branches and even the identity of some of its directors. Functionally, the Bank provided a location for the U.S. Treasury to store money it collected through import tariffs, other taxes, or land sales. In addition, its network of regional branches created a mechanism for merchants to transfer money easily and safely from one place to another. Finally, the Bank helped stabilize the value of the national currency by printing federal bank notes guaranteed by gold and silver deposits. At a time when state-chartered banks routinely issued their own bank notes, currency values fluctuated from region to region, since merchants and bankers distrusted and discounted the face value of bank notes from faraway banks. Promissory notes from the Bank of the United States could be redeemed in silver or gold coin at any Bank branch, creating something close to a national currency.[9]

From the beginning, the Bank typified Hamilton's Federalist vision. Most Americans did not use currency on a regular basis, so most of the Bank's day-to-day operations primarily served the interests of elite merchants. In addition, the Bank's corporate structure reinforced the privileged place of the wealthy: The federal government itself owned 20 percent of the corporate stock, while the other 80 percent was sold to wealthy Americans. Yet this structure was exactly as Hamilton intended. By catering to elite merchants, the Bank wrapped up their financial interests in federal institutions and thus guaranteed that they would continue to lend political, moral, and economic support to the Constitution and its government.

Congress chartered the Bank of the United States for twenty years, after which time that charter would have to be renewed. Yet as we have seen, the political tide changed between 1791 and 1811. Jeffersonian Republicans denounced the Bank as a dangerous concentration of economic power among a few wealthy bankers. What's more, the

Bank disproportionately served the interests of the *northern* mercantile elite, not the *southern* plantation-owning elite, whose wealth was generally illiquid and tied up in land and slaves. With the decline of Federalist political power and the ascent of Jeffersonian Republicans, the Bank was doomed. Congress failed to renew its charter, which expired in 1811.

The War of 1812, however, created a banking disaster that persuaded many Jeffersonian Republicans to put their ideological concerns aside. In the absence of a national bank, the federal government shifted its deposits to a large network of state-chartered banks. When war with Britain came, the Treasury increasingly borrowed from those state banks, which printed more and more bank notes to satisfy the demand for loans. (A bank note, what we consider "cash," is really a debt borrowed from a bank, to be repaid later.) With more currency in circulation, the value of that currency declined. The resulting price inflation destabilized the economy and rendered interstate or international business transactions perilous.

The economy of the early republic depended on networks of credit and debt. As products moved along the distribution chain—from the field to the shipyard, from the warehouse to the mill, and then back again—various middlemen relied on bank notes and other forms of credit to make transactions. From planters to wholesalers to mill owners, people throughout the chain of commerce came to doubt whether those debts would be repaid, or if a note they received on Monday would still have value on Tuesday. That uncertainty compounded the country's economic woes. Finally, the British attack on Washington, D.C., in 1814 sparked a financial panic. Americans rushed to redeem bank notes for gold or silver, draining the banks' supplies. Many banks stopped extending credit altogether, and business dried up.

In 1816, a group of prominent businessmen lobbied the Republican majority in Congress to charter a Second Bank of the United

States. Their hope was to regulate the behavior of smaller state banks by controlling the quantity of bank notes in circulation. Like its predecessor, this new, larger national Bank, which opened in 1817, operated mostly independently of the federal government or the democratic processes. Of its twenty-five directors, only five were government appointees.

Mismanagement by these directors allowed state banks to extend too much credit, particularly to rural, western areas, in 1817 and 1818. When the financial panic of 1819 erupted, the national bank tried to correct this imbalance by calling in its debts, worsening the ensuing economic depression. The consequences in rural areas were especially harsh and the Second Bank repossessed huge tracts of mortgaged land in western cities like Cincinnati. Although the Bank's directors regulated credit more skillfully thereafter, painful memories of 1819 lingered. Many people in the countryside, as well as working-class residents in cities, nursed a fearful grudge against the new Bank.

In the 1820s, popular opposition to the Bank grew ever stronger among cash-strapped farmers, especially in the South and West, aggravating the classic ideological breach between Hamiltonians and Jeffersonians. Manufacturers and financiers, mostly in the North, lauded the Bank for facilitating commerce by creating a stable business environment. Many agrarians, however, saw it as a concentration of power in the hands of an unaccountable elite. With approximately $35 million in outstanding stock, the Bank was easily the largest business enterprise in the country. Most citizens could scarcely understand the Bank's role regulating credit and the overall supply of money, but farmers who needed to borrow money from local banks understood that this far-distant institution held huge power to dictate the terms of their loans. In addition, many workers in burgeoning northern factory communities and others who earned wages paid in paper money, such as self-employed artisans, blamed the Bank for currency inflation and economic downturns.[10]

Political clashes over the Bank dominated national politics in the 1820s and early 1830s, giving rise to an episode often called the "Bank War."[11] On one side, Nicholas Biddle, a lawyer from Pennsylvania who became president of the Bank in 1823, attracted support from the northern financial community and the budding industrialists who depended on loans from wealthy bankers. On the other emerged populist politician Andrew Jackson, a lawyer from North Carolina who moved to the Tennessee frontier before gaining national fame as a military hero in the War of 1812. Preaching the virtues of rural America and the evils of concentrated power—epitomized by the Bank—Jackson campaigned as an outsider and won the presidency in 1828.

Yet the debate over the Bank was not as clear-cut as this account might suggest. In addition to populist agrarian and working-class fears about concentrated power, some members of the northern business community came to distrust the institution as well. Powerful New York–based financiers objected to Biddle's conservative, cautious approach to monetary policy, which limited how much credit banks could extend. Generally younger than Biddle's supporters, such investors knew that more vigorous lending by smaller banks—many of which they held stock in—could mean greater profits. Easy credit could also benefit entrepreneurial industrialists who wanted to expand operations. As a result, these anti-Biddle New Yorkers, as well as owners of state-chartered banks across the country, joined up with agrarians and urban workers in the Jacksonian coalition.[12]

Jackson's election raised the prospect that Bank opponents could finally succeed in destroying the institution. As with the first Bank, Congress had granted the second one a twenty-year corporate charter, which would expire in 1836 unless Congress passed a bill to issue a new charter. Despite Jackson's promise to veto a recharter bill, pro-Bank politicians pushed one through Congress in 1832, hoping that the president's intransigence would backfire and cost him votes and support. Yea votes in Congress came from states with conservative banking traditions in the Biddle mold—including Massachusetts, Pennsylvania, and Connecticut—as well as western states where businesspeople feared the shaky, unstable system of state banks. But southern states aligned against the recharter plan, as did New York's legislators, who represented the large and fast-growing banking community of lower Manhattan.

Although the recharter bill passed both houses of Congress, Jackson vetoed it in the summer of 1832. "It is to be regretted that the rich and powerful too often bend the acts of government to their selfish purposes," he opined in his veto message.[13] The president then won an overwhelming re-election that fall (beating Henry Clay 54 percent to 37 percent in the popular vote and winning sixteen of twenty-two states), and the Bank's supporters lost all hope of redrafting a charter. In 1836, its charter expired and it became a private bank, ultimately going out of business.

The destruction of the Second Bank of the United States had tremendous consequences for American politics and business development. Politically, the Bank War—along with debates over the tariff—ended the "Era of Good Feelings." Jackson's coalition, heirs to the Jeffersonian Republican tradition, renamed themselves as Democrats during the fight. Beginning in 1833, their opponents identified as Whigs, taking the name of the British party that had historically challenged the authority of the king. (The "king," to these American Whigs, was Jackson himself.) America's second party system was born.

The end of the Bank War inaugurated an era of monetary decentralization during which only state legislatures regulated banking. Individual businesspeople launched private banks and issued paper bank notes as currency, the value of which fluctuated. Private New York–based banks grew larger and more powerful, and could soon underwrite investments in new business ventures, particularly railroad construction. Yet these liberal banking policies came at the cost of stability. A tremendous financial crisis rocked the nation in 1837, soon after the Bank of the United States ceased operations, and another hit in 1857. And not until the Civil War did the federal government create a national banking system that could regulate credit and help stabilize the value of paper currency.[14]

The Tariff, the Nullification Crisis, and the Rise of Sectional Conflict

Even as the Bank War raged, the long-standing issue of protective tariffs continued to drive a wedge between northern manufacturers and southern farmers. Agrarians in the South had backed the Tariff of 1816, but their support proved fleeting. In 1824 and 1828, when Congress raised protective tariffs even higher, they returned to their traditional opposition. The struggle over tariffs would lead to a political and military standoff known as the Nullification Crisis. Regional and sectional divisions hardened, foreshadowing the divisions that would lead to the Civil War.

The battle over tariffs reached its peak in the same years as the Bank War. In 1828, President Adams—a Massachusetts native supported by northern industrialists who had little sympathy for the slave-owning South—signed a bill that raised tariffs to their highest point in American history. High tariffs, by design, made foreign-made goods more expensive for American consumers. Northerners were more willing to accept higher prices to protect their industries, but southerners, who had few factories, felt no such inclination. In addition, southerners worried that high American tariffs would prompt their trade partners, especially Britain, to retaliate with tariffs of their own, raising the cost of American-grown products such as cotton for British manufacturers and depressing prices for southern planters.

Outraged over the obvious threat to southern business (not to mention the apparent lack of northern sympathy), southerners blasted what they called Adams's "Tariff of Abominations." Led by

South Carolina planter John C. Calhoun—who served as vice president under Adams and, starting in 1829, Jackson—some southern politicians articulated a constitutional argument known as "nullification." By willingly signing on to a national Constitution that divided power between the states and the federal government, Calhoun argued, individual states such as South Carolina retained the right to "nullify"—or fail to respect—any federal law that its citizens rejected, particularly the 1828 tariff. Since tariffs were collected at ports, such as Charleston, their enactment depended on the willing compliance of local populations. If South Carolinians refused to collect the tariff, the federal government had limited ability to compel them.

Hoping to mollify southern planters, Congress passed, and President Jackson signed, a law to lower tariff rates in the summer of 1832. Enraged politicians in South Carolina still insisted that the rates were too high. In the fall of 1832, South Carolina's legislature passed a law nullifying the federal tariff. In response, a vengeful Andrew Jackson asked Congress for the right to use military force to collect tariffs in that state. Calhoun resigned the vice presidency and declared that any use of force by Jackson would give South Carolina a just cause to declare its independence from the United States.[15]

For a few months, the possibility of armed conflict appeared real. Only skillful diplomacy defused the crisis. Congress passed a compromise tariff that lowered rates, on the condition that South Carolina repeal its nullification statute. Yet the battle lines that formed over the Nullification Crisis, as well as the constitutional and legal theories about the relationship between the federal government and the states, established a powerful precedent.

A generation later, southern politicians again feared a northern assault on their economic livelihood and invoked Calhoun's theories of states' rights to justify extreme action. In the fall of 1860, a lawyer from Illinois named Abraham Lincoln was elected president. The head of the recently formed Republican Party, a coalition of farmers from nonslave states as well as northern industrial and banking interests, Lincoln opposed the expansion of slavery. For the slave-owning elite in the South, Lincoln's election threatened the future of slavery. Again led by South Carolina, eleven states eventually declared independence from the United States in the winter of 1860 and 1861, precipitating a disastrous Civil War.

Why did southern states secede in 1860 and 1861 over the expansion of slavery, but not in 1832 over the tariff? The history of business provides two interrelated answers. First, the economic threat posed by higher tariffs in the 1830s was far lower than the (perceived) threat to slavery in 1860. Second, despite the vitriol of South Carolina's politicians, support for secession in 1832 was tepid. Many southern politicians worried that the tariff debate signaled a broader decline of their political influence that left them vulnerable to the growing strength of northern abolitionism, but they still retained significant control over national politics. Moreover, most southerners did not believe their economy was strong enough to survive without the industrializing North. Both situations had changed by 1860, however. Lincoln's election confirmed that proslavery politicians were outnumbered, and the dramatic rise of the cotton economy in the 1840s and 1850s convinced the planter class of their economic infallibility. Secession and war came when a critical mass of white southerners—both slave-owners and the non-slave-owning majority—concluded both that the threat to their way of life justified secession *and* that they had the ability to pull it off.

Business and the Civil War

The politics of business in the early republic came to a devastating climax in the American Civil War, which raged from 1861 to 1865, at the cost of more than six hundred thousand American lives. After four years of bloodshed, the Civil War ended in defeat for the South and the reunification of the country. Through the complete destruction of the slave South, the liberation of millions of enslaved people, and the partisan realignment it engendered in national politics, the Civil War changed the development of American industry. In addition to losing their political power and the tremendous wealth held in slaves, southern planters lost their dominant place atop the global cotton market, as cotton growers in East Africa, India, and the Middle East filled the void. After decades of single-minded focus on large-scale commercial agriculture, the southern economy would take decades to regain economic viability.[16]

Yet the Civil War also had dramatic consequences for business in the North. The disruption of the cotton trade hurt many members of the merchant class, but—as during the Embargo of 1807—it provided opportunities for businesspeople to shift the focus of their operations. Capitalists who redirected their resources toward industrial pursuits, especially by investing in the stock of railroad and mining companies, found new avenues for profit.[17] Northern and midwestern farmers also benefited from Republican policies, particularly the 1862 Homestead Act, which sold off government land in the West at low prices to white Americans willing to cultivate it. Congress also established a system of national, federally chartered banks that helped stabilize currency after the war, to the benefit of the financial class.

In the end, the Civil War realigned the business world in the United States. The old order gave way to a new political economy, run by Republicans and rooted in the interests of northern and midwestern farmers, manufacturers, and other industrialists, bolstered by a strong and growing federal government.[18] The age-old debate between Hamilton and Jefferson appeared to be settled in Hamilton's favor. Yet American history never escaped the power of the

Jeffersonian vision, either in its politics or in its national mythology. Even as industrial manufacturing, performed at ever-larger and more profitable firms, came to dominate, popular fears of concentrated power and an overwhelming faith in the virtue of rugged independence continued to shape the destiny of American business.

5

BUSINESS GETS BIG

I n the spring of 1980, a network of political activists led by consumer advocate Ralph Nader organized a nationwide event called "Big Business Day" to protest the influence of large corporations on American life. One public interest group in California "celebrated" the day by hosting a mock awards ceremony at the Los Angeles Press Club—the "Cornelius Vanderbilt 'Public Be Damned' Bad Business Awards." The grand prize for "all around worst corporation" went to the Standard Oil Company of California, which received a live, squealing pig as a symbol of its greed. The main charge was extorting high prices from consumers at the gas pumps while boasting record profits in the middle of the late-1970s energy crisis. Naturally, no one from Standard Oil claimed the prize.[1]

This minor episode from 1980 exemplifies the powerful grip that "Big Business" has on the American popular and political imagination. For many people, like the protesters with the pig, those words connote corruption and greed, as well as the exploitation of workers, consumers, and the environment. For others, large corporations represent more positive developments—economic growth, technological innovation, and good jobs, not to mention the philanthropy of the business giants. Debates over concentrated wealth and corporate power have been a constant presence in American history. The protesters in 1980 echoed many of the same charges that Jacksonian Democrats made about the Bank of the United States, or that protesters in the Occupy Wall Street movement made in 2011.

It was no coincidence that the "award" for Bad Business was named after Cornelius Vanderbilt, who amassed one of the largest fortunes in American history in the mid-19th century as a pioneer in the railroad industry. The protesters misquoted him, however. The phrase "the public be damned" came from Cornelius's son William, who took over the business upon his father's death, becoming, in all likelihood, the single wealthiest person in the world. In 1882, a New York–based reporter claimed the younger Vanderbilt uttered those words after being asked about the "public benefit" of his company. A witness to that interview told a different story: A pushy reporter interrupted Vanderbilt during dinner, claiming "the public" wanted to hear from him. According to that account, Vanderbilt exclaimed, "the public be damned," as if to say: "I don't care about your reading public right now; I'm eating."[2]

Whether or not William Vanderbilt wanted the American public to go to hell, many Americans in the 1880s were prepared to believe that he did. An epic public relations disaster unfolded, and the image of the uncaring "big business" executive became further cemented in popular culture.[3]

In addition to recalling Vanderbilt and his poor public relations, the Bad Business Award ceremony in 1980 also recalled long-standing animosity toward the petroleum industry in particular through its decision to honor Standard Oil of California. That company, known today as Chevron, was a descendant of the original Standard Oil Company—the oil-refining giant founded by John D. Rockefeller in the 1880s and broken up by the United States Supreme Court in 1911. Like the Vanderbilts, Rockefeller became one of the richest people on

Earth and left a profound and conflicted legacy. The same newspaper cartoonists who portrayed Cornelius Vanderbilt standing astride the railroad industry like a colossus also helped craft a public image of Standard Oil as a nefarious octopus, its corrupt tentacles strangling the life out of democracy itself. Modern day complaints about the influence of "Big Oil"—from ExxonMobil to Koch Industries—are no more than an updated version of that 19th-century fixture.

Our modern images of "Big Bad Business" embody the enduring cultural power of the large corporations that emerged to dominate American business in the late 19th century. In the three decades after the Civil War, the United States joined Britain, France, and Germany as a world-class industrial power, and it did so through the creation of a specific type of business enterprise: the large-scale, integrated, heavily capitalized corporation.

Compare the big businesses of the late 1800s to what came before. Even the largest textile mills of the 1840s or 1850s provided jobs for fewer than a thousand workers. Their total market value, or capitalization, was perhaps a million dollars. Yet in the late 19th century, manufacturing left that traditional structure behind. Starting with railroads and soon spreading to fields such as oil and steel, corporations grew enormous in scale and scope. In 1901, a series of mergers created the U.S. Steel Corporation with a market value of $1 *billion*, and a workforce in excess of one hundred thousand people.[4]

Today, we take the existence of massive corporations for granted. For Americans in the generation after the Civil War, by comparison, they represented something unprecedented in human history. Within a relatively short period of time, the arrival of big corporations reshaped American business. Single firms operated across multiple states, controlling entire distribution networks, and forged a vast, interconnected national market. From the production of raw materials to transportation, warehousing, refining, and ultimately consumption, big business was everywhere.

Railroads: The First Big Businesses

In early October 1841, two people died and seventeen were injured when two passenger trains owned by the Western Railroad Company collided head-on along a single railroad track that connected Worcester, Massachusetts, and Albany, New York. This event was certainly not the first fatal rail accident in the United States, but it revealed a major structural problem in the railroad industry, one that would only worsen in the years ahead. The Western crash occurred along the 150-mile stretch of track that connected central Massachusetts and the Hudson River, which only the year before had become the country's first "intersectional" rail line—that is, it was built in multiple sections. Each day, the Western sent three trains in each direction along the eight-hour route, at speeds that averaged twenty miles per hour and with no system of signals or other means to communicate between trains coming at each other from opposite directions. A devastating accident was unavoidable.

Yet before 1841, railroad companies had not yet devised a way to structure their operations to prevent head-on collisions, rear-ending, and other accidents. The problem, as the directors of the Western admitted when an outraged state legislature called them to task, was that their company stretched its operations over such a great distance that its traditional method of decision-making and responsibility didn't function well. A railroad manager sitting in the head office in central Massachusetts could not make informed decisions about events a hundred miles away, possibly in another state.

So in response to the accident, the Western created a new organizational structure for itself. It divided the railroad line into three sections, each of which had a local manager who reported to a central headquarters in Springfield, Massachusetts, located in the middle of the line.

The structural changes that the Western Railroad made as a result of its fatal accident were repeated and augmented over the coming decades by other railroad companies. By the 1870s, this practice of dividing corporate activities into separate departments and creating a system of hierarchies among managers became the standard means of organizing railroad companies, which had by then grown to sizes unimaginable in the early 1840s. As the eminent business historian Alfred Chandler showed forty years ago (in his 1977 book *The Visible Hand*), this "managerial revolution" actually *allowed* businesses to overcome the limitations on their growth. Once other types of industries copied the railroad model, business could get big.[5]

The story of the rise of Big Business in America, therefore, starts with the railroads. Steam-powered railroads emerged in the late 1820s as part of a broader revolution in transportation that also brought about improved roads, canals, and steam-powered ships on rivers and lakes. Following the precedent set by the Baltimore and Ohio Railroad in 1828, small groups of businesspeople sought out corporate charters for railroad companies from state legislatures. As the market economy expanded, spreading both commercial agriculture (cotton from the South and grains from the Midwest) and factory-produced finished goods, railroad companies expanded. Intersectional lines such as the Western remained unusual in the 1840s, but they grew more prominent thereafter. In the last ten years before the Civil War, the number of miles of railroad track in America increased from ten thousand to thirty thousand, most quickly in newer states such as Illinois and Ohio. By 1860, a traveler could move from any major port on the East Coast, out to Chicago or St. Louis, and then down the Mississippi at speeds that had been unthinkable a generation earlier.[6]

The federal government promoted the growth of the railroads, particularly through a policy of distributing land to private citizens and companies for development. The first "land grant" law, passed in 1850, designated a line—which would become the Illinois Central Railroad—between Mobile, Alabama, and Chicago, Illinois. The law created a series of six-mile-square land parcels along each side of the proposed track; in an alternating, checkerboard pattern, the federal government bequeathed every other parcel to the states of Illinois, Alabama, and Mississippi, and sold the others off to farmers.[7]

This legislation established a pattern for subsequent laws. During the Civil War, the Republican-controlled Congress changed the plan so that the retained spots went to railroad companies, rather than to the states. Those companies—which lobbied for this type of legislation— retained a right-of-way to the entire line as well as a monopoly of access to the farmers who settled along it. By the early 1870s, when the government ceased making land grants to private companies, railroads had received a total of more than 130 million acres.

The war itself also provided a tremendous boon to the railroad. Both the North and the South relied on railroads to move troops to and from the front, boosting demand. But the uneven sectional development of the mid-19th century, exactly as the railroad industry began to grow rapidly, meant that far more miles of track connected the growing urban centers of the North than the agricultural South. What's more, the North's manufacturing, population, and financial advantages put it in a position to devote considerably more money to expanding its railroad networks during the war.

And expand it did. The number of miles of track doubled from 35,000 to more than 70,000 in the eight years that followed the end of the war, most rapidly in the two years of economic boom that preceded the financial panic of 1873. In 1869, the first transcontinental railroad track was completed, creating a formal link—however treacherous and long—between the two oceans. Although economic recession in the mid-1870s slowed the juggernaut somewhat, Americans laid up to 8,000 miles of track per year through the 1880s. By 1890, the country boasted 166,000 miles; by the early 20th century, there would be 254,000 miles of tracks.[8]

The number of miles of track, of course, tells only part of the story of the railroads' massive size. On any number of metrics, these companies dwarfed all other types of business enterprises. They employed thousands of workers and sold tens of millions of dollars' worth of stock. The inherent barriers to entry in the railroad business were massive—the costs of materials and labor needed to construct and maintain tracks, as well as to build and fuel locomotives. By 1860, several large eastern railroad companies were valued at more than $20 million. In the 1870s, the Pennsylvania Railroad had a market capitalization of $78 million.[9]

But that immense size created challenges on an unprecedented scale. The speed of rail travel generated logistical nightmares for scheduling and safety. Moreover, meeting their capital requirements forced railroad companies to rely on outside investors by selling shares and issuing bonds. Many railroad companies, especially in the far West by the 1860s and 1870s, were leveraged to the point where slight fluctuations in their revenue could—and often did—lead to business failure. At every turn, railroad managers confronted high-stakes decisions: How do we schedule trains safely and efficiently? What rates should we charge for different types of cargo, or different types of customers? Where to expand? When to compete?

Railroad Bosses Invent Modern Management

As American railroad companies expanded in the 1850s and then during the Civil War, the most successful among them pioneered new management strategies that allowed them to handle growing complexity. Consider how one railroad superintendent (a manager in charge of day-to-day operations) described the situation to the president of the New York and Erie Railroad Company in 1856: "The magnitude of the business of this road, its numerous and important connections, and the large number of employees engaged in operating it, have led many . . . to the conclusion that a proper regard to details . . . cannot possibly be attained by any plan that contemplates its organization as a whole." Instead of trying to manage the railroad as a singular entity, the superintendent proposed "a more effective organization" that clearly separated the line into divisions and branches "in charge of superintendents, who are held responsible for the successful working of their respective divisions." This separation and clarification of managerial roles would distribute responsibility and accountability more broadly, to assure efficiency and attention to detail—so that "the most satisfactory results will be obtained."[10]

Within a generation, the traditional model of decision-making had given way to a system of bureaucratic hierarchies. No longer did a small number of owners make all strategic decisions unilaterally; rather, they created structures to delegate responsibility and authority in clear, accountable ways. Railroads became the first "Big Business" because they combined the unique scale and scope of their industry *and* the deliberate choices by their leaders to adopt what we now recognize as a modern system of management.

Of course, railroad managers did not invent the concept of bureaucratic organization from scratch. Rather, they self-consciously copied the internal structure of another vital social institution that also coordinated the activities of vast numbers of people over sprawling territories—the military. The managerial hierarchies adopted at companies such as the Pennsylvania Railroad, and copied by their competitors, mirrored the distribution of authority and chain of command found in the 19th-century professionalized armies of Napoleon in Europe and Lee and Grant in the United States.

In the 1850s, 1860s, and 1870s, railroads were the only private businesses to adopt managerial hierarchies. Establishing managerial bureaucracies necessarily meant that top managers relinquished direct control over day-to-day operations. Stockholders, the ultimate owners of the corporations, had to trust the executives they hired, and those men in turn had to rely on the expertise of sales managers, division superintendents, and others on down the line. Before the 1870s or so, few nonrailroads—including industrial manufacturing and mining—grew large enough to justify the trade-off of control for efficiency.

In addition to operational efficiency, the separation of ownership from day-to-day control had a significant long-term social and economic consequence: the creation of a new class of professional managers. Unlike traditional business owners, the wealthy capitalists who hoped to earn favorable returns on their investments, professional railroad managers were salaried employees. Yet they held far more influence than the laborers who laid the tracks or shoveled the coal. Educated and skilled office workers, they would—along with other professionals such as doctors, lawyers, and accountants—form the heart of a new urban middle class in the modern American economy. Keeping their company in business for years to come meant job security, so professional managers tended to promote stable and less risky business practices.

Integrated Industry

Railroads' contribution to the spread of big business was bigger than just management techniques. By the post–Civil War period, railroads had created a transportation infrastructure that united a rapidly growing population in a national market for goods. Within a few decades, manufacturing, mining, and other industrial companies successfully exploited that market and copied the railroads' organizational plans, growing into behemoths themselves. In addition to expanding their individual productive capacities, 19th-century corporations pioneered new methods of combining with other firms, gaining market share and wielding tremendous political and economic power in the process.

Two of the most famous men in American business history, Andrew Carnegie and John Rockefeller, achieved icon status in the late 19th century by pioneering new acquisition and management strategies and successfully exploiting the new national market. By combining the mass *production* of goods and the mass *distribution* of those products, they created the largest industrial operations—Carnegie in steel, Rockefeller in oil—that the world had yet seen.

As an old man, Andrew Carnegie made his name as a philanthropist. But before he became Carnegie the giver, the Scottish immigrant rose from relative poverty to become one of the richest Americans ever. Starting in the telegraph office of the Pennsylvania Railroad in Pittsburgh in 1850, when he was fourteen years old, he rose to become superintendent of the Pittsburgh Division seven years later, a plum managerial position that paid $1,500 per year. His career as an investor began shortly thereafter. In 1856, he borrowed $600 from a personal mentor (who was also his boss) and bought stock in a transport company that soon paid him his first return: a check for $10. By 1863, still a manager at the Penn Railroad, the $45,000 he made per year from his stock investments far outpaced his salary.[11]

Recalling that first dividend check from the transport company, he gushed that "it gave me the first penny of revenue from capital—something I had not worked for with the sweat of my brow. 'Eureka,' I cried. 'Here's the goose that lays the golden eggs.'" For Carnegie, capitalism—the system where money earns money through profitable investment—was almost magical.[12]

Carnegie's near mystical reverence for the returns on capital guided his business operations and his contribution to the expansion of the steel industry. In 1865, he quit the Penn Railroad to handle his investments full-time, but in 1872 he liquidated all his assets and started building steel mills in western Pennsylvania. To keep all managerial authority to himself, he declined to sell stock, but instead raised funds from a handful of partners, supplemented with his own wealth. As a former railroad man, Carnegie replicated the Penn's commitment to high volume, low-cost production, and he distinguished himself by being fastidious about cutting costs wherever possible. He ordered detailed accounting systems of every department in his factories and negotiated for the raw materials he needed to feed his blast furnaces. And famously, he ruthlessly suppressed a labor strike at his Homestead Steel Works in 1892 to keep wage rates low and profits high.[13]

But there were limits to Carnegie's ability to control his costs, and that fed his desire to expand operations through the strategy of *vertical integration*. In particular, Carnegie was vexed that raw material and transportation costs fluctuated throughout the year, and that he was sometimes unable to purchase what his factories needed. In response, he expanded beyond producing steel and into other, related lines of business up and down the supply chain (hence "vertical" integration). Increasingly, he purchased the mining companies that unearthed the iron, as well as transportation companies and factories that transformed raw steel into finished deliverable products (such as rail tracks and beams for buildings in the growing cities). In addition, he financed all this expansion through his own profits, cutting out bankers. By the 1890s, the integrated Carnegie Steel Company produced more pig iron than all of Great Britain.

Like Andrew Carnegie, Rockefeller did not come from inherited wealth. (Carnegie emigrated from Scotland as a boy; Rockefeller grew up in rural New York state.) However, also like Carnegie, he was white, English-speaking, and male—historically the three greatest determinants of upward mobility in America.[14] Rockefeller entered the business world as a teenaged bookkeeper, and in 1859 founded an agricultural wholesale company at the age of twenty. In 1867, he and a handful of partners launched an oil refinery in Cleveland, just as the commercial petroleum industry was beginning to grow. Their capital-intensive refinery converted raw oil into usable forms such as kerosene, which factories and homes used increasingly instead of whale oil for heat and light, as well as by-products of petroleum such as tar for paving, paraffin for candles, and grease for machines. In search of greater capital to pay for expansions of the refinery, they incorporated as the Standard Oil Company in 1870.

Like Carnegie, Rockefeller developed an intense focus on cost-cutting and efficiency. In the competitive oil industry, that fixation on lowering costs allowed him to reduce prices and expand sales. But the intense competition also set off ruthless price wars—great for oil consumers, but bad for the producers. Rockefeller saw price wars as a disastrous waste of potential profits. He reasoned that if oil producers worked collaboratively rather than competitively, they could keep prices (and profits) higher.[15]

In that spirit, Rockefeller pursued a vast strategy of *horizontal integration.* "The day of combination is here to stay," Rockefeller reportedly stated in 1880. "Individualism has gone, never to return."[16] In that spirit, he used his mastery of cheap production to force his competitors into an impossible position, where they either closed up shop or sold out to Standard Oil. More formally, he established a collaborative agreement among approximately forty oil producers in 1882 known as the Standard Oil Trust. A 19th-century "trust" resembled what we would call a holding company today. As a legal entity distinct from any of the member companies, the Standard Oil Trust controlled all the stock of those corporations, centralizing control over prices, distribution schedules, and other business decisions. By the 1890s, more than 90 percent of the oil produced in the United States was refined through Standard Oil.[17]

In addition to its horizontal mergers, Standard Oil also pursued vertical integration, expanding to take over various aspects of the petroleum industry in addition to refining. By the height of its power (before the Supreme Court ordered it broken up in 1911), Standard Oil united in one organization the production and distribution of petroleum, as well as oil drilling and ultimately the retail sale of finished products.

In 1901, Carnegie Steel played a key role in one of the largest acts of horizontal integration in American history when the financier J. P. Morgan merged it with several large (though smaller) competitors to create the United States Steel Corporation. The combined entity included hundreds of plants and mines, and it accounted for 60 percent of all the steel produced in the United States. It was also the first business enterprise in the world valued at more than $1 billion. That's 1901 dollars. As a percentage of gross domestic product, which at the turn of the last century was about $21 billion, the merger that birthed U.S. Steel would be worth about $1 trillion today.[18]

By the turn of the 20th century, U.S. Steel and Standard Oil had become two of the largest corporations in the United States. Joining them at those top ranks was the American Tobacco Company, founded by North Carolinian James Buchanan Duke and several business partners. That firm, capitalized at $500 million by 1904 (when Standard Oil was worth just over $120 million), reaped immense profits first by mechanizing the production of cigarettes and then by systematically underpricing and absorbing its competitors. The rise of large, integrated industrial firms in the last quarter of the 19th century saw the birth of hundreds of major corporations that would endure throughout the 20th century and remain vital today, from Johnson & Johnson and Coca-Cola to General Electric and Goodyear.[19]

Finance Kings and the First Merger Wave

The largest and fastest-growing corporations in the decades after the Civil War were typically more *capital-intensive* than *labor-intensive*. From railroads to refineries, pig iron to cigarettes, these industries confronted hefty up-front costs that presented significant barriers to entry for newcomers and privileged established companies. And getting established, as the story of Carnegie shows, depended to a great extent on access to capital.

It is no coincidence that the rise of big industrial manufacturers occurred alongside a major transformation in financial services. As with heavy industry, the rise of finance had important roots in government policy. During the Civil War, the Republican-controlled Congress passed the National Banking Act, allowing the government to charter national banks to compete with state banks. Although it only barely passed over the objections of state banks and other neo-Jacksonians who feared the concentration of power, the national banking legislation forged a key compromise between the decentralized system that had existed since the destruction of the Second Bank of the United States in the 1830s and a truly nationalized central bank, which major European countries already employed and which the United States would eventually adopt with the creation of the Federal Reserve System in 1913.[20]

One important consequence of the newly stabilized financial order was the massive proliferation of commercial banks, whether chartered nationally or by states. These commercial banks performed the types of duties we associate with everyday consumer banking today: They accepted people's deposits, exchanged bank notes, and made small loans. From about two thousand in 1860, the number of commercial banks reached almost twenty-five thousand by 1910. In the same years, other types of financial services also flourished, including stock exchanges, credit-rating agencies, and insurance companies. All financial institutions played an important role in re-allocating capital toward business enterprises. An insurance company would take the money a farmer spent on a policy and purchase railroad securities through a stock exchange, after first receiving information about that railroad through a credit-rating agency such as Dun and Bradstreet.[21]

No financial institutions had as great an effect, however, as investment banks, which rapidly increased in size and scope in the last few decades of the 19th century. Unlike commercial and savings banks, which managed the deposits and savings of small companies and individuals and issued loans for things like equipment and home mortgages, investment banks dealt primarily with the large-scale capital needs of large corporations. First pioneered to organize the financing of the expanding railroads in the 1850s, these institutions grew alongside big business itself. By the 1880s and 1890s, they supported a wide array of large corporations by amassing the funds necessary to underwrite industrial securities—stocks and bonds—that permitted steel, oil, and other industrial companies to grow.

Just as important, these investment banks (or "houses," as they were somewhat quaintly known) played a major role in the mergers and acquisitions through which industrial corporations integrated their operations. Perhaps no single institution better typifies these trends than the one that boasts the name of the grandfather of investment banking himself: J. P. Morgan.

Hailing from an old-money New England merchant family, Junius Morgan moved to London in the 1850s to help manage a private bank. During the Civil War, his son, John Pierpont (J. P.) Morgan, built up the family bank's operations in New York; afterward, he took the bank national. Upon his father's death in the 1890s, the younger Morgan renamed the firm "J.P. Morgan and Co."; by that time, the Morgans had joined European families like the Rothschilds as the epitome of elite finance, loaning to governments and railroad tycoons alike.

Morgan had an extremely conservative disposition toward risk, even by the standards of bankers, who were traditionally averse to excessive gambles. In his view, successful investing required a stable business and economic environment, free of rapid value swings or foolish speculation. And like John Rockefeller, Morgan viewed unbridled competition as the most pernicious threat to business stability.

Price wars, underbidding, and business failures all generated chaos, he insisted, and hampered his ability to achieve a steady return on his investments. Business fared better when industries were controlled and concentrated into large, centralized operations such as Rockefeller's Standard Oil Trust. Monopoly, not competition, was the key to success.

The disastrous financial Panic of 1893 created new opportunities for Morgan to put his vision of corporate control into action. The economic collapse, precipitated by overspeculation in railroads, crippled the nation. More than fifteen thousand companies, including six hundred banks, failed in what became the worst economic depression to that point in U.S. history. As countless railroad companies teetered on the verge of bankruptcy, Morgan and a handful of his partners engineered a series of takeovers and mergers. Shareholders in those failing companies surrendered their stocks in exchange for "trust certificates," and the House of Morgan took control of the companies' assets. In the aftermath of the Panic of 1893, approximately thirty-three thousand miles of railway track (one-sixth of the total) was "Morganized."[22]

Along with the Standard Oil Trust, J.P. Morgan became one of the most notorious monopolists of the 1890s. In the aftermath of the panic and depression, many other industries faced similar consolidation, and horizontal combinations grew common. The result was the country's first "merger movement," a period of massive consolidation among capital-intensive, mass-production companies. At the peak of the wave in 1899, about three hundred companies per year merged, and the most famous occurred two years later when J. P. Morgan offered Andrew Carnegie a lucrative ticket to retirement and created U.S. Steel. By 1904, some two thousand companies had been absorbed into others.[23]

A New Landscape in American Business

With the finance-fueled merger wave of the late 1890s, the era of big business had come of age. In only a few generations, the American economic landscape had been transformed. Smokestacks and oil tanks dotted the countryside, which was crisscrossed by railroads and telegraph wires. Cities boomed, and factories churned out all manner of goods, from steel and oil to rubber, gunpowder, and cigarettes. And atop this new mass-production economy sat a handful of the most powerful and wealthy business leaders known to history.

Yet the rise of big business came at a cost to many Americans. For urban workers—white and black, immigrant and native born—as well as rural farmers and middle-class professionals, the rise of mass production, mass distribution, and big business brought a pronounced sting. In the same years that giants of railroads, manufacturing, and finance built their corporate empires, other political forces took shape in response. Through the clash of big business and its discontents, America entered the modern world.

6

WARRING WITH THE OCTOPUS— WORKERS, FARMERS, AND TRUSTBUSTERS

The Great Railroad Strike of 1877—the first major industrial strike in American history—began in July, when workers on the Baltimore and Ohio Railroad in West Virginia walked off the job. Their specific grievances were local—a series of sharp pay cuts as the B&O struggled through the protracted economic depression that followed the Panic of 1873—but their fury echoed across the industrial heartland.

Within days, thousands of railroad workers from cities such as Pittsburgh, Chicago, and St. Louis launched strikes of their own to demand better pay and safer conditions. Countless nonrailroad industrial workers joined in solidarity, extending material complaints to a wide-ranging attack on the exploitative power of unchecked and ever-growing corporations. Week after week, the nationwide strike raged, pinching off vital nodes within the transportation infrastructure and nearly bringing rail commerce to a standstill. After forty-five days, railroad owners and their political allies struck back. Under orders from U.S. president Rutherford B. Hayes, federal soldiers moved from city to city to break up the strikes by force. Violent clashes rocked the country before the movement was broken. More than a hundred workers died.[1]

Nearly two decades later, in 1896, a charismatic thirty-six-year-old politician from Nebraska ascended the stage of the Democratic National Convention to accept that party's nomination for president. Representing a new political union between the Democrats and the southern- and western-based People's Party, also known as the Populists, William Jennings Bryan delivered a powerful rebuke to the industrial and financial interests that, he claimed, oppressed and exploited rural farmers and poor workers alike. In passionate oratory that became an iconic episode in American rhetoric, Bryan denounced the monied interests of big eastern cities for their "hard money" policies: the gold standard that pushed down prices and punished debtors. "You shall not press down upon the brow of labor this crown of thorns," he thundered, evoking Christ's sacrifice for humanity. "You shall not crucify mankind upon a cross of gold!" Bryan went on to lose the presidential election of 1896 to Republican William McKinley, but his fiery rebuke marked a pivotal moment in the growing critique of financial capitalism.[2]

Just a few years later, in 1902, another American with a gift for rhetorical flair—writer and activist Ida Tarbell—began to publish a series of articles that exposed the unscrupulous business practices of John Rockefeller's Standard Oil Trust. When published together as *The History of the Standard Oil Company* in 1904, Tarbell's pioneering work of investigative journalism exposed the dark underside of Rockefeller's monopoly. She offered vivid details of price manipulation, coercive underselling, and forced buy-outs that allowed Standard Oil to secure near total control over the American oil industry. In addition to inspiring further journalistic investigations of large corporations, Tarbell's book helped inflame public opposition to monopolies and, according to many historians, hastened the Supreme Court's 1911 decision to break up the Standard Oil Company into dozens of smaller companies. Along with fellow muckrakers, Tarbell galvanized a nationwide antitrust movement in the early 20th century devoted to reining in the power of large industrial corporations by bolstering the regulatory power of the government.[3]

In the last three decades of the 19th century, the rapid rise of big business prompted a powerful critique of corporations' size, scope, power, and operations. Industrial workers decried hazardous working conditions and low wages and began to organize into labor unions to push back against employer exploitation. Politicians such as Bryan built careers condemning eastern bankers for the string of depressions that drove many farmers to destitution. And intellectuals and urban activists such as Tarbell exposed and attacked the organizational structure—the integrated, monopolistic firm—that threatened the existence of small and medium-sized enterprises while gouging consumers with inflated prices.

Yet despite the variety of their grievances, these opponents of big business shared a common enemy. Discontent bubbled over as critical constituencies grew convinced that corporate capitalism posed a profound, even existential, threat to workers, farmers, small business operators, and democracy itself. The concentration of wealth in the hands of a few, in the words of one prominent union, would "invariably lead to the pauperization and hopeless degradation of the toiling masses."[4] Confronting the entrenched power of railroad giants, industrial tycoons, and international financial houses was a daunting task, and reform was often halting and incomplete. Yet big business's discontented antagonists—workers, farmers, and trustbusters—mobilized into a wide-ranging coalition at the turn of the 20th century, reshaping national politics at the dawn of the Progressive Era.

Labor Gets Organized

Industrial laborers confronted working conditions in the mid-to-late 19th century that their parents and grandparents—even those who had worked at menial tasks or in humble shops—could not have imagined. Men, women, and children by the thousands toiled in dirty, dark, dangerous environments in factories and mills, quarries and mines, rigs and rail yards. The spread of mechanization and chemical technologies made work itself more boring and, simultaneously, more dangerous. Booming industry drew rural Americans away from farms and into cities, where they competed with a massive influx of European immigrants in a flooded labor market.

At the center of this new social order lay the large, integrated industrial corporation. As its technological, organizational, and financing prowess expanded, big business employed a rising share of the American workforce. In 1850, for example, historians estimate that 21 percent of American wage laborers were employed in mining, construction, or manufacturing; in 1900, that figure had risen to 32 percent, and it hit 38 percent in 1920.[5] The most successful corporations kept costs low—by combining with their suppliers, distributors, and competitors; by producing goods more efficiently; by improving production processes; and, most important for the millions of Americans who labored under their shadow, by pushing down wages.

The labor movement emerged from this new industrial environment. Following a pattern set in Britain (like so much else in the story of industrialization), the earliest American labor unions brought together skilled craft workers such as carpenters and shoemakers. Like medieval guilds, these early organizations aimed to preserve a monopoly of knowledge concerning their specific trade. As mass production in factories reduced the need for specialized skills, craft unions controlled access to their knowledge, regulating the supply of skilled workers to keep compensation high.

Unionization accelerated in the decades after the Civil War as the number of Americans engaged in wage labor increased and large industrial plants created an environment favorable to the formation of a working-class identity.[6] In traditional small shops, even low-skilled and wage-earning workers had labored in close contact with owners, and in relatively small groups. Under mass production, however, workers increasingly labored in large, homogeneous units, quite removed from a company's wealthy owner. This new social order generated a sense of class consciousness and solidarity, which in turn strengthened workers' commitment to collective action.[7]

One of the earliest and most dramatic manifestations of class tension between laborers and economic elites was the creation of a national labor union in 1869 called the Knights of Labor. Officially called "The Noble and Holy Order of the Knights of Labor" and first organized as a secret society, the Knights of Labor grew into a major voice for the wholesale reform of the industrial system. Unlike most trade unions, the Knights welcomed both skilled and unskilled workers from the craft, retail, and manufacturing sectors, and, quite notable for their day, they encouraged membership by both African Americans and women. Central to the Knights' social vision was the notion of the *producer*. So long as you made something, they reasoned, you served a social good, regardless of your race, sex, or relationship to the means of production. The only people the group actively *excluded* were "nonproducers"—liquor dealers, gamblers, lawyers, and bankers, for example.

By the 1870s and 1880s, the Knights had become a widely recognized champion of a radically new vision of industrial society. Boasting some seven hundred thousand members at the height of its influence, the organization campaigned for an eight-hour workday (when ten- and even twelve-hour shifts were common), an end to child labor, equal pay for women, and a graduated income tax. Most important, they insisted that workers should not be separated from ownership and control of factories. To overcome the often violent clashes in capitalist society—including episodes such as the Great Railroad Strike of 1877—they promoted (and in many cases operated) cooperative business enterprises, including collectively owned and operated factories, stores, mines, and newspapers.[8]

Despite its widespread appeal, this radical social vision faced obstacles that proved fatal. Most business owners and other members of the financial elite viewed trade unions as a threat. Collective action by workers or prolabor public policy—whether to increase wages, shorten the workday, or improve conditions—appeared to violate the sacred tenets of the free market, as well as menacing employers' bottom lines. A few months after the Great Railroad Strike of 1877, a New York silk merchant declared: "No trade-unions, or riotous strikes, or leveling legislation, can suspend the operation of the inexorable law that has determined that labor . . . must be sold for what it will bring."[9]

To most employers, the socialist vision that animated the Knights of Labor—as well as other radical organizations and intellectual circles spreading around industrializing Europe as well as the United States—was pernicious. Unlike conservative craft unions that wanted to limit access to their skills to keep their wages high, socialists challenged the very structure of capitalist ownership.

A horrific incident in Chicago in the spring of 1886 helped cement the link between the Knights of Labor and radical, often violent, socialism in the minds of many business leaders. Amid a labor protest in Haymarket Square, someone threw a bomb that killed ten people. Eight suspects, all loosely affiliated with the Knights and variously described as anarchists, were convicted of murder. The Knights themselves were not involved, but their public image never recovered. Membership peaked in 1886, and the group declined in size and influence thereafter.[10]

Philosophical opposition to socialism wasn't the only reason for the fall of the Knights of Labor, however. Fierce competition from within the ranks of organized labor, particularly from the American Federation of Labor (AFL), likewise fueled its collapse. Founded in 1886 as a federation of craft unions (not a union itself, a structure it retains today), the AFL rose just as the Knights faded. Its first leader was Samuel Gompers, an English immigrant and president of the Cigar Makers' International Union. Although Gompers believed in improving working conditions, he was far from radical. Labor, he argued, could achieve its goals not by collective ownership, but by collective bargaining. Instead of undermining capitalist property relations, Gompers' AFL sought to gain a stronger negotiating position for unions, whose leaders would sit down with management to hammer out wage agreements, contracts, and other deals. Unions might engage in strikes or boycotts as a bargaining tactic, not because they wanted to disrupt the fundamental structure of business. And although radical alternatives persisted in the first few decades of the 20th century, the AFL under Gompers became the preeminent voice and model of organized labor.[11]

That Gompers and the AFL appeared moderate compared to the Knights of Labor or other socialist labor groups did not diminish employers' anxieties about unions' growing collective power. Labor clashes were vicious and violent. In the summer of 1892, the Carnegie Steel Corporation put down a strike by the Amalgamated Association of Iron and Steel Workers at its Homestead Steel Works outside Pittsburgh by hiring a private security force. For hours on end, Carnegie's personal soldiers, known as the Pinkertons, engaged in a bloody shoot-out with workers and townspeople. The state militia curtailed the violence, siding with the company and charging strike leaders with murder. Within months, public support for the Amalgamated collapsed, and any hope of unionizing the steel industry, at least for the foreseeable future, fell along with it.[12]

The hostility between workers and corporate employers spilled into the political arena. In the decades after the Civil War, the Republican Party dominated national politics and established itself as the party of business—from industrialists in the North to railroads in the West. So strong was the pull of probusiness politics that Democrats such as New York governor Grover Cleveland embraced the GOP's fiscally conservative and business-oriented policies. Cleveland became the only Democrat elected president (for two nonconsecutive terms—the only time in U.S. history that's happened) between the 1850s and the 1910s largely because of his close ties to Republican positions.[13] It was no coincidence that he also presided over one of the most brutal and emblematic instances of collusion between the federal government and industrial business interests: the violent repression of the Pullman Strike in 1894.

The labor violence that began at the Pullman Palace Car Company of Illinois grew out of the hardships that befell the overextended railroad industry after the Panic of 1893. The ensuing depression weakened demand across all industries—especially among railcar manufacturers. Facing falling revenue, the Pullman Company cut wages for its workers. No one likes to see a pay cut, but Pullman workers were especially aggrieved because most of them lived in the Pullman company town, where they paid rent to the corporation—and those rents remained at precrisis levels. In the spring of 1894, more than three thousand nonunionized workers walked off the job in protest.

Within weeks, the strikers attracted the support of the burgeoning American Railway Union (ARU), the first industry-specific nationwide union. The ARU had been founded the previous year by Eugene V. Debs, a labor organizer from Indiana who would later—after his imprisonment for leading the Pullman Strike—become the country's most prominent socialist politician and activist. The entry of the Railway Union nationalized the Pullman strike, as union members far removed from Pullman itself refused to work on railcars that had been manufactured there. Worker solidarity, sophisticated organizing, and long-simmering anger united a quarter-million workers in more than twenty-five states. They brought the nation's rail system to a halt.[14]

The Pullman Strike encapsulated the "labor problem"—the term used at the time—that vexed the entire capitalist system. Mass production and mass distribution, the hallmarks of industrial capitalism, depended on an extraordinarily large workforce. Complying with workers' demands for higher wages or other concessions, business owners insisted, would raise the costs of production and threaten their profitability. Faced with steep competition and a weak economy, many railroad companies would be forced to close—costing workers and owners alike their livelihoods.

Unable to appease labor while retaining their prerogatives as owners (including profits and high stock dividends), corporate leaders turned to their allies in the government. In the end, that alliance paid off. President Cleveland accused the striking unionists of illegally hampering trade and threatening public safety, and invoked his constitutional duty to see that the mail was delivered. With vocal support from Samuel Gompers of the AFL, he dispatched twelve thousand federal soldiers to break up the strikes by force. Troops killed several dozen strikers in clashes before the strike ended. Eugene Debs served six months in jail for violating a federal injunction to allow rail traffic to resume. During his imprisonment, he became a committed Marxist and later converted his American Railway Union into a socialist political party.[15]

Despite clear support from state and federal government officials in their clashes with strikers, many business leaders were unsettled by the newfound power of labor unions—whether radical or moderate, skilled or unskilled. While some employers sympathized and agreed with the need to increase pay and workplace safety, most people who ran large industrial corporations feared that organized labor threatened their ability to manage their companies profitably, not to mention their social and personal stature. During the Pullman Strike, company president George Pullman expressed his incredulity, in a speech to shareholders, at the suggestion "that this company ought to have maintained the scale of wages existing in the car manufacturing department in April, 1893, without regard to the *current selling prices* for cars." More than half of the labor force had worked for him less than five years, he explained. "Had all of them earned a guaranty of uninterrupted, undiminished wages?"[16]

In addition to arousing the ire of corporate leaders, the rise of organized labor led to notable changes in the business community. Social clubs such as Rotary and the Kiwanis emerged, businesspeople founded local chambers of commerce, and many of the most successful tycoons—such as Andrew Carnegie and John Rockefeller— devoted vast funds to universities, hospitals, and charities. Then as now, people argued over what exactly to make of such philanthropy. Carnegie gave away hundreds of millions of dollars after he sold out to Morgan in 1901. Did some of that flow from guilt over episodes such as Homestead? Or a strategic move to preempt the push for public, government-funded facilities?[17]

In addition to philanthropy and civic engagement, many companies tried to blunt labor's power by undercutting the central issues that drove labor organization. Through the strategy known as *welfare capitalism*, corporations found ways to respond to workers' complaints yet retain their managerial authority by handling everything in house. Business leaders improved safety conditions, created recreational facilities, offered pensions and health benefits, and formed company-based "unions" to hear complaints.[18]

As with philanthropy, we can interpret the rise of welfare capitalism as either deeply cynical or genuine and beneficent. Either way, it embodied a common reaction to growing concerns about the social consequences of industrial working conditions as well as the growing role of labor in national affairs.

Farmers Fight Back

When William Jennings Bryan delivered his fiery "Cross of Gold" speech at the Democratic National Convention in the summer of 1896, he brought national attention to a political movement that had been brewing in the nation's agricultural heartland for several years. The movement historians refer to as "Populism" (with a capital *P*) found its greatest support among white farmers in the South, Midwest, and Great Plains states. While the movement took on a variety of institutional forms in the latter decades of the century, it was most commonly invoked as a nickname for the Nebraska-based "People's Party," which joined the Democratic Party in nominating Bryan in 1896. (Bryan accepted both nominations and appeared on the ballot of both parties, albeit with different vice presidential running mates.) The People's Party disbanded in 1908, by which time the national Democratic Party had embraced many of its positions and co-opted much of its rural constituency. Nonetheless, agrarian opposition to big business, especially banking, left a profound legacy for Progressive Era politics.[19]

Much of the Populists' platform overlapped with the aims of left-leaning workers' parties, including structural reforms to the business system and an expansion of democratic governance. Agrarian reformers pitted themselves against unregulated capitalism and decried concentrations of wealth and power. They called for a graduated income tax, government ownership of utilities such as railroads, telegraphs, and telephone lines, direct election of U.S. senators, a one-term limit on the presidency, a voter referendum system, and a shorter workday. They also promoted restrictions on immigration, partly to restrict the labor supply (and keep wages higher) and partly due to racist, xenophobic, and anti-Semitic beliefs that many of them harbored. Populists also wanted lower tariffs, echoing the old Jeffersonian concern that high tariffs drove up the prices farmers had to pay for manufactured goods.

Yet the most distinctive aspect of the farmers' political program, and the issue with which Bryan launched his career, was their attack on eastern banks and the influence of financiers over the national government. Monetary policy, in particular the question of the *free coinage of silver,* was their primary focus. The "silver question" often strikes history students as esoteric, obscure, and technical, yet it was one of the single most important political issues of the late 19th century. The struggle split the country between those who favored minting coins only in gold—monometallists—and those who wanted to use both silver *and* gold—the *bi*metallists. As a political rallying cry, the silver debate proved instrumental to a larger critique of corporate capitalism.

Bimetallists, or "silverites," like William Jennings Bryan saw their mission as nothing less than rescuing the country from the antidemocratic machinations of the "money trust" of Wall Street bankers. They called on Congress to reverse the Coinage Act of 1873, which had ordered the U.S. Mint to issue dollar coins only in gold, not in silver. This law had made gold the de facto metal currency, reducing the total amount of money circulating in the economy. A smaller money supply led to economic contractions, including the prolonged depression of the 1870s, and long periods of deflation. Debtors, including many farmers, suffered disproportionately in a deflationary economy, because the value of their crops fell even as the amount they owed to creditors remained constant. At the same time, bankers benefited from the price shifts: If I loan you one hundred dollars and prices are falling, I can buy *more* with the hundred dollars you pay me a year from now than I could when I loaned it to you. Thus, as a political issue, silver united debtors across the country (as well as the owners of silver mines in the West, who stood to profit if the value of silver increased) against what they saw as the duplicity of scheming bankers.[20]

The election of 1896 represented the high-water mark of the Populists in American politics. The Republican nominee, former Ohio congressman William McKinley, toed a traditional line in favor of the gold standard, high tariffs, opposition to labor unions, and other probusiness policies. The Democratic Party, in contrast, was in disarray. The outgoing president was Grover Cleveland, the conservative and business-oriented politician who had earned the ire of workers through his repression of the Pullman Strike and generally anti-labor positions. No real distinction existed between Cleveland's wing of the party and the Republicans. (Indeed, historians generally agree that those similarities were critical to Cleveland's electoral successes.) A fierce schism between the Populists and conservatives rocked the party as it headed toward its nominating convention.

Bryan's nomination marked the bimetallists' successful takeover of the Democratic convention and, in the following months, his energetic Populist campaign alarmed the nation's conservative business community. Led by McKinley's savvy campaign manager Marcus Hanna, the Republicans raised unprecedented levels of campaign funds from wealthy eastern bankers. In some cases, business owners shored up support for their candidate by deploying their market power, drawing up contracts with their suppliers that were contingent on a Republican victory.[21]

Just as important, the McKinley campaign convinced a significant percentage of the working-class voting population in industrial centers to support the GOP ticket. Workers' livelihoods, Republican partisans argued, depended on a strong business climate, which in turn depended on hard money and a stable currency. Politically, this tactic cleaved the left. Urban laborers may have had more in common ideologically with the Democrats and Populists, but they earned their paychecks from the wealthy business establishment. And that's largely where their votes went.

McKinley delivered a clear defeat to William Jennings Bryan in

November 1896, besting him by nearly one hundred votes in the electoral college and 5 percent of the popular vote. Nationwide, Bryan captured nearly as many states as McKinley (twenty-two to twenty-three), but the Republican's support was far stronger in the more populous East and Midwest, while the Democrats held the South and West. Yet by incorporating farmers' critique of capitalism into the national Democratic Party, the Bryan campaign helped recast national politics. The cause of free silver was forever lost, but the Populist attack on monopolistic banks and railroad corporations became central parts of the Progressive platforms of both major parties in the decades ahead.[22]

Slaying the Octopus: Regulation and Antitrust

If the "silver question" ended in defeat for anti-big-business reformers, the broader antimonopoly impulse, which coalesced around the so-called trust question, left a longer-lasting mark on American business and public life. As contemporaries framed the issue, the "trust problem" resulted from the tendency of companies in a state of free competition to increase in size and market power to the point where they deliberately *prevented* free competition. Ida Tarbell's exposé of the Standard Oil Trust offered a compelling depiction of the dilemma: By outcompeting his rivals, Rockefeller created an oil industry in which none could challenge his dominance. Free competition had extinguished itself. The struggle to confront this new reality of industrial capitalism drew on a broad-based political and intellectual movement and proceeded along several distinct tracks. The result, however, was significant institutional and structural change to both the legal and business systems. The struggle against monopolies, in short, laid the foundations for the government regulation of business.

As with everything in the history of big business, the story of regulation begins with the railroads. The midcentury expansion of railroads had created robust new markets as farmers moved west along rail and telegraph lines. Although those agrarian settlers owed their communities and livelihoods to the success of the railroads, they resented the industry's monopolistic pricing power. Particularly galling was the practice of *price discrimination*, the system by which railroads charged higher rates per mile for shorter routes than for longer routes. Such fluctuating price schemes made sense from the railroad's perspective—given the high fixed costs of loading and unloading freight, the cost per mile went down on longer hauls. Yet many farmers and other commercial shippers objected that the system privileged larger operations that shipped goods greater distances, and disproportionately raised the shipping prices paid by people in more remote areas.

To rein in railroad companies' economic power, the state of Massachusetts established a national model for state-level regulation in 1869. Headed by Charles Francis Adams Jr. (grandson and great-grandson of two former presidents), the Massachusetts Board of Railroad Commissioners investigated how railroad companies conducted their business, including how they determined what rates to charge for freight and passengers. Other states created similar investigatory commissions, in hopes that the threat of negative publicity would compel railroads to lower their prices.

A stronger and alternative vision of railroad regulation took shape in midwestern states, where legislatures were more willing to take on the task of actually *prescribing* the rates railroads could charge. A political movement among farmers known as the Granger movement coalesced in the years after the Civil War, and in 1871 the states of Illinois, Iowa, Minnesota, and Wisconsin passed so-called Granger laws. Arguing that railroads served a public function by facilitating commerce, the state governments set up administrative agencies to balance the bottom-line interests of the railroad companies with the public interest in safe, affordable, and fair transportation. Railroad companies pushed back, urging state legislators to repeal the laws. In addition, the Panic of 1873 and the ensuing economic depression pushed prices down rapidly, weakening political support for maintaining the agencies. However, even in death, the Granger laws set a vital precedent for regulating railroads in the name of the public good.[23]

In 1877, the U.S. Supreme Court upheld the constitutionality of the Granger laws in *Munn* v. *Illinois*. However, just nine years later, the Court revised its ruling in *Wabash Railway* v. *Illinois* (1886), declaring that, where railroads crossed state lines, state-level laws improperly usurped the constitutional right of the federal Congress. (Article I, Section 8 of the Constitution gives Congress the unique right "to regulate commerce with foreign nations and among the several states.")

The *Wabash* decision led to the passage, the next year, of the Interstate Commerce Act of 1877—a piece of legislation that created the country's first federal regulatory agency, the Interstate Commerce Commission (ICC). To keep prices low for farmers and commercial shippers, the commission banned certain forms of price fixing as well as price discrimination between short- and long-haul routes. However, it also included a major loophole: The ICC was charged with ensuring that freight rates were "reasonable and just," but the act gave no guidance about what those words meant in practice. The law also gave the ICC little in the way of enforcement power. Thus, until Congress expanded its regulatory purview with the Hepburn Act of 1906, the ICC was little more than an information-gathering agency, rather than a forceful regulator.[24]

Using government agencies to regulate business activities in the public interest represented one avenue to rein in the new power of late-19th-century corporations. Another strategy, which took aim at the rise of corporate monopolies more explicitly, led to the passage of the Sherman Antitrust Act in 1890. If the ICC had represented an effort to *regulate* monopolistic behavior, the antitrust movement endeavored to *disband* monopolistic companies entirely. Named after its chief proponent, Ohio senator John Sherman (brother of Union general William Tecumseh Sherman), the act sought to preserve the benefits of free competition by cracking down hard on anticompetitive behavior. It criminalized "every contract, combination in the form of trust or otherwise, or conspiracy, in restraint of trade or commerce." Instead of prescribing rules and procedures to mitigate corporate power, as the ICC did, the law required the criminal prosecution of "every person who shall monopolize, or attempt to monopolize, or combine or conspire with any other person or persons, to monopolize any part of the trade of commerce."[25]

Yet while the new law declared monopolistic activity illegal, actually prosecuting offenders proved to be challenging for antimonopolists. To enforce the Sherman Antitrust Act, the U.S. Department of Justice (founded in 1870 and headed by the president-appointed attorney general) had to initiate the proceedings. With probusiness Republicans such as Cleveland and McKinley holding a firm grip on the presidency in the decade after 1890, the Antitrust Act's immediate impact was muted.

The task of enforcing prohibitions on anticompetitive behavior thus fell to a new generation of Republican politicians, particularly Theodore Roosevelt (who ascended to the presidency upon the assassination of McKinley in 1901) and his successor William H. Taft. Younger, brasher, and less beholden to deep-pocketed financiers than his predecessors, Roosevelt sensed the shift in public opinion against flagrant monopolists. Ida Tarbell's scathing book had portrayed Rockefeller as cold and unfeeling, particularly when it came to undercutting and destroying the life's work of small, independent oil refiners. The disastrous Panic of 1907, sparked by the collapse of unregulated financial firms, likewise cemented the public case against the monopolists. Roosevelt began his term in office cautiously, leery of offending the business community, but he quickly directed the Justice Department to set its sights on the most egregious violators of the Sherman Act.[26]

Standard Oil was top of the list. By the early years of the 1900s, John D. Rockefeller's horizontally integrated enterprise had taken near total control of the petroleum market. Surely if anyone had run afoul of the Sherman Act, it was Rockefeller. Going after anyone else would expose the entire enterprise as corrupt. Yet Rockefeller was the richest man in the country, and possibly, depending on how you calculate inflation, the richest person of *all time*.* His resources to fight an antitrust lawsuit were nearly bottomless. If he beat the case, the Justice Department worried, would the government be able to retain public support? If you shoot at the king, as they say, you best not miss.

In 1910 and 1911, by which time Roosevelt had left the presidency and Taft had assumed the office, the Justice Department argued its case against the Standard Oil Trust. On May 15, 1911, the Court ruled that Standard Oil met the definition of "restraint of trade" by engaging in anticompetitive behavior. Writing for the majority, Chief Justice Edward White concluded that Standard Oil "charges altogether excessive prices where it meets no competition." In the face of competition, however, "it frequently cuts prices to a point which leaves even the Standard little or no profit" to drive its competitors under. Judging Standard Oil to be an illegal monopoly, the Court ordered it broken up. It was forcibly divided into thirty-four regional companies, many of which—like ExxonMobil, Marathon, and Chevron—persist to this day.[27]

The Taft administration pursued other successful antitrust law-

---

* At the time of Rockefeller's death in 1937, his assets equaled approximately 1.5 percent of the nation's total economic output. As a share of today's GDP, that would be approximately $270 billion, several times the wealth of the richest people on Earth. Carl O'Donnell, "The Rockefellers: The Legacy of History's Richest Man," *Forbes*, July 11, 2014.

suits as well, including the breakup of the American Tobacco Trust (decided on the same day as the Standard Oil case). Those 1911 decisions, as the historian Louis Galambos has argued, "put large corporations and their legal advisors on an antitrust alert."[28]

Yet the assault on monopoly was far from complete. In 1911, the Justice Department opened an antitrust case against J. P. Morgan's U.S. Steel. After years of legal maneuvering, however, the Supreme Court ultimately ruled in 1920 that "the power attained by the United States Steel Corporation, much greater than that of any one competitor, but not greater than that possessed by them all, did not constitute it a monopoly."[29] For the antimonopoly forces, U.S. Steel's survival exposed the limitations of the antitrust movement. The Sherman Act successfully attacked cartels and price-fixing schemes, but because it banned *restraint of trade*, not market dominance in general, it did nothing to curb corporate mergers or stem the tide of industrial concentration.[30]

The Progressive Era: A Response to Industrialism

The public discontent with industrial capitalism—from the predations of giant corporations and price-fixing to the exploitation of workers and deflationary monetary policy—launched one of the most important political reform movements in American history. Historians of the period have long used the phrase "Progressive Era" to describe the years between the turn of the century and the onset of World War I, defined by a political and intellectual response to the rapid rise of industrialized society. Rooted neither in radical socialism nor in unfettered laissez-faire economics, Progressivism sought to mitigate capitalism's excesses while retaining its benefits. In the process, the Progressive period both reaffirmed classical elements of the American political tradition and established new institutions, government agencies, and expectations about the promise of democracy.

The Progressive Era inaugurated major changes in the role the federal government played in Americans' daily lives. At the national level, reforms included the 1906 Pure Food and Drug Act, which established nationally applicable rules about the contents of food and medicines. In 1909, Congress passed the Sixteenth Amendment to the Constitution, authorizing the income tax. Ratified four years later, this measure provided a constitutional funding stream for both federal and state governments that required wealthier individuals *and* more profitable corporations to contribute higher percentages of their income. Also in 1913, another constitutional amendment established the direct election of U.S. senators by voters, rather than by state legislators. This reform reflected widespread concern about corruption and favor seeking by well-connected financial elites, as well as a resurgent faith in popular democracy. And in 1914, Congress—with the backing of the country's most powerful business leaders—established the Federal Trade Commission, institutionalizing and bureaucratizing the process of antitrust enforcement to make competition policy more transparent and nonpartisan.[31]

Through these and other structural and legal reforms, Progressives confronted the problems of corporate size and economic centralization while reaffirming the private business system itself. Some of the most influential Progressives—such as the Boston retailer Edward Filene—were prominent businesspeople who saw regulation, at both the state and federal levels, as an indispensable tool for creating a stable, predictable, and growth-oriented business climate.[32] By addressing the critiques of big business's most ardent discontents, Progressives aimed to impose a sense of order on the chaotic world of industrial capitalism.

7

THE DAWN OF MODERN LIFE

I n 1908, a carmaker named Henry Ford—who at the time was trying to keep his third automobile company from following his first two ventures into insolvency—devoted himself to producing exactly one model of vehicle: the Model T. Ford had grown convinced that the key to the auto business was to sell high-quality, low-cost products. While most of his competitors made expensive cars in a batch process—only a few at a time—Ford pioneered a new strategy that brought the efficiencies of mass production to a consumer product. A 1908 Model T cost $850, but by the early 1920s, the price had fallen to under $300.* Sales boomed as the price dropped: Ford set a record by selling nine thousand cars in 1907, but by the late 1910s, he sold nearly a million a year.[1]

Sales were great, and the Model T made Henry Ford one of the richest men in the country. More important, it also launched an entire

---

*When you take into account the massive price inflation that accompanied World War I (1914–1919), the difference is even more striking. Three hundred dollars in 1924 dollars might have bought what $120 did in 1908, so the real price of the Model T fell by up to 75 percent!

industry—soon to include the giant General Motors Corporation, which eventually outcompeted Ford—that rivaled the railroads, refineries, lending houses, and mining corporations as the definition of big business in America. The mass-produced automobile also signaled something new: the growing importance of the *consumer* market for major industries. Earlier titans had focused on filling the needs of fellow industrialists, but automobile makers targeted the end user—the driver. Ford had one vision for what the consumer wanted, while his competitors disagreed. But they all believed in applying the technique of mass production to serve a growing consumer market.

This new approach transformed American life. The first few decades of the 20th century witnessed a dramatic growth of consumer-oriented goods that revolutionized American life. By the 1920s, as automobiles flooded city streets and rural lanes, advertisements for national brands such as Coca-Cola dotted store fronts, and private homes buzzed with new electrical conveniences such as radios and toasters. As one journalist put it in 1924: "The American citizen has more comforts and conveniences than kings had 200 years ago."[2] The mass consumption economy had arrived.

So Long as It Is Black: Standardized Production at Ford

The mass production of consumer goods, which came to define modern life in the early decades of the 20th century, grew from the innovations in production pioneered by the giants of industrial capitalism in the previous generations. As we saw in earlier chapters, the move toward rationalizing business operations had been the key to large-scale production in the railroad, oil, steel, and other heavy industries. That trend included not only the adoption of clear managerial hierarchies and strategic decision-making, but also a decisive move toward standardizing production itself. From steel rails to firearms, the most successful and profitable 19th-century firms found ways to streamline their processes, moving away from the "batch method" and toward mass production.

One of the most important innovators in this move toward standardized production techniques was a mechanical engineer turned management guru, Frederick Winslow Taylor. Taylor was not the only prophet of standardized production in the late 19th and early 20th centuries, but he was perhaps its most famous spokesperson. First as a steel plant manager and later as an author, public speaker, and paid business consultant, Taylor demonstrated how manufacturers could bring order, efficiency, and profit to the chaotic and poorly organized factory system. Such was his advocacy that the word "Taylorism" became a shorthand for many people to explain a methodical, hyper-rationalized, and—certainly from the perspective of workers—repressive and unforgiving approach to shop-floor management.

Born in Pennsylvania in 1856, Taylor began his rise to national prominence in the 1880s. Working as a manager at Pennsylvania's Midvale Steel Company, he became a fixture in a national conversation among industrial manufacturers over how to manage workforces and design work-flow procedures. In the wake of the long economic recession that began in the early 1870s, owners and managers debated how to increase the efficiency and productivity of their factories. And while the previous generation of industrial leaders had placed their faith in the promise of new *technologies*, the cohort of men in Taylor's circles focused more pointedly on the question of *organization*.

In the 1890s, Taylor began publishing a series of papers that introduced the term "scientific management" to the business lexicon. The latter decades of the 19th century were marked by a growing public faith in rational, methodical, and scientific approaches to all aspects of human life, from medicine and biology to social relations and race. Traditional shop-floor conditions were chaotic, disorganized, and grossly inefficient, and Taylor preached that scientific management—careful measurement, clear-cut models, and rigorous testing—was the cure. For more than two decades, he promoted his ideas through writings and public lectures. Four years before his death in 1915, he published what would become the most influential of all his works, a book called *The Principles of Scientific Management*, which brought his ideas to a broad audience.[3]

Taylor argued that managers should observe how long a worker took to perform a given task and use that metric as a standard for all workers to match. Output, in other words, could be set "scientifically" through testing and measurement. Taylor became famous for the stopwatch he used to time individual tasks as he consulted with factory managers who hoped to rationalize their workforce.

Since most factories had expanded organically over time, machines and workplaces were frequently laid out haphazardly, with little deliberate planning. Workers, Taylor explained, "wasted" time moving from place to place or waiting for bottlenecks to clear before they could proceed with the next step in a production line. In response, the principles of scientific management called for redesigning the workflow by positioning equipment rationally and deliberately, creating a line of workers each of whom was timed by a stopwatch.

The scientific management approach did not stick in all industrial settings, but a significant number of factories, especially in metalworking, adopted Taylor's prescriptions to various degrees. Yet reworking a shop-floor design, even in the interest of raising productivity, was an expensive undertaking, as it often required taking the factory off-line for some time. Larger companies could absorb that cost better and see the benefits more clearly, so Taylor's techniques took hold more quickly among big businesses than among smaller manufacturers. Nonetheless, the basic notions propelled changes across the country (as well as in other industrialized nations), bringing greater order, productivity, and profits through mass production.[4]

The spirit of scientific management and standardized production found perhaps its clearest expression in the Detroit-based work-houses of America's first automobile giant, the Ford Motor Company.[5] Henry Ford didn't invent the car—there were already six different models on display at Chicago's Columbian Exposition in 1893—but his devotion to the Model T starting in 1908 revolution-ized the industry. Standardization was key: Ford simplified the design of his "Tin Lizzie" and used a bare minimum of parts (about five thousand). Those mass-produced parts were also interchangeable between cars—any wheel would fit any body. "The way to make auto-mobiles," Ford explained, "is to make one automobile like another automobile . . . to make them come out of the factory just alike."[6] Standardized production led to Ford's famous boast that customers could buy one in any color, "so long as it is black."[7]

The notion of standardized mechanical production did not orig-inate with Henry Ford, of course. Throughout the 19th century, manufacturers had found ways to create a variety of components in standardized, repeatable ways, from textiles to revolvers.[8] The factories that produced the screws, nuts, and bolts that held together railroads likewise produced their parts in a standardized fashion. Ford's real contribution came in applying the philosophy of stan-dardized production to such a large, complex piece of machinery as the automobile. Putting Frederick Taylor's insights into prac-tice, Ford introduced the first *moving* assembly line in 1913 at his River Rouge plant in Michigan. Seizing on a long-standing notion of arranging workers in a line and adding a little bit at a time to a product, Ford added a crucial element: a rotating conveyer belt to move the parts from worker to worker, whose very pace the factory managers could control. By stripping down the car's design and standardizing the assembly process into discrete and repeatable steps, Ford reduced the time it took to assemble a car from twelve hours to two hours.

Because the Model T required less steel and less labor than its competitors, Ford could undercut his competitors' prices and still make tremendous profits by selling high volumes at (relatively) low profit margins. Yet the rapid pace of work on the assembly line created harsh working conditions, even by the already exploitative standards of early-20th-century manufacturing. Ford's plants suffered from high employee turnover. To entice his workers to remain, Ford also pioneered labor policies that appeared progressive to many. In 1914, the company introduced the "five-dollar day," when two dollars a day was more typical.[9] In the next few years, Ford reduced the workday to eight hours and the workweek from six to five days, goals long championed by the labor, populist, and socialist movements. His business success, his personal austerity (especially when compared to the flamboyant wealth of men like J. P. Morgan), and his public devotion to the ideal that industrial workers should be able to afford the fruit of their labors—that a car should be inexpensive enough for the masses—contributed to Ford's personal popularity around the world.[10]

That luster didn't last, either in business or in the public imagination. In the decade after World War I, General Motors overtook Ford in market share, in part by realizing that the "any color so long as it is black" monotony did not appeal to an increasingly discerning consuming public or the vibrant, energetic culture of the Roaring Twenties. Henry Ford's stubborn refusal to change his marketing approach led the company to slip, and it barely survived the Great Depression. At the same time, his hateful racial views turned many off. Ford was a vicious anti-Semite and broadcast his hatred of Jews through his company-owned newspaper, the *Dearborn Independent*. He helped circulate the false and anti-Semitic text known as the *Protocols of the Elders of Zion*, which proclaimed a (nonexistent) Jewish conspiracy bent on world domination. And by the late 1930s, he attracted the open admiration of Nazi dictator Adolf Hitler, who praised the virtues of what the Germans called *Fordismus*—or Fordism.[11]

Fordism has a conflicted place in the lexicon of American business, economics, and labor history. Ford's devotion to ruthless order and opposition to individuality or diversity appealed to fascists such as Hitler, who applied the mechanical efficiencies Ford pioneered to murder millions. But Fordism also reflected a populist devotion to improving the lot of the downtrodden through the "miracle" of mass production.

Historians themselves are divided about the term "Fordism." For some, it connotes a system that lowers the costs of production and distributes benefits widely. In that sense, laborers are no longer "alienated" from the product of their labor in the way Karl Marx described, but can earn enough to purchase it. That framework may help us make sense of the industrial economy that came of age during the 1930s and continued to prosper during the twenty-five years following World War II, until the "post-Fordist" period that began in the 1970s.[12]

Other historians eschew the term and prefer other ways of characterizing labor-management relations and the distribution of wealth during the 20th century. They point out that Henry Ford himself, in addition to his association with the horrors of World War II, only adopted worker-friendly practices out of dire necessity. Yet whatever we make of the term, the Ford Motor Company's contribution not only to the practice of mass production but also to the burgeoning consumer-based economy in the first decades of the 20th century was undeniable.

Consumers Everywhere

Mass production lowered the prices of manufactured products, from reapers and rifles to automobiles and radios. In the early decades of big business, most production was aimed at other companies—"business-to-business" transactions, to use today's term. Steel mills bought from iron mines, and sold to railroad companies, which transported freight for farmers and merchants, for example. Yet as the 20th century dawned, the advances of mass production—more and more goods and lower and lower costs—spread beyond the business world and revolutionized everyday life, creating the modern mass consumption society. But the mere *availability* of newer, mass-made, and cheaper goods did not lead by itself to a culture of mass consumption. This revolution in consumption came about through the deliberate choices of capitalists, entrepreneurs, and savvy marketing specialists.

Revolutions in business practices have historically relied on developments not only in *production*, but also in *distribution*. Just as the Market Revolution in the early 19th century relied on improvements in roads, shipping routes, and ultimately railroads, so, too, did the mass consumption economy in the early 20th century depend on new ways of moving goods to consumers. In short, generating consumption *by* the masses meant that businesses had to make their products available *to* the masses. Tremendous changes in sales and distribution altered the ways Americans consumed everyday items as well as their ideas about modern life, nowhere more powerfully than in the fields of retailing and advertising.

Today, the notion of buying products from retailers is commonplace—whether from brick and mortar stores or online purveyors. Before the rise of industrial capitalism, however, retail outfits were only found in cities and mostly sold specialty items such as books and furs. The idea of shopping for a variety of grocery or household items—or the notion that stores themselves could be big businesses—didn't develop until the late 19th century.

Since the colonial period, urban merchants with international connections had made up the core of the nation's wealthy elite. They purchased large quantities of items from abroad and, during the cotton boom, the American South, which they then supplied to shop owners in smaller towns. Many of the most successful merchants also retained flagship stores in New York, Boston, and Philadelphia, where customers could purchase goods directly. During the massive economic expansion after the Civil War, merchants transformed themselves into mass retailers by cutting out intermediaries and purchasing from manufacturers. Larger stores grouped dry goods—such as clothing, leather, foodstuffs, and farming equipment—into discrete sections, or departments. By the late 19th century, these *department stores* had become common in major cities, including companies such as Macy's and Bloomingdale's in New York and Jordan Marsh in Boston. By the first years of the 20th century, the model had spread to smaller cities as well.

Another harbinger of the spread of mass retailing was the growth of the mail-order business. As expansive railroad networks linked the hinterland to large cities, merchants took advantage of those new distribution channels. In 1872, a Chicago-based traveling salesman named A. Montgomery Ward launched the country's first mail-order firm. He published an illustrated catalog and mailed it, free of charge, to small-town farmers, who could then order products at lower prices than what local merchants charged. In 1886, another Chicagoan—a twenty-three-year-old man named Richard Sears—imitated Montgomery Ward's success and started selling pocket watches by mail. Within a few years, Sears partnered with Alvah Roebuck, a watch repair specialist, providing both sales and maintenance services, all remotely. The pair broadened their offerings to compete directly with Montgomery Ward—their catalog became known as "the Farmer's Bible," and their Chicago warehouse filled orders from around the country. In rural America, mail-order companies quickly outcompeted local merchants, who could not match their price, reliability (such as money-back guarantees), and variety.

Incorporated in 1893, Sears, Roebuck supplanted Montgomery Ward and became the country's biggest mail-order company by 1900.[13]

In addition to department stores and mail-order houses, a new type of retail model—the *chain store*—also helped spread mass consumption. Unlike traditional shops or city-based department stores, chains operated many storefronts in different locations, all under the same name and a single corporate ownership. The earliest and most famous pioneers of this model were F.W. Woolworth's, which operated from 1878 to 1997, and the Great Atlantic and Pacific Tea Company, which survived until 2015 as the A&P supermarket. Formed in 1859, the A&P opened its doors in New York as a discount purveyor of teas and coffees, which its founders purchased in bulk straight from ships (allowing them to offer cheaper prices). Within twenty years, the A&P offered a wide variety of grocery products and owned stores in more than one hundred locations, stretching from Minnesota to Virginia. Combining efficient distribution channels, inventory management, and low costs—the hallmarks of Taylorism—grocery chains like the A&P grew prominent in the early 20th century.[14]

The success of the retail revolution, and the chain store model in particular, changed the way Americans identified as consumers, but it came at a cost. By the end of World War I, the chain store model had grown widespread, and traditional, local stores faced destructive competition. Political opposition to the "chain store menace" mirrored the types of moral and anti-elitist arguments marshaled by populist crusaders against industrial monopolies. National chain stores, critics claimed, drove small stores out of business and syphoned profits away from local communities and toward "absentee owners" in large cities such as Chicago and New York. Integration among grocery stores, they feared, created monopoly pricing environments that raised prices for consumers even as the quality of the goods and services declined.[15]

Beyond financial concerns, anti–chain store advocates worried that the rise of impersonal, national sellers threatened traditional American values. Retail, they argued, was the economic and social lifeblood of small-town America. One lobbyist representing small grocers made the case against chains in 1930: "Is there not something lost of individual initiative, responsibility, self-reliance, citizenship and relations between the individual and his community that after all is essential to America?"[16] In the midst of a consumer revolution, Americans laid vital groundwork for decades of criticism of the depersonalizing effects of mass retailing—decades before similar arguments against giant sellers such as Walmart became a permanent part of the national debate.

The Birth of Advertising

The mass consumption economy brought Americans more goods, as well as easier and cheaper access to them. But the presence of consumer products did not mean that people would buy them. The art of attracting consumers and shaping their buying habits turned into a business opportunity in its own right and, in time, gave birth to the modern advertising industry.

As more and more companies competed for loyalty from the consuming public, specialized advertising agencies provided a way for businesses to outsource the task of attracting customers. Many of those agencies were located on Manhattan's Madison Avenue, a street known since the mid-19th century as a hub for advertising and image making. The number of advertising agencies exploded—professionals handled 95 percent of all national ads by 1917. American companies spent more than a billion dollars per year on advertisements by the time of World War I, and major firms like Quaker Oats and Goodyear spent a million dollars on magazine ads in 1920.[17]

Advertisers played a critical cultural as well as economic role, linking the new consumerism with evolving ideas about how Americans should relate to the products they purchased. Before World War I, most ads used large amounts of text to explain the benefits of a product and to offer a compelling, rational reason why a consumer should purchase it. (Those reasons weren't always *accurate*, but they nonetheless *explained* the product.) Text-heavy ads persisted for decades, but ad makers began to alter their content strategically in the 1920s. Increasingly, ads stressed the way products made customers *feel* or what they signaled about a person's social position. Ads during World War I put a major focus on patriotism and loyalty, for example. In the years to come, producers of new conveniences such as radios, gramophones, and automobiles used art and photographs to convey a sense of luxury and modernity.

The advertising business expanded through its ability to *create* a consumer need where one had not existed, as the Lambert Pharmaceutical Company did in the 1920s with Listerine mouthwash. Invented in the mid-19th century, Listerine was an alcohol-based chemical designed as a powerful antiseptic for use during surgery. In 1920, advertising copywriters for Lambert launched a marketing campaign that proposed a new use for this old product—as a solution to bad breath (when taken in small quantities and not swallowed!). In its ads, Lambert introduced Americans to the word "halitosis," an obscure but clinical-sounding, scientific word for "bad breath," giving the impression that Listerine addressed a pressing medical problem. By 1927, Lambert's profits, driven by Listerine sales, had skyrocketed from one hundred thousand dollars a year to more than $4 million, in the process changing the daily ablution habits of millions of people.[18]

General Motors and Modern Corporate Organization

The 1920s, for many people, conjure images of tremendous energy and excitement—wild "Great Gatsby"–style parties, in spite of national alcohol Prohibition, or all-night dance marathons, flappers, and jazz. This popular memory reflects the tremendous economic boom that the United States experienced, following a brief postwar slowdown, when the forces of mass production and mass consumption came together. Not everyone benefited equally, however, and long-standing grievances among farmers and the urban working class persisted, as did racial violence and the hardening of Jim Crow racial segregation. The very forces that propelled the economic boom exacerbated these clashes: industrial concentration and the integration of a national market for consumer goods and services.

Advances in agricultural technology, to take one example, boosted crop yields but pushed prices down—good for urban consumers, but challenging for the agricultural community. Facing stiff competition and declining profits, many farmers felt they had no choice but to sow more than their fields could bear. Overplanting not only strained the productivity of the soil, but flooded the market with excess crops, driving prices down even further. At the same time, the tremendous successes of the industrial manufacturing community gave management even greater leverage over factory workers, and organized labor confronted fierce opposition in its efforts to unionize. The conservative political climate, itself a response to the aggressive reforms of the Progressive moment, routinely supported the prerogatives of management over labor, as it had for decades.

In the years after World War I, the dominant economic force remained large, integrated manufacturing firms like General Electric, U.S. Steel, and Du Pont, which prospered from a more fully integrated national market and sophisticated management. Big industries grew increasingly consolidated in those years, and many of today's well-known corporations emerged and expanded, including IBM, *Time* magazine and Warner Bros. (now Time Warner), and Disney.[19]

The 1920s also marked the moment when the Ford Motor Company—the market leader and innovator in rationalized production during the 1910s—began to falter. In 1924, two out of every three cars built in the United States were Model T Fords. In the next two years, the Model T slipped to account for only one-third of total production, while its chief competitor, General Motors, doubled its sales. According to one commentator in 1927, Ford was like the famous white whale Moby Dick—once "autocratic master of the seven seas of automobile selling," but now "wounded, spouting blood," with rivals looking to "fry his fat."[20] And indeed, General Motors did just that (with much more success than Captain Ahab ever had!). It matched Ford's market share by 1929 and has reigned as the largest American carmaker ever since.[21]

To pull off such a coup, GM successfully pursued two strategies that marked the triumph of the modern form of corporate organization and strategy in the 1920s.

General Motors was founded in 1904 when William Durant, a carriage maker in Flint, Michigan—just seventy miles northwest of Henry Ford's headquarters in Detroit—took over a small and failing car company called Buick. Over the next several years, Durant expanded his production of Buicks and absorbed dozens of other car manufacturers under his corporate umbrella, following the model of horizontal integration pioneered by large extractive companies such as Standard Oil. That rapid growth created organizational and managerial confusion, because the various constituent companies (Oldsmobile, Cadillac, and so on) each had their own internal structure, products, and corporate culture. Many of General Motors's cars targeted the same type of consumer, leading to a frustrating internal competition that hurt profits. In the mid-1910s, Durant set his company on the road to resolving these problems by launching an important collaboration with executives from the DuPont Corporation.[22]

DuPont was a family-owned company (founded in 1803 to produce gunpowder) that embarked on a massive transformation in management and strategy during and after World War I. Taking advantage of massive demand from the military between 1913 and 1919, a young generation of DuPont executives took the company in new directions. Their workforce rose sixteenfold to 85,000, and their capital expenditures quadrupled as the company expanded beyond explosives to a variety of chemical products, including artificial fibers. Yet throughout this expansion, the company retained its traditional management structure, centralizing functions such as sales, production, research, and accounting. With an ever-rising number of products designed for different markets, the sales staff became overstretched and uncoordinated. And top-level decisions about company-wide investments—which markets to pursue, where to invest in new research—suffered from poor communication.

DuPont and General Motors each resolved these structural issues in the 1920s by pioneering a new strategy known as "decentralized management." In essence, they redrew their companies' internal organizational charts based on products (dyes, paints, and so on for Du Pont; Chevrolet, Buick, and so on for GM), rather than functions such as "sales" and "accounting." Under a decentralized management structure, each *product* had its own sales force, marketing team, accountants, and research arm, and those managers reported to a higher-level executive who could now see how individual units performed. This decentralized approach allowed companies to expand with logistical ease. Adding a new product, or absorbing a competitor, no longer required integrating all aspects of that new business piece by piece; instead, the company could just add another column to its management chart.

It is no accident that business historians give both General Motors and DuPont credit for this advance, because the fortunes—literally and figuratively—of the two companies were bound up with each other during the 1910s and 1920s. In the late 1910s, General Motors president Durant brought in Pierre du Pont (one of the young du Ponts leading that company's expansion) as a major investor and chairman of the board of directors. In 1920, with GM still struggling, Durant resigned from the company he built, yielding his presidency and stock shares to Pierre du Pont. Shortly thereafter, Du Pont hired a young engineer named Alfred Sloan to bring decentralized management to the car company.

Like Frederick Taylor, Alfred Sloan had both an engineering background and a fierce devotion to rational organization and planning. He laid out chains of accountability among managers and facilitated communication. On the production side, General Motors differentiated its various makes and models, aiming its cars at distinct sections of the consumer market. No longer were GM automobiles in direct competition with one another: Cadillac, for example, attracted a wealthier clientele than Chevrolet did. And the cars were produced, marketed, and priced accordingly. By the mid-1920s, under Sloan's decentralized management structure, GM surpassed Ford as the country's largest automaker.

Sloan also rejected Henry Ford's belief that all cars should look alike, "just like one pin is like another pin when it comes from a pin factory," as Ford put it. The GM boss understood far better than Ford did that popular tastes were evolving as the mass consumption society blossomed in the 1920s. Car buyers would pay extra for style and fashion, he concluded. As a result, General Motors pioneered the practice of rolling out new models of its automobiles each year, and making them available in different colors and trims. Only after the death of Henry Ford in the late 1940s would the Ford Motor Company start to catch on to the modern strategy for marketing cars.[23]

By the end of the 1920s, institutions on a scale previously unknown in human history reached into all facets of daily life. Corporations employed workers by the thousands and wielded immense sway over prices, products, and politics. Yet for all their ubiquity, modern firms were less personal—more detached—than their predecessors. Such was the central tension of modernity: Americans were simultaneously more interconnected and more atomized; more beholden to material goods and more removed from their production. From cars to radios, Listerine to razor blades, the modern business firm and the triumph of mass consumption had profound consequences for American life. As the following two chapters explore, the "corporation" became a full-fledged social and political institution by the middle of the 20th century, spawning opportunity and prosperity as well as deep discontent and strife.

8

∽

FROM ROOSEVELT TO ROOSEVELT: BUSINESS AND THE MODERN STATE

In the summer of 1907, just a few months before a financial panic swept Wall Street and plunged the United States into yet another horrific depression, President Theodore Roosevelt traveled to Cape Cod, Massachusetts, to lay the cornerstone for the Pilgrim Memorial Monument. There to praise the past—and particularly values such as hard work and thrift that Americans had long associated with the early English colonists—Roosevelt used the occasion to speak to the present.

Industrial capitalism and the large-scale corporation, the president explained, had created both opportunities and challenges that earlier generations could never have conceived. The "great aggregations of capital" that were the hallmark of industrial society posed existential threats to the virtues he had come to honor. The rugged individualism and self-reliance of the Pilgrims and Puritans (however misremembered) had given way to a corporate culture of excess and corruption. The once-scrappy entrepreneurs of the past had been replaced by "malefactors of great wealth," unethical capitalists who could "amass a great fortune by special privilege, by chicanery and wrongdoing." The consequences for democratic rule and America's moral fabric were grave.

If the problems created by the industrial economy were historically unique, so, too, were the solutions. To cope with the modern market, Roosevelt and other reformers called for a modern regulatory state—a powerful administrative bureaucracy to regulate the affairs of private businesses in the public interest. Their vision found a clear articulation in Roosevelt's Pilgrim Memorial speech. Calling for real enforcement of the Sherman Antitrust Act of 1890, as well as a "national incorporation law for corporations engaged in interstate business" and national control of utilities such as railroads, the president laid bare the Progressive solution to the problems of monopoly. It lay, he insisted, with the national government.[1]

Nearly thirty years later, another President Roosevelt—Theodore's fifth cousin Franklin—picked up where his predecessor had left off. Before a roaring crowd at New York City's Madison Square Garden in October 1936, a week before the first of his three re-elections, the younger Roosevelt took aim at the predations of unscrupulous capitalists. In populist language that echoed his Progressive Era cousin, Franklin Roosevelt attacked the "economic royalists" who stood in the way of his New Deal reforms. They were "the old enemies of peace," he charged, guilty of "business and financial monopoly," "reckless banking," and "war profiteering." And in the face of real progress to regulate business and confront the disaster of the Great Depression, those forces were now "united in their hatred" for him. Convinced that taking on big business was a smart political strategy, Roosevelt taunted his critics, declaring: "I welcome their hatred."[2]

In their public bravado, the two Roosevelts deployed similar political language, despite the decades that separated their presidencies. Their furious and unequivocal condemnation of certain business leaders typified the contentious politics surrounding political and economic reform, and especially the state regulation of private enterprise, in the first third of the 20th century. The birth of the modern corporation and the rapid spread of industrial capitalism gave rise to a powerful political movement to expand the power of the administrative state as a bulwark in defense of democracy and equality. Put together, the Progressive Era and the New Deal period bookend a remarkable moment of political reform, as well as the emergence of a potent backlash.

For many business leaders, the expansion of the regulatory power of the government represented both an affront to their character and a challenge to their business. While some made their peace with new regulations, and even found ways to profit from them, others drew a hard line against progressive politics. Unfettered capitalism, they charged, cleared the path toward freedom and growth, while government rules and regulations were un-American and even seditious. The New Deal, according to Irénée du Pont (younger brother of Pierre and president of the family company from 1919 to 1925), was "nothing more or less than the Socialistic doctrine called by another name."[3] Many of the leaders of the country's largest corporations agreed, banding together into political clubs and trade associations to defend their economic interests.

Yet too much focus on fiery terms such as "economic royalists" and "Socialistic" suggests an overly simplified debate that pitted "free markets" against "government regulation." The history of American business shows that reality was far more complicated. Political tempers flared, but the relationship between the federal government and the business community—between the regulators and the regulated— was in fact marked by important episodes of accommodation and negotiated compromise. What made the years framed by the Roosevelt presidencies so pivotal for business history was not the flamboyant rhetoric, but the long-term dance between two emerging giants of the 20th century: the massive integrated corporation and the administrative, bureaucratic state, which developed an essentially *associational* relationship with each other.[4]

The Rise of Business Associations

One of the most important ways in which businesspeople engaged with the new, modern state was through business associations. Municipal chambers of commerce and boards of trade—relatively small operations during the 19th century—grew larger and attracted new members, particularly among midlevel businesspeople. As business enterprises became more specialized, so, too, did their associations, and trade groups dedicated to the interests of retailers, manufacturers, and other sectors proliferated. At the same time, large national organizations also came together to unite the financial, intellectual, and political power of the business community.[5]

Two primary factors propelled this new associational life among businesspeople: the growth of the regulatory state and the increased power of organized labor. To many business owners, managers, and investors, the swift rise of unions and regulations—themselves a response to the emergence of large, integrated firms—presented major obstacles to doing business. Labor activism, business leaders charged, drove up costs. Economic regulations, although aimed at stabilizing the economy and mitigating the destructive effects of unbridled competition, likewise aroused the ire of many business leaders, who saw the intercession of the government as a direct threat to their prerogatives.

Just as skilled craftsmen banded together to promote their interests, so too did businesspeople create new organizations. Whether they represented particular industries or sectors or the national business community, these associations helped solidify a new relationship between business and the modern state during the 1910s and 1920s.

The story of the National Association of Manufacturers (NAM), which continues to lobby for small and midsized industrial firms today, illustrates the important role that the politics of labor played in propelling pan-business unity. Formed in 1895, the NAM pushed for high protectionist tariffs on imports, following the script prepared by Alexander Hamilton a century before. At the same time, the organization operated as a vital tool of the Republican Party's efforts to attract the voters of small and medium-sized manufacturers in the Democratic-controlled South. Indeed, one of its founders was Ohio governor William McKinley (and his campaign strategist Marcus Hanna), who relied on support from the manufacturing community to defeat the populist Democrat William Jennings Bryan in 1896.

A few years after the group's founding, however, the NAM's leaders shifted their focus from tariffs, where they had only limited success. They reasoned that their manufacturers' association could attract more members and greater influence by turning its political fire on labor unions. Soon, the NAM distinguished itself in political battles against organized labor's efforts to achieve real shop-floor gains, such as higher wages and shorter working days. By the 1920s, the NAM acquired a permanent reputation as a conservative antagonist to the labor movement.

NAM had a lock on the antiunion position, but for Republican president William Taft—who assumed office in 1909—the group was too narrowly focused. Concluding that no association represented business's broader interests, Taft called for a conference of business leaders in Washington, D.C., in 1912, which led to a new, national business organization: the Chamber of Commerce of the United States. The National Chamber (as it was also known) cast itself as a centralized and more influential version of state- and city-based chambers of commerce, which had promoted local trade and industry across the country since the 19th century. Unlike the NAM, which limited itself to the manufacturing industry, the National Chamber included representatives from across the business world—from chain stores and hotels to steel companies and Wall Street banks.

By the late 1920s, the organization boasted nearly fourteen thousand members (NAM had about five thousand) and played an active role in public policy. (Indeed, it remains the most powerful and best-funded business lobbying organization in the country today.)[6] By taking an inclusive view toward the business community and representing more than just the narrow positions of elite industrialists and financiers, the Chamber promoted a singular vision of the business community. As the self-styled "voice of business," the chamber embodied President Calvin Coolidge's famous maxim that "the business of America is business." Indeed, Coolidge himself praised the Chamber for "very accurately reflect[ing] . . . public opinion in general."[7]

Unlike the NAM, the Chamber of Commerce did not focus solely on the labor question. Instead, it devoted its resources to a wider range of issues. By the 1910s, as companies grew larger, more integrated, and more complex, the quantity of economic statistics—about production costs, productivity, prices, supply chains, and other factors—expanded. Business leaders in the Progressive Era grew increasingly interested in understanding and analyzing the new data. "It is now generally agreed by students of the subject that the ups and downs of business prosperity are due to deep-seated influences," Harvard Business School's Melvin Copeland explained in 1915. To succeed, businesses had to understand the intricacies of complex markets, not just worry about such external factors as "tariff acts, political happenings, or court decisions." More specifically, University of Chicago economist Frank Knight wrote in 1921, a businessperson had to "*estimate* (1) the future demand which he is striving to satisfy and (2) the future results of his operations in attempting to satisfy that demand."[8] In addition to advocating for or against specific regulatory or labor policies, business associations such as the Chamber of Commerce scientifically assessed and distributed expert economic analysis.

In addition to improving managerial decisions, this devotion to collecting and studying economic information served an important political function as well. By drawing on the expertise of corporate executives, Progressive-Era business associations cemented a collaborative relationship with government policymakers. As rules about fair trade practices, product safety, price discrimination, and labor policies proliferated in the early decades of the 20th century, business leaders secured a prominent seat at the table.

In the years after World War I, this collaborative relationship between government policymakers and prominent leaders of the business community coalesced into a philosophy of government known as "associationalism"—the voluntary collaboration of self-governing organizations. The most famous apostle of this philosophy was Herbert Hoover, who directed the Commerce Department under Presidents Harding and Coolidge from 1921 until 1928, when he resigned to seek the presidency himself.[9]

Hoover had been a mining engineer before he entered public life, and he applied that rational, scientific mindset to political problem solving. Moreover, he had faith that collaboration between private firms and the government would lead to efficient results. As commerce secretary, Hoover brought government agencies and trade associations together to collect economic data that businesses could use to improve and standardize their practices. State and local governments also reflected this collective approach, passing licensing laws that regulated, professionalized, and standardized many business practices.

Today, many people think of the 1920s as a time of unfettered laissez-faire capitalism, when large combinations of industrial firms dominated the economy, and consumer goods such as radios and cars brought the promises of mass production to an ever-larger segment of the population. Yet a parallel expansion of the state accompanied the growth of business, and trade associations worked in collaboration with government agencies and officials such as Hoover in the interest of a shared general prosperity. Defenders of this new, progressive model of business-government relations believed they had struck a vital balance—they respected the traditional autonomy of private enterprise and the sanctity of private property while containing the destructive vicissitudes of the marketplace.

Business in the Roaring Twenties

The booming economy in the decade after World War I seemed to affirm Hoover's "associational" vision, and business leaders in those years achieved a prominent place in American culture, law, and politics. After a brief recession at the end of the war, the business cycle entered a prolonged period of expansion in 1922, and the next six years earned the nickname "the Roaring Twenties." Efficient mass production and mass distribution techniques, sophisticated organization, and the proliferation of consumer-oriented products all fueled the economic growth. Flush with new technological wonders and weary of foreign entanglements after the devastation of World War I, many Americans in the 1920s rejected the spirit of reform that had animated the Progressive period and embraced a political culture in which conservative attitudes flourished, particularly toward business.

For many businesspeople, this "retrenchment" meant a renewed defense of laissez-faire capitalism and an ever-stronger commitment to using their relationship with the government—on the local, state, and national levels—to promote business-friendly policies. As the *Wall Street Journal* gushed by mid-decade, "Never before, here or anywhere else, has a government been so completely fused with business."[10]

Nowhere was this fusion more evident than in relations between business and organized labor. Vladimir Lenin's Bolshevik Revolution in Russia in 1917 propelled a "Red Scare" over radical leftism. And a nationwide strike wave at the conclusion of World War I convinced many conservative politicians and business leaders that domestic union activism represented as grave a threat as communism abroad.[11]

The most dramatic labor activism unfolded in the steel industry. In September 1919, approximately 350,000 steelworkers walked off the job at mills across the country, from Colorado to New York, after months of fraught and ultimately futile negotiations with management. With support from the American Federation of Labor, the steelworkers mobilized around cries for higher wages—in the face of stark postwar price inflation—as well as safer working conditions and an eight-hour day. Most important, they demanded formal recognition of their union, the Amalgamated Association of Iron, Steel, and Tin Workers, with which the steel companies refused to negotiate.

The Great Steel Strike was one of the most powerful demonstrations of labor power in the nation's history, yet it met an inglorious fate. Just as they had during the Pullman Strike of 1894 and countless others, corporate owners used their political clout and influence over local, state, and national law enforcement to violently put down the strike within a few months. Unions failed once again to secure a recognized seat at the bargaining table.

The post–World War I strikes strengthened anti-labor sentiment within both the business community and the public at large. Many Americans feared that industrial unions, whose members were more likely to be unskilled immigrants and racial minorities, represented a fifth column attack by international communism—a radical threat to public safety, property, and core American values. Business leaders led the antiunion charge and public hostility to radical politics flourished, pushing unions to the point of impotence. As a prominent labor historian, David Brody, put it: "Organized labor posed no threat in the postwar decade."[12]

The Red Scare, antiunionism, and general retrenchment contributed to a revival of a political culture that rejected many of the reform- and regulation-oriented principles of the previous two decades. The Republican Party overcame the divisions between its progressive and conservative wings and returned to its roots as the party of business when it took control of Congress in 1919 and the White House in 1921. Such business-friendly conservatism shaped policy in several important areas, not least on the old issue of tariffs. The Republican-backed Fordney-McCumber tariff of 1922 raised import taxes to extraordinary levels. To the chagrin of rural producers, the high tariff not only protected manufacturers but also signaled a broader American desire to pull back from engagement with the wider world.[13]

Taxation was another issue where probusiness politics shaped national life. Ratified in 1913 at the height of the Progressive Era, the Sixteenth Amendment to the Constitution gave the federal government the power to collect taxes on income from both individuals and corporations. During World War I, income taxes provided vital revenue for the government, but the tax regime was steeply progressive, applying only to the top earners. Only approximately 15 percent of American households paid any income taxes at all in 1918; the richest 1 percent contributed about 80 percent of all revenue and paid effective tax rates of about 15 percent of their total income.

During the 1920s, Treasury Secretary Andrew Mellon—who paid the fourth-largest tax bill in the country, behind John Rockefeller, Henry Ford, and his son Edsel Ford—launched an antitax movement that would come to shape tax debates for generations to come (and down to the present). Outlining what later came to be known as the "supply-side" critique of progressive taxation, Mellon argued that high income taxes on the rich put a drag on economic growth by curtailing investment. Moreover, high taxes gave the wealthy a powerful incentive to hide their income or otherwise cheat the system. Lowering the tax rate, Mellon maintained, would both increase compliance and allow rich Americans to spend more on productive economic activity. During the Coolidge administration (1923–29), Mellon achieved many of his goals, and the top rate paid by individuals declined from 73 to 25 percent. Republicans in Congress, following Mellon's prescriptions, also lowered the tax on inherited property, known as the estate tax. They increased the exemption (the value of an inherited home below which one did not pay taxes) and lowered the top rate paid from 25 to 20 percent. By the late 1920s, only one half of one percent of inherited property was subject to taxation.[14]

Not every issue unified businesspeople and policymakers in the 1920s, however. Probably the most divisive issue was the national prohibition of alcohol, which cleaved the political world—business included—into the wets and the dries. In 1919, the Eighteenth Amendment launched an extended social experiment by barring "the manufacture, sale, or transportation of intoxicating liquors." The politics of Prohibition have long intrigued historians, since the movement to ban booze simultaneously represented a conservative (and anti-Catholic and anti-immigrant) effort at social control and a progressive impulse for reform in the name of public health. Although many corporate leaders agreed with the moral and social arguments, many also saw Prohibition as an unjust intrusion by the federal government into the private sector. (Not for nothing, this view was especially common among major beer manufacturers in the Midwest, such as Schlitz and Anheuser-Busch.) In fact, some of the most active supporters for the *repeal* of Prohibition, which took place in 1933, were business leaders who worried that it set a dangerous precedent for the government's ability to control business activity.[15]

But the twenties still roared, and political debates over taxes and alcohol did little to dampen widespread enthusiasm among industrial leaders, trade associations, and Wall Street investors. "American capitalism," in the words of economist John Kenneth Galbraith, "was in a lively phase." Production of manufactured goods was high, particularly in automobiles, and employment figures rose steadily from 1925 to 1929. The extended economic boom joined bootlegger parties and flappers among the decade's most iconic images.[16]

The roar of the decade was perhaps most evident in the spectacular rise of the stock market. Although stock trading had existed throughout the 19th century—the New York Stock Exchange was founded on Wall Street in 1792—the business really took off as railroad corporations expanded, using stock to raise capital, in the 1840s and 1850s. Speculation in stock prices had been central to the expansion of big businesses in the late 19th century, and by the early 20th it was a fixture of the financial world.

From its low point in the summer of 1921, the Dow Jones Industrial Average increased fivefold during the decade. The fastest increases in overall stock valuations took place in 1928 and the first half of 1929. A growing middle class with greater expendable income for consumer products certainly fueled corporate profits and stock prices, but the driving force of the stock expansion was speculation—investors hoping to buy low and quickly sell high. By the late 1920s, Wall Street investment houses developed a system known as "buying on margin," which made investing far easier. Under this system, investors could buy stock with only a small percentage in cash, and borrow the rest from a broker. The "margin" was the difference between the down payment and the purchase price of the investment. If the stock price increased, the investor could sell at a higher price, repay the broker for the margin loan (plus a bit more), and walk away with a profit. If and when the broker wanted to call in the loan, he would make a "margin call" to the investor, compelling repayment.[17]

As risky as this practice seems in hindsight (if stock prices decreased, investors might be unable to pay the brokers back), it appeared logical in the boom market of the 1920s. And as stock prices rose, so did margin buying. Galbraith estimated that the total amount of money loaned by brokers in the early 1920s ranged from $1 billion to $1.5 billion. In 1926, that total reached $2.5 billion and then $3.5 billion by the end of 1927. From $4 billion in June 1928, the volume of loans to stock purchasers spiked to $6 billion by the end of the year. By October 1929, brokers had made more than $8.5 billion in loans.[18]

This general prosperity convinced many Americans that modern business practices had conquered the vicious swings of the boom-and-bust cycles that had rocked the economy throughout the nation's history. A handful of voices urged restraint—including that of Republican president Herbert Hoover, who took office in March 1929 and, despite his public optimism, privately urged Wall Street investment houses to curb their enthusiasm and rein in margin lending. Yet such notes of caution were the exception, and most businesspeople believed the good times would last. "Stock prices are not too high and Wall Street will not experience anything in the nature of a crash," declared Yale economist Irving Fisher in response to market jitters on September 5, 1929. "We are living in an age of increasing prosperity and consequent increasing earning power of corporations and individuals," he continued. Just over a month later, Fisher reaffirmed that stocks had reached "what looks like a permanently high plateau."[19]

Business Gets a Black Eye: The Great Depression

The good times did not last. From the heights of the 1920s, the United States tumbled into one of the greatest economic catastrophes in history in the 1930s, dragging most of the world's economies along with it. Between 1929 and 1933, stock market values plunged, banks failed, savings were wiped out, farms and homes were foreclosed on by the thousands, and millions of citizens were out of work. As the country stumbled through the long financial crisis and into the despair of Depression, the glory days of American business looked like a relic.

Economic historians continue to debate the causes of the Great Depression. What is not debated is that the national economy entered a cyclical contraction at the end of the 1920s that spiraled into a global economic catastrophe. Signs of instability had been apparent for several years by 1929, including declining agricultural prices and massive, albeit localized, losses in real estate speculation. Most Americans, and especially most businesspeople, failed to take notice, however, until the stock market crash of October 1929.

After hitting a high in early September, the stock market started to stutter. Brokers and banks that had loaned money on margin worried that even small reductions in stock prices would leave investors unable to pay them back. They began calling in loans. Stock owners, in turn, tried to sell off what they had before prices dropped too low. This massive sell-off turned into a self-fulfilling prophecy, pushing prices down.

Leaders of the financial community worked to shore up the nervous markets. On Thursday, October 24, the stock market lost more than 10 percent of its value as the trading day began, and a cadre of top financiers sprang into action. Meeting at the offices of J.P. Morgan, this group of bankers agreed to pool as much capital as necessary to send reassuring signals to other investors. They sent a representative to the floor of the stock exchange, where he made a number of large, overvalued bids for high-profile stocks such as U.S. Steel. Their goal was to demonstrate confidence and convince others to stop the sell-off. For a brief moment, the plan appeared to work, but it soon became clear that there was no way to head off a full panic.

Fear spread over the weekend when the market was closed, and an even larger sell-off began when trading resumed on Monday. The floodgates opened the following day—October 29, 1929 (quickly dubbed "Black Tuesday"). Frenzied traders sold stocks for whatever price they could get. There appeared to be no bottom. Eight million shares changed hands by noon and 16 million trades were made by closing, setting a record for volume traded that stood until 1968.[20]

Yet the stock market crash was only the beginning, and the economy only grew worse in the months and years that followed October 1929. As investment wealth disappeared, consumer demand declined and prices dropped, pushing many businesses to ruin. Total corporate profits fell from $10 billion to $1 billion, a drop of 90 percent. As workers lost their jobs, consumer spending declined even further in a vicious cycle. By 1932, more than one hundred thousand businesses had closed. Unemployment reached 30 percent of the "civilian private nonfarm labor force" by 1933, or 11.5 million people. By the time the market bottomed out in 1933, nominal gross domestic product was nearly half what it had been in 1929.[21]

Speculative investment and the oversaturation of consumer products certainly helped bring about the Depression, but the muted policy response was critical as well. President Hoover, against his better instincts, was hamstrung by a Republican political tradition that favored a "laissez-faire response." Treasury Secretary Andrew Mellon insisted that the only course was to "liquidate labor, liquidate stocks, liquidate farmers, liquidate real estate . . . it will purge the rottenness out of the system." (The quotation attributed to Mellon comes from Herbert Hoover's memoir, written decades later; whether Mellon uttered those exact words or not, the sentiment was real.)[22]

A similar disposition at the Federal Reserve—the institution created in the Progressive Era to stabilize the economy—left policymakers unable to cope with the massive systemic failure of the banking system. American banks had never been especially stable, even in good times. Around five hundred failed every year throughout the 1920s. And for about a year after the stock market crash, the failure rate remained only slightly above average. Starting in the last two months of 1930, however, a protracted series of runs shuttered thousands of local banks, particularly in the Midwest. Bank runs spread on panic, much like the stock market sell-off. As people who had borrowed money from banks failed to pay it back—and the value of their homes and farms declined—banks' income declined. Worried that their bank would go bust and take their savings with it, depositors rushed to withdraw their money. The early arrivals were lucky, but those who came too late found that the banks were out of money.

With no lending from the Federal Reserve to prop up the struggling banks, thousands of financial institutions went bankrupt. In 1931, nearly 2,300 banks went out of business. Some 1,450 went under in 1932. The next year, 4,000. In the days before government-sponsored insurance on banking deposits (created in response to this disaster in 1933), these failures took personal and business savings with them, driving the country further into Depression.

The onset of the Great Depression brought the probusiness ebullience of the 1920s to a dramatic and rapid close. Public outrage against the excesses of capitalist greed pushed President Hoover in 1932 to launch an investigation of Wall Street investors, whom he blamed for causing the stock market crash. In addition, the 1930 midterm election brought to Congress large numbers of Democrats who did not share Andrew Mellon's desire to "liquidate" and backed more aggressive federal intervention. In 1932, Congress passed and Hoover signed a law to create the Reconstruction Finance Corporation (RFC). This new federal agency provided government-backed loans to creditworthy businesses and state and local governments that, because of the failing banking system, were unable to get loans they would qualify for otherwise. An inherently conservative institution that only made the safest loans (and therefore made back the money it loaned out), the RFC did nothing for the millions of Americans left unemployed or homeless by the Depression. It also came far too late to save Herbert Hoover's political career. The thirty-first president became synonymous with widespread destitution—unwillingly lending his name to slums called "Hoovervilles" and gestures such as the "Hoover flag," an empty pocket turned inside out.[23]

The economic crisis challenged not only Americans' vision of business leaders, but also their belief in the legitimacy of private enterprise. As William Leuchtenburg, one of the most famous historians of American politics, summarized: "If businessmen had caused prosperity, who but they must be responsible for the depression?" For their part, business leaders did little to improve their public standing. Many clung to the old nostrums of laissez-faire and self-reliance, blaming the poor and the unemployed for their plight. In the fall of 1930, just as the banking system began its epic collapse, the president of the National Association of Manufacturers asked if the jobless failed to "practice the habits of thrift and conservation . . . [was] our economic system, or government, or industry to blame?"[24] If the 1920s had marked a conservative moment of faith in business and a rejection of Progressive Era reforms, the 1930s would bring about a resurgence of regulation.

Business and the New Deal

After flying to Chicago to accept the Democratic Party's nomination for president in the summer of 1932 (the first candidate to do so in person), New York governor Franklin D. Roosevelt promised that, if elected, he would offer "a new deal to the American people." During the campaign, Roosevelt offered only vague strategies for fighting the Depression, and even once he took office the next March, his policies reflected an emergency mindset (which he called "bold, persistent experimentation") rather than a coherent political philosophy. Nonetheless, the phrase "New Deal" stuck, and within a few years came to represent a new approach to government that forever recast the relationship between American business and the American state.[25]

In his first two years in office, Roosevelt pushed through a wide-ranging series of reforms to stanch the economic bleeding, provide material relief to millions of suffering Americans, and shore up the nation's ailing financial markets. Among the longest-lasting reforms to emerge from this period, which historians often call the "First New Deal" (1933–34), were key provisions of the Banking Act of 1933. This legislation created the Federal Deposit Insurance Corporation (FDIC), which prevented bank runs by providing a government backup to consumer bank deposits. In addition, four provisions of the law (often referred to as the "Glass-Steagall Act" after its Congressional sponsors) legally separated the functions of commercial and investment banks.

The most important part of Roosevelt's first year in office, however, was more short-lived. In June 1933, Congress created the National Recovery Administration (NRA) to revive the national economy.* The NRA brought together representatives from the business community as well as organized labor to create "codes of fair competition," setting standards for prices, distribution schedules, and wages in an effort to limit further business failures. Such top-down planning— instructing firms and industries how much to produce and telling workers how much they'd be paid—represented a radical approach to economic policy. By involving the leaders of large firms and labor groups, the NRA represented a model of "corporatism" that was far more common in European economies than in the United States. Yet

---

* The National Rifle Association, founded in 1871 as a sports and hunting association, did not achieve national prominence as a gun-rights lobbying group until the 1960s. In the 1930s, the acronym "NRA" would not have held a dual meaning for most Americans.

big manufacturers largely supported the NRA, since it allowed them to remain profitable and reduced the threats of excessive competition. The president of the U.S. Chamber of Commerce wrote to Roosevelt: "The psychology of the country is now ready for self-regulation of industry with government approval of agreements reached either within or without trade conferences."[26]

If the NRA represented a power-sharing agreement between big business and the federal state, its dissolution by the Supreme Court marked a premature end to that compromise. In 1935, the Court ruled the NRA unconstitutional on two grounds. One, by giving the executive branch rule-making power, the law usurped the legislature's constitutional authority. Two, by setting standards, such as minimum wages, that applied *within* states, the law overstepped the bounds of the Interstate Commerce Clause.[27]

The destruction of the NRA, as well as calls from organized labor and other groups for even more aggressive business regulation, pushed President Roosevelt to the political left in 1935. His public speeches, such as the 1936 Madison Square Garden address, expressed Roosevelt's willingness to attack entrenched wealth. Likewise, his policy agenda reflected a renewed defense of the economically powerless, particularly the poor, the elderly, and workers. A major cleavage quickly emerged between the business community and the political coalition increasingly identified as "New Deal liberalism."

The New Deal's labor policies marked a profound historical departure. In 1935, organized labor won a major victory with the Wagner Act, which enshrined in law workers' right to organize and bargain collectively. The law created the National Labor Relations Board (NLRB), a regulatory commission that ruled on whether employers practiced unfair labor policies, such as discriminating against union members, trying to dominate union activities, or refusing to bargain. In addition, the NLRB guaranteed that workers could conduct open elections to decide on a union to represent them. Radical workers' parties, including socialist and communist parties, protested that the Wagner Act was too moderate because it focused on the procedural rights to bargain collectively but left the general positions of management and labor intact and brought no structural change to workplace dynamics. On the other hand, many business leaders objected to the institutionalization of labor rights and worried that collective bargaining weakened managers' autonomy.

The Social Security Act of 1935 represented a second source of schism between business and New Deal liberals. By creating federal pension payments for the old, widowed, disabled, and poor families with young children, Social Security put the government in the business of providing for the nation's neediest. The fruit of tremendous compromise and political effort, the act proved to be one of the most contentious policies of the New Deal (and debates over it rage to this day). Some traditionalists charged that paying people who didn't work would fuel what Herbert Hoover called "a cult of leisure," and many others worried about what social insurance payments would do to the strained national budget.[28]

Roosevelt agreed that regular treasury funds should not be spent on pensions, and worried that future legislatures could vote away any plan he enacted. To solve both problems, he favored a program funded by separate, specific taxes on earned income (a "payroll tax") that linked future pension payments to a worker's lifetime contributions—half the tax paid by the worker; half by the employer. As he put it: "We put those payroll contributions there so as to give the contributors a legal, moral, and political right to collect their pensions and their unemployment benefits. With those taxes there, no damn politician can ever scrap my social security program."[29] Social Security was highly popular (rising from a 68 percent approval rating in 1936 to 96 percent in 1944), but many large corporations and business associations recoiled at the new expense employers faced.[30]

By the mid-1930s, the New Deal inaugurated a variety of important regulations over business activities that recast the political relationship between corporations and the state. In the aftermath of the stock market crash, a congressional investigation concluded that certain bankers had manipulated the financial system in the interests of insiders, leading to the bubble and the financial ruin that followed. If the financial community could not be counted on to police itself, the Roosevelt administration reasoned, the government would do so instead. And with Wall Street so discredited by the Depression, Roosevelt faced little opposition. In 1934, Congress created the Securities and Exchange Commission to take over what had previously been the domain of private actors—ensuring the integrity of corporate affairs. Signaling a new approach to business regulation, the SEC required publicly traded companies to disclose financial information and created new legal prohibitions against profiting from insider information.[31]

Other New Deal regulations also sought to improve fairness and transparency, as well as economic efficiency. Improvements in road quality and automotive technology gave the trucking industry an advantage over the heavily regulated railroads, whose rates and routes were governed by the Interstate Commerce Commission. In response, Congress expanded the ICC's purview to regulate trucking. To regulate the new business of commercial air flight, Congress created the Civil Aeronautics Board to set prices and control entry to the industry, deciding who was allowed to be an airline company. In similar ways, the government also regulated water companies and energy companies, setting policies for oil, coal, natural gas, and electricity.

Many prominent business leaders had supported Franklin Roosevelt during the election of 1932 and backed the National Recovery Administration between 1933 and 1935. By the middle of the decade, however, those relations had grown strained. The years 1935 and 1936 saw the blossoming of a reinvigorated labor movement. Emboldened by the Wagner Act and organized by effective and powerful leaders, workers forced major employers such as General Motors and U.S. Steel to bargain with industrial unions. The Social Security program created a new and intimate financial relationship between the American people and the federal government, on which many—particularly the old and disabled—now depended for their livelihoods. And new regulations reinforced the public's distrust of corporate leaders.

In response, many businesspeople turned away from Roosevelt and condemned the New Deal. The U.S. Chamber of Commerce broke with Roosevelt over Social Security in 1934. That same year, a bipartisan organization called the American Liberty League—funded by the DuPont Corporation—formed to oppose the New Deal; it would later endorse Republican challenger Alf Landon for president in 1936. (Its effectiveness was quite muted; Landon suffered one of the worst defeats in American presidential election history.)[32] Those defections help explain Roosevelt's choice to rail against the "economic royalists" who united in their hatred for the president and his New Deal policies. The relationship between the state and the private sector in the United States had changed for good.

9

IN LOVE WITH BIGNESS:
THE POSTWAR CORPORATION

I n 1956, a reporter from *Fortune* magazine named William Whyte dropped a bombshell on the culture of Corporate America with a book that would become a best seller, *The Organization Man*. Modern life, Whyte argued, was dominated by large, impersonal organizations that stifled individuality and creativity under the boot of their hierarchical structures. Although government agencies, religious and educational institutions, and the military all reflected this trend, Whyte singled out the business corporation as the most pernicious example of the oppressive weight "the organization" placed on American life. Unlike earlier critics of big business, who focused on its effect on consumer prices, smaller competitors, and traditional society, Whyte worried most about the effects of modern firms on the men who worked in them. (And in Whyte's gendered and 1950s formulation, his book was all about men.) Like the mass-produced housing developments that dotted the American suburban landscape in the 1950s, he argued, the modern corporation created a stultifying culture of conformity and thwarted the entrepreneurial spirit that had once defined America.

Whyte's social criticism sprang from his life experience. Born to a wealthy Pennsylvania family in 1917, he spent most of the Great Depression at St. Andrew's preparatory school in Delaware and then Princeton University. After working as a traveling salesman for Vick Chemical Company, he joined the Marines during World War II and fought in the Pacific, including at Guadalcanal. His privileged background, as well as his experience within one of the most hierarchical and anti-individualist organizations known to history—the U.S. war machine—shaped his work as a journalist when he joined *Fortune* at war's end. Fascinated with the link between corporate structure and the new culture of consumerism and suburbia, he dedicated himself to creating a descriptive taxonomy of the business world.

Drawing on interviews with a wide range of businesspeople, Whyte concluded that large institutions, particularly corporations, discouraged risk-taking and bred complacency by rewarding those who fell in line. Gone was the fabled "Protestant work ethic" and its faith in individual initiative, hard work, and personal sacrifice. In its place a "social ethic" had arisen that valued group effort, group thinking, and collective work. By "collective," Whyte did not mean to suggest that corporations were run like communist governments, but rather that the way people related to each other and their work reinforced a set of values that put the whole above the parts.

The primary practitioner of this new ethic was the "Organization Man" himself, that young manager or executive whose identity, Whyte argued, was subsumed by the collective mission of the corporation. In this diagnosis, Whyte borrowed from the popular critique of the sociologist C. Wright Mills, whose 1951 book *White Collar* had identified the choking and even dehumanizing nature of corporate office work. Despite their comfortable paychecks, the men Mills and Whyte profiled—typically denizens of cookie-cutter suburbs to match their cookie-cutter, gray-flannel-suit jobs—felt bereft of purpose or individuality. These overwhelmingly white, college-educated, and privileged young men (like Whyte himself) risked losing their individual identities.[1]

What most concerned cultural critics such as Whyte and Mills was that most Americans seemed to prefer the new business culture. During and after World War II, the economic recovery had lifted large businesses in particular to unprecedented heights; by 1948, corporations—not individuals or small businesses—held a clear majority of the nation's wealth, and the largest two hundred firms accounted for one out of every five nonagricultural jobs.[2] In the 1940s and 1950s, young men graduating from elite universities overwhelmingly declared their desire to join a company like General Motors or U.S. Steel and work their way up the corporate ladder. One survey found that three-quarters of Americans believed that "the good things outweigh the bad things" when it came to big business's effects on society.[3]

The deep critiques of intellectuals, juxtaposed against the pervasive public acceptance and even embrace of large corporations, exposed the central tensions of post–World War II American society. Many of our classic images of the 1950s—suburbs, nuclear bomb shelters, and quaint, family-oriented TV sitcoms such as *Father Knows Best*—reflect a spirit of social retrenchment and conservatism. As the Cold War between the United States and the Soviet Union developed in the years after World War II and the threat of nuclear war hung overhead, many Americans longed for security and predictability. The dominance of large, integrated corporations—from chain stores to heavy industry, from technology to entertainment—meant less turbulent market competition and greater economic stability. As consumers as well as employees, many Americans found solace in the uniformity.

At the same time, American business in the postwar years reinforced the new ties between the government and the private sector created during the New Deal of the 1930s. Entangled in the Cold

War arms race, as well as the space race, with the Soviets, the United States directed unprecedented resources to scientific research and development, forging vital partnerships with American industry. The triumph of the large corporation at midcentury shaped the direction of technological development as well as the structural relationships between public and private entities.

From the 1940s through the 1960s, the dominant trend in both American society and American business was toward bigness—big corporations, but also big government programs (from the Apollo mission to the War on Poverty). Some critics, such as William Whyte and C. Wright Mills, worried that corporate culture eroded such traditional values as thrift, hard work, creativity, and individualism. Other public intellectuals who identified themselves as politically liberal, including the economist John Kenneth Galbraith, lauded the benefits that big social institutions created, but warned that material prosperity and consumer culture blinded Americans to social problems—including persistent poverty and racism—and weakened civic engagement.[4] And still other critics from the political left as well as the right worried that the close ties between the government, the military, and the industrial community threatened individual freedoms and democratic governance. Yet underlying all these critiques was the undeniable new reality: From industrial revival during World War II to the rise of the tech-infused knowledge economy, from the "organization" to the conglomerate merger wave of the 1960s, American corporations wielded dominant power over postwar culture.

World War II and a New Start for Business

The United States officially joined World War II the day after Japan attacked Pearl Harbor in December 1941, but the war began reshaping the American economy years before American GIs deployed to the battlefields of Europe and Asia. Long-standing alliances with

France and Britain meant significant military contracts for American manufacturers as Hitler's armies overran Europe in 1939 and 1940. By the time Congress passed the Lend-Lease program to supply war matériel to the beleaguered British in March 1941, both business and the political establishment had switched to a war footing. Anticipating the major new expenditures war would bring, Congress enacted two Revenue Acts in 1940 to increase individual and corporate tax rates and—to head off charges of war profiteering—imposed an "excess profits tax" on corporations. All told, the United States government spent approximately $320 billion (in 1940s money) on World War II, about half of it borrowed from the public through bond sales and the other half raised in taxes. That spending provided a massive boost to the gross national product, which shot up from $88.6 billion in 1939 to $135 billion in 1945.[5]

During the war, the U.S. government hired private companies to produce hundreds of thousands of aircraft, millions of trucks, and billions of rounds of ammunition. Shipyards produced thousands of warships, merchant ships, and smaller vessels. After Germany invaded France in the spring of 1940, President Roosevelt called on American manufacturers to boost their production numbers from 13,000 to 50,000 planes a year; those demands hit 60,000 per year in 1942 and 125,000 in 1943. Aircraft companies ultimately built about 300,000 airplanes during the war.

In the interest of secrecy and efficiency, the military preferred to contract with relatively few private manufacturers, rather than pit competing firms against each other. As a result, war procurement led to a major consolidation in manufacturing. According to some estimates, the hundred largest American industrial companies had accounted for 30 percent of the country's output in 1939, but by 1943 they produced 70 percent.[6]

With the boom in industrial production during the war, the U.S. economy slipped the shackles of the Great Depression. Employment rebounded, both because of the millions of Americans enlisted in the armed services and because of renewed demand for manufacturing. The civilian workforce expanded, and the number of hours available to work went up. The average length of a workweek in manufacturing rose from thirty-eight hours to more than forty-five hours. One of the more important changes during the war was the massive increase in employment by women, particularly in manufacturing. By 1944, unemployment had fallen to just over 1 percent (remember that the official rate hit 25 percent in 1933). Within the span of eleven years, in other words, the country had seen both the highest and lowest levels of joblessness of the century.

Perhaps the most significant aspect of the economic recovery during World War II was the relative independence that business leaders managed to secure. Unlike in other warring countries, where the government effectively took over industrial production, the Roosevelt administration consciously permitted private firms to remain private and did not construct its own production facilities. Wartime regulations placed severe limitations on economic activity. Companies with government contracts had to honor wage pledges to workers and price controls set by the Office of Price Administration, just as consumers had to make do with rations on products such as meat and gasoline. The excess profits tax likewise limited the wealth individual businesspeople could reap, even as production ramped up. Yet the American economy remained fundamentally market-oriented during the war. In the end, World War II helped cement the New Deal's experiment with managed capitalism—neither unfettered laissez-faire nor state-run industry.

The recovery appeared miraculous, but many experts worried about what fate would befall the national economy when the war ended. Perhaps the war economy—with its massive outlays for industrial production, strict price controls, and patriotic spirit of cooperation between business, government, and labor—was a temporary deviation from the norm. In the 1930s and 1940s, many prominent economists blamed the Great Depression on a mature and oversaturated industrial economy: The speed, scale, and efficiency of modern production methods had maxed out, leaving no more room for growth or profitable investment. A growing number found hope in the theories of British economic John Maynard Keynes, who argued that government spending could drive demand and revive a stagnant economy, but nonetheless worried that the end of wartime expenditures would lead to renewed hardship.[7] As the war ended, many business leaders and policymakers came to believe that postwar prosperity would depend on fostering a vibrant consumer culture, with a focus on spending.[8]

Science, R&D, and the Rise of the "Knowledge Economy"

If World War II saved the economy and revived the public's faith in business, it also cemented the might of the American industrial system. During the war, American manufacturers perfected their mass production and distribution techniques, putting themselves in a position to expand into colossi of global commerce. After 1945, as Europe and Asia struggled to dig themselves out from beneath the rubble of war and remake their political, cultural, and economic lives, American business stood nearly unchallenged as the world's foremost producer of industrial goods. What's more, within a few years, a new international crisis—the Cold War with the Soviet Union—created an even more advantageous environment for business. That conflict fueled not only proxy wars in Korea and Vietnam, but also a technological space and arms race, all of which tied the national government ever closer to business. Benefiting from their size and structure, as well as federal grants, subsidies, and tax breaks, large American corporations pioneered opportunities in science and technology.

Before the 1940s, the biggest American businesses had been large, capital- and labor-intensive firms that dealt in industrial products—steel, petroleum, automobiles, and chemicals. Those industries persisted and grew after World War II, but newer fields emerged and became dominant parts of the American economy. The early Cold War period sparked developments in areas such as advanced telecommunications, electronics (including the earliest computers), pharmaceuticals, and synthetic chemicals. Whereas mechanized mass production firms invested huge sums in equipment and relatively unskilled labor, these new high-tech firms relied to an unprecedented degree on "intellectual capital" to create new and complex processes and technologies. This premium on scientific research—often performed by highly educated employees and funded in part by government grants—marked the beginning of what we have come to call the "knowledge economy."[9]

During the early Cold War period, the most prosperous economic sectors—in addition to home goods and new home construction—were high-tech. The aviation industry thrived during the war and also transitioned afterward to become a major part of postwar American business. Commercial and military air travel was in its infancy in the 1930s but expanded mightily during the war. As the Cold War began, Boeing Corporation emerged as a major supplier to the Department of Defense (as the country optimistically renamed the War Department in 1947). By the 1950s, Boeing had developed the B-52 bomber, which became a mainstay of Cold War strategy and played a major role in military campaigns beginning with the Vietnam War.[10]

Boeing's lucrative government contracts allowed corporations to translate those technological advances to the civilian sector. In the 1950s, the company introduced a four-engine passenger jet airplane called the 707, which became the basic model for private commercial airlines around the world. It updated that model with the 737 and 747 in the 1960s, the 757 and 767 in the 1980s, the 777 in the 1990s, and more recently the 787.

And Boeing was far from the only firm to reconfigure military technology for civilian purposes. In the chemical products field, DuPont—an old lion of 19th-century industry—reinvented itself through its expansive research and development (R&D) efforts. As a pioneer of the diversified and decentralized management structure that defined postwar firms, DuPont incorporated R&D programs in its corporate structure. Its early successes provided a financial cushion that allowed the company to fund research efforts that could take years to generate anything marketable. Its smaller competitors could not afford such risks. Indeed, many of the products that DuPont researchers created turned into commercial flops—such as synthetic silk and leather, for example. Nonetheless, the company learned that a single hit could offset any number of duds.[11]

The pharmaceutical industry also experienced a boom as the knowledge industry expanded at midcentury. Biomedical research, funded by corporations as well as universities, both of which received vital government grants, led to remarkable advances in life-saving and life-improving drugs. Antibiotics and vaccines wiped out many diseases that had plagued humanity for thousands of years, including such scourges as polio. The rise in prescription-only medications illustrates the rapid transformation of the pharmaceutical industry: In 1929, prescription drugs accounted for only 32 percent of all medicines purchased in the United States (by cost); by 1969, that figure reached 83 percent. Drug companies such as Merck and Pfizer, which held valuable patents, profited immensely. In those same years, the federal government committed itself to improving public health by subsidizing medical care for the poor and elderly (through the Medicare and Medicaid systems created in 1965), expanding the market for pharmaceutical products as well as health care services.[12]

Perhaps no industry illustrates the massive changes the knowledge economy brought to American business better than electronics. Although Japanese companies such as Sony would become the leaders in consumer electronics by the end of the century, American companies such as RCA led the way between the 1940s and 1970s. Originating as a radio broadcaster in 1919, RCA (the Radio Corporation of America) began conducting research on the new medium of visual television in the 1930s. By the 1940s, the Camden, New Jersey–based corporation made 80 percent of the TVs sold in the United States (at two hundred thousand per year). The rapid adoption of televisions in middle-class American households in the 1950s and the innovation of color TV in the 1960s brought tremendous profits to RCA, which moved from New Jersey to Indiana, Tennessee, and ultimately Mexico in search of less expensive labor environments.[13]

Equally important was the electronic computing industry. As with all major technological developments—from the steam engine to the automobile—the "computer" was not invented by any one person. During the 1940s and 1950s, engineers in universities, government research settings (in a variety of countries, including Nazi Germany), and private corporations devoted immense amounts of time, money, and intellectual energy to creating an electronic device capable of storing information and performing calculations. In 1946, a team of researchers at the University of Pennsylvania announced the ENIAC (Electronic Numerical Integrator And Computer) machine, the fruit of a project funded principally by the U.S. Army to calculate trajectories for artillery and, ultimately, nuclear weapons. About the size of a large room (8 feet by 3 feet by 100 feet) and weighing more than twenty-seven tons, the ENIAC included thousands of vacuum tubes to conduct electrical current. In 1947, researchers at Bell Laboratory—a private research facility that had been spun off from AT&T's research and development program in 1925—invented the electronic transistor, a conduit for current that replaced the clunky vacuum tubes.

In 1950, a typewriter manufacturing company named Remington Rand acquired the patent right to the ENIAC design and soon released the first marketable mainframe computer, the UNIVAC

(UNIVersal Automatic Computer). At first, Rand sold its machines, which were about the size of a small truck, to government agencies to perform tasks such as sorting census data or cataloging Social Security information. In 1954, however, General Electric became the first private firm to own a mainframe computer when it bought a UNIVAC.[14]

Not every major contributor to the burgeoning computer industry was a young upstart, however. In the 1950s, no company did more to make computer technology widely available than IBM. That iconic American corporation, originally International Business Machines, began in the 1910s manufacturing machines that sorted punch cards, which the large industrial and financial corporations of the Progressive period used to feed their growing fixation with data analysis. In the 1930s, the company sold its increasingly sophisticated sorting machines, which depended on a complex system of hydraulic tubes, to government bureaucracies that had a newfound demand for organizing massive quantities of information.

In 1952, IBM introduced its version of an electronic computer and took the lead in bringing them to market. As new technologies emerged, IBM integrated them into its products. The most significant was the integrated circuit, invented in 1958 by an engineer at Texas Instruments, an electronics manufacturer that sold primarily to the military and received vital research funding from the U.S. Army. That invention—essentially a set of small transistors carved from a piece of semiconducting material—eliminated the need to solder multiple transistors together and allowed far higher volumes of current to pass through the circuitry, increasing computing power exponentially. Using Texas Instruments' breakthroughs, IBM cemented its status as the leader in mainframe computer manufacturing in 1964 when it released its signature machine, the System/360. That computer, the first designed to perform a wide range of functions and thus fill a variety of corporate and governmental needs, marked the arrival of the modern computer industry in the business world.[15]

The knowledge economy that underlay the development of electronic computing in the mid–20th century grew from vital collaborations between the private sector, universities, and the federal government. Starting during World War II and continuing with gusto through the Cold War, the government served not only as a major consumer of new technology but also as a principal underwriter. Government grants—both to university research centers and to private firms—fueled the technology boom. Public-private partnerships also led to the creation of major research hubs. The combination of defense spending, private capital, and top-notch research facilities at Stanford University, for example, created a hub for information technology that, in the 1970s, would be nicknamed "Silicon Valley"—after the semiconducting material used in the integrated circuits that helped create the information technology industry.[16]

The Conglomerate Wave

The dominant theme in American business after World War II was bigness—large-scale, integrated, multidivisional organizations run by professional managers and executives, yet owned by a diverse array of shareholders with relatively little control over day-to-day operations. The roaring postwar economy and a soaring stock market created an environment ripe for continued expansion, and many successful corporations redirected their profits toward acquiring other firms. Beginning in the late 1950s, a merger wave developed, mirroring in many ways the experiences of the late 1890s and late 1920s. The total number of mergers per year jumped from just over one thousand in 1963 to six thousand when the wave peaked in 1969. Thereafter, a declining stock market, the onset of a recession, and tax reforms made mergers less attractive.[17]

The merger wave of the 1960s reshaped corporate America not only through the raw *number* of mergers, but also through the specific *way* many corporations fused themselves together. Many mergers followed the traditional patterns of horizontal and vertical integration—buying up one's competitors or suppliers—but a substantial number of corporations departed from their traditional field of operations. Taking the logic of impersonal efficiency, rationality, and decentralized management to at times perverse lengths, individual corporations used their merger activity to enter unrelated sectors or industries, transforming themselves into *conglomerates*.[18]

Roughly defined, a conglomerate is a corporation that conducts business in a wide range of markets and industries that have little or no relationship to one another. Berkshire Hathaway, the company founded by billionaire investor Warren Buffett, provides a familiar example of the form today—it acts as a holding company that owns and operates an array of disparate businesses, from GEICO insurance to Jordan's Furniture to Fruit of the Loom.

Identifying conglomerates in history presents a challenge, because the label itself is open to interpretation. Whether any particular merger created a "pure conglomerate," in which the parties truly had nothing in common, depended on how one defines "nothing." Since the legal and regulatory systems do not distinguish between corporations based on the logical compatibility of their internal holdings, "conglomerate" status is often in the eye of the beholder.

Nonetheless, scholars widely agree that the conglomerate model became increasingly widespread during the merger mania of the late 1960s. In 1968, as the merger wave approached its highest point, approximately 84 percent of large corporate mergers either created a conglomerate or occurred when a conglomerate expanded. Within the mining and manufacturing sector alone, the value of mergers totaled $12.6 billion—and $11 billion of that involved conglomerates.[19]

The level of merger activity in the 1960s was only possible because of the triumph of structural changes to corporate organization pioneered by firms such as DuPont and General Motors in the 1920s.

Decentralized management and smooth coordination among various business units became commonplace in nearly all large corporations in the postwar period. These complex but well-designed structures not only allowed companies to establish new product lines, research and development programs, and sophisticated marketing; they also freed executives to pursue new lines of business. Executives searched for ways to circumvent the curse of mature or stagnant markets and position themselves for permanent growth. In 1956, Textron—a company begun as a textile manufacturer in the 1920s that diversified into a range of manufacturing fields after World War II—printed a single phrase on the cover of its annual report: "Stability through diversification."[20]

If structural developments were a precondition for the merger wave, a combination of a robust postwar economy, large-scale investment in the stock market, and executives' newfound willingness to engage in creative financing all encouraged the conglomerate mania. Rather than save up accumulated profits from the past to finance expansion, as they had traditionally, postwar executives borrowed and raised money more aggressively through private capital markets, bonds, or stock sales, all underwritten by investment banks. Conglomerate chiefs deployed complex financial schemes that often relied on manipulating accounting figures to minimize losses and inflate profits in order to maintain investors' confidence. For many corporate leaders, faith in financial and accounting practices solved the perennial problems of business stagnation by allowing companies to expand constantly.

Gulf+Western, one of the most infamous conglomerates formed during the midcentury wave, provides a telling example of how the process operated. The firm began life in 1934 as the Michigan Bumper Company, which manufactured metal bumpers for automobiles out of Grand Rapids. Facing falling revenues in the early 1950s, the company's managers expanded into the related field of metal plating and stamping, changing the name to Michigan Plating & Stamping in 1955. The next year, a young New Yorker named Charles Bluhdorn, who had fled anti-Jewish persecution in Austria as a teenager and started his career in the coffee import business, acquired enough of the company's cheap stock to get himself put on its board of directors. In 1957, Bluhdorn orchestrated a merger with an auto parts distributor from Houston, expanding the company but still maintaining its general focus on the automotive services sector. In recognition of the company's new geographical spread, however, he changed the name to Gulf+Western—a title that specified neither product nor location—and set his eyes on expanding beyond the automotive support industry. Beginning in 1959, Bluhdorn acquired a new company roughly once every quarter. Within ten years, he had executed seventy-two mergers and expanded annual sales from $10 million to $1.3 billion. A full-fledged conglomerate, Gulf+Western now dealt in entertainment, clothing, mass media, publishing, and real estate. By the late 1960s, it owned Paramount Pictures, the South Puerto Rico Sugar Company, Simon & Schuster, and Madison Square Garden.

The rise of the conglomerate form reshaped managerial culture. Conglomerate builders such as Charles Bluhdorn succeeded, at least for a time, because they were experts at managing their company as an investment portfolio, not as a productive entity. They relied on financial and accounting metrics—such as stock valuation and earnings reports—rather than sales or production figures, to gauge the health of their operations and determine where to go next. Working in many different industries meant that some fields could do well while others struggled, and managers could reallocate capital and even personnel where they could be most profitable. Bluhdorn's favorite expression, according to those close to him, was "What's the bottom line?"

The shift in focus within conglomerates shaped and accelerated a broader trend in managerial culture, eventually redefining the character of the business executive. Traditionally, top managers and executives had been specialists in their particular corner of industry—they were unrivaled experts in the ins and outs of jet engines, children's toys, or synthetic rope. As corporations adopted the conglomerate mindset, if not always the exact form, a new mentality began to replace those old notions. From the 1960s onward, boards of directors increasingly sought to hire men (and let's not forget that occupying the corner office was a nearly exclusively male privilege) who were experts not in a particular industry or niche, but in *business management* itself. Versatile generalists, holding degrees from the newfangled business schools mushrooming throughout the country, could adapt their broad understanding of business principles to any specific managerial problem they encountered. Conglomerate executives in particular often bragged that they could manage their companies through financial controls and measurements, remaining disconnected from the actual product or service the company provided.

The conglomerate wave did not last forever, however. By the mid-1970s, economic recession and the inflation and energy crises led the merger mania to peter out. As credit dried up, many found themselves overextended and ultimately collapsed. Gulf+Western managed to survive by calling a halt to its expansion by the mid-1970s and, by the early 1980s, recasting itself nearly exclusively as a media corporation. By selling its other holdings off, the company refocused on its "core competencies." Bluhdorn's successor (he died of a heart attack in 1983) renamed the company Paramount Communications in 1989 to take advantage of one of its highest-profile holdings, Paramount Pictures. The entire operation became part of the media giant Viacom in 1994.[21]

On the whole, conglomerates during the midcentury merger wave appear to have fared no better or worse than other large corporations. In both cases, fortune favored firms well managed by people who paid attention to production efficiency, technical innovation, and marketing. Yet by the end of the 1970s, the exuberance that underlay the conglomerate craze had passed. Merger and acquisition waves swept corporate America again in the late 1980s and have done so roughly every decade since, but none have witnessed the ideological fervor for extreme diversification—the unabashed zeal for bigness—that marked the conglomerate wave of the 1960s.

Corporation Nation

In 1938, the famous publisher of *Time* magazine, Henry Luce, predicted the arrival of what he called the "American century"—a period when the United States would dominate global politics, diplomacy, culture, and economics. The decades during and after World War II appeared to bear out Luce's prediction, as America emerged as a global superpower holding together an alliance of noncommunist nations. In business as well, the United States reigned unchallenged. Atop this economic superpower sat the modern corporation, distinguished by its size, scale, scope, and structure. As both an economic and a social force, American enterprise embodied both the triumphs and challenges of the postwar experience.

Bigness, in other words, was the cardinal feature of postwar American life. In 1952, the liberal economist John Kenneth Galbraith praised the stabilizing role that these new patterns of social and economic organization could play. His theory of "countervailing power" argued that Big Business, Big Labor, and Big Government all kept each other in check, preserving both economic efficiency and social justice. Galbraith even defended chain retail stores, the bête noire of small business advocates, for their role in keeping prices down for consumers. Just the next year, the lawyer, public servant, and later international businessman David Lilienthal made headlines with his defense of big business. During the New Deal, Lilienthal had helped run the massive federal agency that served as a socialized electrical utility, the Tennessee Valley Authority. In the postwar period, however, he came to embrace the efficiency and potential of modern business techniques. As he wrote, he had learned to let go of the "old dream: the independent man in his own little shop or business." In its place rose "a new dream: a world of great machines."[22]

Yet many Americans bristled. From its inception, America's political tradition has hailed the virtues of smallness—the independent farmer, the local store operator, the town hall meeting. The organizational bigness that defined the mid-20th-century cut against these received traditions. Social critics bemoaned the dehumanizing, antidemocratic effects of bigness and lumped massive institutions like the government, the military, the church, and the corporation into a common basket.

No less a figure than President Dwight Eisenhower—perhaps most famous for leading one of the largest "organizations" in world history during the D-Day invasion of 1944—invoked a growing sense of foreboding at the perils of large corporate interests in his famous "farewell address" from the White House in January 1961. Having presided over eight years that saw the massive escalation of Cold War tensions, including the proxy war in Korea and the acceleration of U.S. military involvement against communists in Vietnam, Eisenhower warned of the deep links between an increasingly militarized society and the growing might of large corporations, particularly those that profited from military spending.

"In the councils of government," he warned, "we must guard against the acquisition of unwarranted influence, whether sought or unsought, by the military industrial complex. The potential for the disastrous rise of misplaced power exists and will persist." If decisions of war and peace depended in any way on the profit motives of wealthy private citizens, he argued, the cause of freedom, security, and justice for all could only suffer.[23] Eisenhower's famous admonition about the threat massive institutions—"organizations," in Whyte's terms—posed to democracy would be echoed later in the decade by antiwar protesters and anticorporate activists. If World War II and the Cold War pitted, at least in Americans' eyes, the totalizing political ideologies of fascism and communism against liberal democracy and individual freedom, many wondered what place large, bureaucratic, depersonalized business corporations would occupy in that struggle.

10

THE PERSONAL, THE POLITICAL,
AND THE PROFITABLE

I n the fall of 1964, students at the University of California at
Berkeley launched a series of sit-ins, walk-outs, and rallies to
protest the university's policy prohibiting political activism on campus grounds. Young people, joined by like-minded allies in the area,
clashed with police and challenged the authority of university admin-
istrators and the political establishment that ran the university system.
Berkeley's "free speech movement" rocked the campus and drew
national attention. Hollywood actor and budding politician Ronald
Reagan won the governorship of California two years later in part by
demonizing student protesters as entitled brats. "No one is compelled
to attend the university. Those who do attend should accept and obey
the prescribed rules or get out," he said.[1] Although university leaders
eventually modified their position on campus speech, the firestorm
of activism persisted and inspired national protests in the years to
come—first focused on civil rights and then expanding to include
opposition to U.S. involvement in Vietnam.

The critiques that the Free Speech Movement leveled at the University of California extended far beyond specific policies, reflecting instead a fundamental—and generational—challenge to the power structure that defined American society. Specifically, students called out their educational leaders for complicity in an antidemocratic, dehumanizing corporate machine that compelled conformity. Taking the microphone at a campus rally in December, Berkeley student and civil rights activist Mario Savio gave voice to the sense of oppression and helplessness many young people felt in the early 1960s.

"We have an autocracy which runs this university," Savio declared. Student leaders had asked whether Berkeley's president Clark Kerr had convinced the university's governing trustees (known as "Regents") to liberalize the school's policies on political activism. Savio continued: "And the answer we received—from a well-meaning liberal—was the following: He said, 'Would you ever imagine the manager of a firm making a statement publicly in opposition to his board of directors?' That's the answer!"

Savio seized on that comparison—by a "well-meaning liberal," or someone the students felt should have been an ideological ally—between higher education and the faceless, bureaucratic corporation.

"Now, I ask you to consider: if this is a firm, and if the Board of Regents are the board of directors, and if President Kerr in fact is the manager, then I'll tell you something: the faculty are a bunch of employees, and we're the raw material!"

But students weren't just passive cogs in an all-powerful, faceless machine. "We're human beings!" Savio yelled to applause. More important, they weren't helpless. They could do more than just rage against the machine. They could resist, defending their humanity, individuality, and democratic rights.

"There is a time when the operation of the machine becomes so odious, makes you so sick at heart, that you can't take part; you can't even passively take part, and you've got to put your bodies upon the gears and upon the wheels, upon the levers, upon all the apparatus, and you've got to make it stop. And you've got to indicate to the people who run it, to the people who own it, that unless you're free, the machine will be prevented from working at all!"[2]

Mario Savio's call to action on the steps of Sproul Hall on the Berkeley campus is often cited as an example of early student protest in the 1960s—the launching point for a decade of struggle, both political and philosophical, led by passionate and often radical young people who would help end a major war (Vietnam) and bring about the downfall of two presidents (Johnson and Nixon). It did all that, but it also exposed the particular *way* that protesters in the 1960s understood the challenges before them. Savio's analogy—which saw the university as a corporate machine and students as raw materials who had thrown their bodies upon its inner workings—grew from a profound sense of unease over the role of business corporations in American society. Political activists in the 1960s—from civil rights advocates to antiwar protesters to more radical and often violent groups such as the Weather Underground—viewed the business corporation as an integral part of the "system" or "establishment" that crippled dissent, promoted imperialism abroad and injustice at home, and stifled free expression.[3] Never removed from issues of war and social justice, business was at the heart of the tumult of the 1960s.

Corporate executives came to understand the very real threats to their political power, social standing, and economic success that political and social unrest augured. Business leaders responded to what they believed were "antibusiness" politics in the 1960s and well into the 1970s with deliberate action to bolster their support and institutionalize their influence with policymakers. Powerful businesspeople had always played an important role in national affairs, of course, but the turmoil of the 1960s and 1970s created a particularly powerful moment of mobilization that, combined with a burgeoning conservative political movement, had long-lasting consequences for American politics.

Business and Protest in the Late 1960s

The social unrest that engulfed the United States had its roots in the civil rights struggle, whose "high phase" of in-the-streets activism peaked between the mid-1950s and the 1965 Voting Rights Act. By the late 1960s, the country had been rocked by an onslaught of public protests, riots, and political assassinations. The rapid escalation of U.S. military activity in Vietnam beginning in 1965 accelerated the turmoil. Opposition to the war (and equally powerful opposition to that opposition) deepened generational and ideological schisms.

America's official military involvement in Vietnam developed over the course of the late 1950s and early 1960s. After Vietnamese nationals ousted the colonial French military in 1954, a civil war broke out between Western-backed anticommunists, predominantly in the southern part of the country, and socialist nationalists (the Viet Minh), supported by the majority of the Vietnamese people. Most American policymakers understood the war through a stark Cold War framework and thus supported the anticommunist regime in South Vietnam, first with military "advisors" and increasingly with regular troops. An alleged "incident" involving a U.S. Navy ship in Vietnam's Gulf of Tonkin in 1964 led Congress to authorize President Lyndon Johnson to escalate U.S. troop presence in the country. (Johnson claimed the North Vietnamese fired on the U.S. ship; while that assertion has been debunked, historians disagree about whether Johnson knew that the report was false.) By 1968, half a million American soldiers were fighting in Southeast Asia, where fifty-eight thousand would die before the United States withdrew completely in 1973.

The escalation of the war prompted a powerful and pointed antiwar movement in the United States, spreading from college campus "teach-ins" to historic protests and marches on the Pentagon and White House. Just as Mario Savio had linked his opposition to Berkeley's anti-free-speech policy to a larger critique of corporate culture, so, too, did many Vietnam War protesters draw a clear line between a war they decried as murderous and imperialistic and the business climate that nurtured it. Invoking Eisenhower's now-famous warning about the "military-industrial complex," protesters charged that America's most successful capitalists bore responsibility for the carnage in Asia. The nation's war machine, they argued, generated military contracts for everything from ammunition and aircraft to the jellified flaming gasoline known as napalm that U.S. bombers poured on the Vietnamese jungles and the people who lived there.

Antiwar demonstrators aimed their protests not only at the military and the government, including President Johnson and later Richard Nixon, but also corporations whom they labeled as war profiteers. "Why . . . do we continue to demonstrate in Washington as if the core of the problem lay there? . . . We need to find ways to lay siege to corporations," one activist wrote late in 1969.[4]

On April 28, 1970, thousands of antiwar activists converged on the annual shareholder meeting of the Honeywell Corporation, an energy-oriented conglomerate that manufactured, among many other products, cluster bombs and other weapons for the Pentagon. Facing the jeers and accusations of murderous complicity from the furious crowd, Honeywell's president adjourned the meeting after only fourteen minutes. Firms such as Dow Chemical Company, producer of napalm, also confronted angry protesters, especially when their corporate recruiters arrived on college campuses. Perhaps most tellingly, antiwar protesters even targeted corporations, such as banks, that lacked any *explicit* connection to Vietnam but represented the entire system, the "Establishment" or the "machine," that put profit before people. In the winter of 1970, protesters near the University of California in Santa Barbara burned down a branch of Bank of America, whose very name, at least to the arsonists, evoked the hubris of capitalist imperialism.[5]

Corporate and political leaders understood that the anti-

Establishment angst was particularly strong among young people. In recent years historians have shown that plenty of the "baby boomers" who came of age in the 1960s were quite conservative and favored the war, the business establishment, and capitalism in general, but many corporate executives at the time were convinced that generational changes were afflicting the nation's youth en masse. The same types of college students who, in the 1950s, headed to stable careers in middle management were, by the late 1960s, committed to upending the society that had nurtured them, taking over college campuses, organizing protests and boycotts, or turning to the counterculture—the "hippie" movement—and rejecting traditional society altogether.[6]

At the same time, corporate executives understood the degree to which they and their businesses had become the scapegoats for dissatisfied and disaffected youth. Public approval of business as a social institution, particularly among young people, declined throughout the war-torn years of the late 1960s and early 1970s. In one commonly cited 1973 survey of students at Oklahoma Christian University— by all counts a conservative place far from radical hotbeds such as Berkeley or Columbia—undergraduates gave businessmen the lowest ranking for ethical standards of all major groups of leaders in the country (including politicians, the military, and doctors). And this poor view of business translated into political leanings that tended to grow more intense as students moved through college—in the early 1970s, one-third of college freshman described themselves as leftists, yet more than half of seniors did.[7]

Corporations in the Crossfire:
The Environmental and Consumer Movements

Business leaders had more to fear than young people raging against the Establishment and the war. America in the 1960s and 1970s witnessed a massive outpouring of political activism focused on public-interest issues, especially protecting the natural environment and safeguarding consumer products. The rising strength of those two movements convinced vast numbers of business leaders that their public support was declining. Combined with the more generalized anti-Establishment critique that the war brought out, consumerism and environmentalism seemed to represent a wholesale loss of public faith in private enterprise. To many businesspeople (and their political allies, especially conservatives), the obstacles represented a profound, even existential, threat. They believed that the political climate of the early 1970s was deeply hostile to the executive class and, by extension, the business system itself.

The modern environmental movement emerged as a powerful force in American politics in the early 1960s (although many scholars have pointed to its origins in the conservationist ethos of the Progressive Era). As we saw in the previous chapter, scientific research boomed in the postwar decades, fueled by a powerful collaboration between private corporations, universities, and government agencies. By the 1950s, scientific research led to greater public awareness of the consequences of human behavior for the natural environment. Experts began to establish clear empirical links between industrial production and increasingly hazardous pollution of the air, water, and soil. A growing chorus of scientists warned that the marvels of modern society—including plastics, automobiles, chemicals, and pharmaceuticals—came at a real cost.

In 1962, a marine biologist named Rachel Carson brought the problems of industrial pollution into the public consciousness with a powerful and popular book. Carson's *Silent Spring* traced the flow of industrial pollutants through the ecosystem. She argued that synthetic pesticides, especially the popular anti-insect chemical known as DDT, had far-reaching negative effects on entire ecosystems. Even though farmers applied only small amounts to protect their crops,

Carson demonstrated, the toxic chemicals grew more concentrated as they made their way up the food chain—ultimately killing birds that ate the poisoned insects (creating the "silent spring"—devoid of birdsong) and posing clear health risks to humans.[8]

The chemical industry responded, and producers like DuPont challenged the extent of *Silent Spring*'s conclusions. Yet the scientific community backed up Carson's analysis and policymakers responded with new restrictions on pollutants. Even more important than its immediate policy effects, the book raised public awareness about the devastating consequences of unchecked industrial activity and increased public acceptance of environmental regulations. It also provided an organizational focus for a broader social movement that pressured lawmakers to expand the government's regulatory oversight. The environmental movement won a number of legislative victories in the decade after Carson's book came out, including the Clean Air Act of 1963 and the creation of the Environmental Protection Agency in 1970, which became the centralized regulatory body for environmental issues within the federal government.[9]

Industrial leaders, as well as conservative politicians, bristled at the environmental movement. In part, their opposition was straightforward and self-serving—large companies reaped huge profits from activities that entailed pollution, and finding cleaner ways to produce would severely damage their bottom line. Not for nothing, the primary corporate antagonists to the environmental movement were the biggest polluters—oil and gas, automotive, mining, and chemicals—while retailers and high-tech companies were less active. In response to new standards that limited automobile emissions, enacted through amendments to the Clean Air Act in 1970, Chrysler Corporation claimed that "citizens have been needlessly frightened" about air pollution. Oil titan Mobil took out national newspaper ads decrying the legislation as a "$66 Billion Mistake."[10]

But corporate opposition to environmentalism ran deeper than the bottom line or quibbles over emissions standards. Antienvironmentalists, both in the corner offices and in conservative political organizations, argued that the spirit behind the movement itself rejected a cornerstone of capitalism—the quest for economic growth. Since the industrial revolution of the 19th century, and particularly since the triumph of modern corporate capitalism in the early 20th century, the pursuit of "more" had animated all aspects of political and economic thought: more people, more goods, more technology, more money. Both political parties, as well as organized labor, embraced the growth ethos, because it promised a higher quality of life for both business owners and working people. Critics of the environmental movement, conservatives as well as many labor unions, argued that its supporters came disproportionately from well-off backgrounds and did not understand the social costs—shuttered factories or higher-priced products—that stricter environmental regulations would entail. They were "zero-growth zanies," according to Edwin Feulner, president of the conservative think tank Heritage Foundation. "Zero growth may help the elites, who can go out and till their organic gardens and watch the sun come up from the serenity of their redwood hot tubs, but it doesn't do much for those among us who are still trying to make it up the economic ladder."[11]

Alongside the environmentalists, the push to protect consumers—both their pocketbooks and their bodies—also fueled national politics in the 1960s. And just as with *Silent Spring*, a single book raised a popular outcry by exposing the detrimental power of large corporations over human life. In 1965, a young lawyer named Ralph Nader published a best-selling critique of the automobile industry called *Unsafe at Any Speed: The Designed-In Dangers of the American Automobile*. Self-consciously tapping the spirit of muckraking journalism against Big Business during the Progressive Era (such as Ida

Tarbell's *History of Standard Oil* and Upton Sinclair's *The Jungle*), Nader accused American automakers in general, and General Motors in particular, of selling cars they *knew* to be dangerous because altering the design would be too expensive. He drew specific public attention to the phenomena of the "second collision" (where the human body hits the interior of the car after the car hits an outside object) and design elements that could reflect into a driver's eyes and cause accidents, as well as the pollution caused by auto emissions.[12]

Nader's advocacy and the popularity of his book led to legislative action. In 1966, Congress passed the National Traffic and Motor Vehicle Safety Act, which gave the federal government broad powers to set regulations on the design and production of cars, including mandatory seatbelts. Nader used his fame to launch a number of legal and political organizations dedicated to discovering and publicizing corporate malfeasance and bringing suit against corporations that violated laws protecting the public interest. Automaker General Motors ironically abetted Nader's rise through a clumsy and hamhanded effort to defame the consumer advocate. Company leaders hired private investigators to look into Nader in hopes of besmirching his character. Nader sued for invasion of privacy, settled with the auto giant, and used the settlement money to further his advocacy organization.[13]

Although Nader received the bulk of industrialists' condemnation, he was only part of a much larger wave of consumer protection sentiment that swept the American public and the halls of Congress in the 1960s and 1970s. This consumer wave corresponded with, and indeed outlasted, Lyndon Johnson's "Great Society"—a set of liberal policies aimed at improving the lives of Americans through civil rights protections, increased medical access and insurance coverage, jobs training and education, urban redevelopment, and antipoverty programs. In those years, Congress passed dozens of consumer protection bills, dealing with such issues as harmful and undertested pharmaceuticals, flammable fabrics (notably in products such as pajamas for children), and auto safety. Consumer protection laws insisted on truth in advertising, required drivers to purchase automobile insurance, created new and more stringent rules about food safety, and set rules for fair debt collection and bank lending practices.[14]

The rise of the environmental and consumer movements added to many corporate leaders' conviction that American business was under political assault. They did not necessarily disagree with the movements' goals—after all, nobody *wanted* to poison the Earth or peddle products that caused death and mutilation—but a growing number feared the antibusiness spirit that they believed guided these movements. In the minds of many corporate executives, consumer and environmental activists demanded new and far-reaching regulatory powers for states and the federal government because they had no faith that corporations would, of their own free will, act in the best interest of society. Business leaders understood that support for new regulations rose as the public's faith in large corporations declined. Public opinion polls showed that Americans' confidence in the leaders of major firms declined from more than 50 percent in the mid-1960s to 15 percent by the mid-1970s. The head of aluminum giant Alcoa summed up the problem in 1976: Public opinion mattered because "what the public thinks . . . has a decided effect on the kind of legislation that comes out of Congress."[15]

Public distrust of business changed the character of the regulations Congress passed. Since the late 19th century, government regulations had been overwhelmingly concerned with economic stability and, frequently, protecting certain types of businesses from others. Antitrust law, for example, promoted competition and limited the predations of monopolistic companies. Utilities and transportation regulations aimed to keep certain industries profitable while also keeping their costs down. In short, the dominant regulatory trend had been *economic regulation*.

In contrast, the trend in the 1960s and 1970s was toward *social regulations*, rules that, by design, targeted aspects of business behavior not traditionally considered "economic"—public health and safety and, quite literally, the downstream consequences of companies' production processes. There had been earlier examples of social regulation, including the Pure Food and Drug Act of 1906, which led to the creation of the FDA to improve the safety and quality of food and medicine. Yet the scale and scope of this new type of regulation exploded in the late 1960s, reinforcing a cultural and political distinction between protecting *the economy* and protecting *people from business*.

Perhaps no government agency or regulatory movement proved more odious to wide swaths of the business community than the Occupational Safety and Health Administration, or OSHA, which Congress created in 1970. Birthed the same year as the EPA, OSHA reflected much of the same spirit that drove labor laws—such as the right to organize, minimum wages, and overtime—but shifted the focus from pay and representation to workplace conditions. Charged with maximizing worker safety, OSHA used its authority to issue thousands of pages of rules concerning such topics as how high up a ladder a worker could climb or where factories had to post safety signs. Business owners, particularly at smaller firms that had to devote a higher portion of their budgets to complying, howled in protest. OSHA rules were both unreasonable and indecipherable, they charged, and the costs of compliance were onerous. National business organizations such as the U.S. Chamber of Commerce publicized stories of small companies forced to close because they could not afford to change their practices in accordance with the new safety rules. "Did you know," the president of the Chamber asked audiences in the mid-1970s, "that Agents of the Occupational Safety and Health Administration can raid a place of business any time they want?"[16]

And as with consumer and environmental regulations, workplace safety rules represented a personal affront as well as a business cost. A growing number of businesspeople came to believe that social regulation proliferated because Americans no longer trusted companies to regulate themselves. If a cornerstone of democratic capitalism had long been the belief that free markets created free people, or that a rising economic tide lifted all boats, the politics of the 1960s called those maxims into question. If people had to be protected *from* business—if private actions no longer promoted the *public interest* (the term Ralph Nader and others used to promote their goals)— business itself faced a serious threat.

Business's Countermobilization

"The American capitalist system is confronting its darkest hour," one corporate executive declared in 1975.[17] He wasn't alone. By the mid-1970s, a refrain echoed across corporate America—from top executives to small shop owners, from conservative politicians and attorneys to journalists and academics. The onslaught of social regulations, anticapitalist culture, and a struggling economy (the boom of the 1960s ended with a recession in 1970, followed by a prolonged energy crisis marked by high inflation and slack growth) meant that business itself was under attack. To defend their bottom lines and capitalism itself, business leaders had to strike back.

In 1971, a corporate lawyer named Lewis Powell—soon to become a Supreme Court justice—gave voice to this rising demand for a political countermobilization with a confidential memo to the United States Chamber of Commerce. A well-connected attorney in Virginia and former president of the American Bar Association, Powell wrote the memo at the request of his friend Eugene Sydnor, who owned a chain of department stores and chaired the Chamber's "Education Committee" (by which the group meant "public education"). The document, called "Attack on American Free Enterprise System," explained the widespread belief that anticapitalist forces—from the universities to the pulpits to public-interest law firms—were waging a cultural assault on business, and that groups such as the Chamber of Commerce had no choice but to become politically active. "Business," Powell wrote, "must learn the lesson, long ago learned by labor and other self-interest groups . . . that political power is necessary . . . and that . . . it must be used aggressively and with determination."[18]

Powell's memo crystallized the growing sense that collective action by business was essential. Circulated throughout the Chamber of Commerce, the "confidential" memo landed on the desks of conservative writers and public figures, and snippets from it peppered the speeches of probusiness activists. About a year after Powell wrote it, and nine months after Richard Nixon appointed him to the Supreme Court, the liberal *Washington Post* columnist Jack Anderson learned of the memo and "outed" Powell, implying that the document represented a subversive plan by high-powered businesspeople to take control of American politics. In reality, Powell's contribution was more rhetorical than conspiratorial. He put into words what many people had been saying privately for years: Businesspeople had to become more involved in national politics. But how?

In addition to holding political office (which a relatively small number of active business leaders did), there were two primary avenues for effecting real influence in national affairs: funding political campaigns, and direct and focused lobbying. American companies dramatically expanded their use of both strategies in the 1970s.

In the early 1970s, Congress overhauled the laws governing campaign finance contributions. The federal government had regulated campaign giving to various degrees since the Tillman Act of 1907, which barred corporations and unions from donating to political campaigns on the rather explicit grounds that they were not humans.[19] Yet both businesses and unions had found end-runs around the law, the latter by creating separate committees, known as political action committees, or PACs, as early as the 1940s. Early PACs existed on the margins of legality, and while organized labor relied on political clout to avoid trouble, corporations generally did not form them. Instead, with minor exceptions, businesspeople preferred other, less official ways to skirt the campaign finance laws. Executives, for example, routinely arranged for special bonuses to top managers, with the clear expectation that those managers would donate their windfall to the candidate of the corporation's choice.[20]

In the early 1970s, a coalition of lawmakers worked to reform the campaign finance system. The Watergate scandal that unfolded between 1972 and 1974 further catalyzed that movement by opening the country's eyes to the shady practices by which wealthy corporations funneled money to campaigns—through redirected checks, bags of cash, secret slush funds, and the like. Out of that mess, Congress created the Federal Election Commission (FEC) and a system for public campaign financing, instituted reporting requirements, and limited expenditures.

In 1975, the FEC clarified that political action committees were legally legitimate, and an explosion in corporate-backed political action committees followed. In the four years between 1974 and 1979, the number of business PACs increased tenfold, from 89 to 950, while the number of labor PACs barely budged, rising only from 201 to 226. The number of corporate PACs continued to soar, peaking around 1,800 in the late 1980s before declining slightly and largely leveling off. In the winter of 2016, the Federal Election Commission counted 1,621 political action committees affiliated with businesses, and 278 for labor.[21]

In addition to engaging in campaign financing, businesses also mobilized in the 1970s by hiring talented people to represent their interests to government officials (both elected politicians and bureaucrats within the ever more complex regulatory apparatus). Lobbying, of course, is an ancient profession, and corporations had a long history of paying well-connected people to sway politicians their way. The presence of paid lobbyists followed the growth patterns of American business itself. The railroad boom of the mid-19th century, which depended on government largesse, led to an uptick in lobbying, as did industrial manufacturing in the following decades. By 1946, Congress first tried to regulate the practice with the Federal Regulation of Lobbying Act, which required all lobbyists to register; six years later, the Supreme Court narrowed the law's scope to require registration only for people whose *primary business* was lobbying. But the method of determining what constituted "primary business" remained vague.[22]

As American companies became larger and more diversified, particularly after World War II, they became more sophisticated in their lobbying capacity. By the 1960s, most big firms had "Washington representatives"—paid permanent employees who lived in Washington and lobbied on their company's behalf.

But small and midsized firms couldn't afford permanent lobbyists. Instead, they relied on trade associations to represent the general interests of their industry. Grocery stores might join the National Grocers Association, for example. With the proliferation of trade associations in the 20th century, including such pan-industry "peak associations" as the National Association of Manufacturers and the U.S. Chamber of Commerce, a legal conflict began to emerge. On one hand, the First Amendment protected the right to free speech and to "petition the government for a redress of grievances," as lobbyists do. On the other, the old Sherman Antitrust Act of 1890 prohibited "any conspiracy in restraint of trade."

Many businesspeople worried that certain types of lobbying might push trade associations over a legal line. "When a 'combination,' such as a trade association, obtains favorable governmental action that results in an illegal 'restraint of trade,'" wondered one writer in 1971, "can the association be held to violate the Sherman

Act, or is the approach to government within the right guaranteed by the First Amendment?"[23]

In the early 1970s, the Supreme Court ruled that the First Amendment speech and petition protections superseded the question of restraining trade. Those rulings gave trade associations far more latitude to represent multiple businesses within an industry, and the amount of trade association lobbying increased markedly.

Leading the charge of coordinating collaborations across companies, and sometimes across industries, were major national associations that had been around for decades. Both the National Association of Manufacturers and the U.S. Chamber of Commerce responded to this new culture of business activism by reinvigorating themselves and broadening their activities. They expanded their political purview to include a broader array of issues—rather than just concentrating on organized labor and workplace issues, they lobbied for and against issues related to consumer protection, environmental regulation, foreign trade, tax policy, and policies concerning inflation and unemployment.

And even as these old groups reinvented themselves, a new force emerged to unify the nation's largest and wealthiest industrial manufacturers, called the Business Roundtable. Founded in 1972, the Business Roundtable comprised approximately one hundred corporations, all of which were in the Fortune 500 and most of which dealt in heavy industry such as steel, aluminum, chemicals, and automotive. (The group has closer to two hundred member corporations today, representing a somewhat wider range of industries, including high-tech, retail, and finance.) While the U.S. Chamber of Commerce tried to appeal to all corners of the business world, from Wall Street to Main Street, the Business Roundtable focused on political issues that directly affected big businesses. What made the organization unique—and particularly powerful—was that its members included *only* the chief executive officers of those companies, not vice presidents, lawyers, or professional lobbyists. When the Round-table wanted to target a certain politician on a certain vote, it would send powerful corporate leaders—the CEO of Ford, or Citibank, or AT&T—to the politician's office.[24]

Business and Conservative Politics

By the late 1970s, the political mobilization of American businesses had begun to redirect the nation's economic policies in ways that pleased conservatives and disappointed progressives. Organizing around a commitment to free market capitalism and an opposition to social regulation, business groups lobbied successfully during a number of key legislative battles that helped stem the tide of liberal policies. In 1978, for example, corporate lobbyists were decisive in the defeat of legislation spearheaded by Ralph Nader to reform the process for regulating consumer protection within the federal government. That same year, the Business Roundtable led the charge against reforms to the National Labor Relations Act, which would have improved labor unions' ability to organize workplaces and created greater oversight and transparency in employee-worker relations. By the 1980s, these groups joined with increasingly active conservative policy groups to promote tax reform, oppose environmental regulations, and urge a balanced federal budget. Despite frequent policy and strategy disagreements among conservative activists and corporate lobbyists, they shared a vital perspective: a dispositional opposition to the liberal state. By lending their organizational, financial, and influential strength to legislative politics, business groups helped secure important policy victories for conservatives.

11

AFTER THE INDUSTRIAL ECONOMY

O n April 1, 1998, the last television set rolled off an assembly line in Bloomington, Indiana. Soon-to-be-unemployed workers sang "Happy Trails to You" as they walked out of the factory gates first erected by electronics giant RCA in 1940. In 1986, longtime competitor General Electric had purchased RCA and sold the company to a French firm called Thomson. By the 1990s, Thomson had moved its North American manufacturing to Juárez, Mexico, where RCA had set up a small plant in 1968. In an era defined by lower trade barriers under the 1994 North American Free Trade Agreement (NAFTA), Thomson and other manufacturers found the appeal of far cheaper labor outside America's borders irresistible. "They got all they could out of us, and now they're going somewhere else," said the president of the Indiana AFL-CIO. But could you blame the Mexican workers who now held their jobs? many asked. "It's not *their* fault," one former RCA worker insisted. "If you didn't have a job and someone built a factory here, what would you do?"[1]

A similar story unfolded in other industries that relied on relatively low-skilled manufacturing. The American furniture industry pivoted away from domestic manufacturing between the 1990s and 2000s. Long-standing firms such as Bassett and Hooker had helped North Carolina and Virginia supplant the Midwest as the home of furniture making in the early 20th century, largely because prevailing wages were much lower in the rural South. By the early 21st century, those firms had recast themselves as importers and retailers, outsourcing the labor of producing the goods to factories in China. As in Indiana, displaced workers in the former furniture belt tried to wrestle with the conflicts the new world of global trade had created. "I guess we traded our jobs for somebody elsewhere in the world to have a better life, I don't know," reflected an ex-sawmiller.[2]

By the turn of the century, global capitalism was undergoing a tumultuous revolution. Between 2001 and 2012, sixty-three thousand American factories shut, taking 5 million jobs with them, even while Chinese manufacturers added 14.1 million new positions.[3] "Deindustrialization" and its cousin phenomena—"outsourcing" and "globalization"—were the new buzzwords. Fierce debates erupted, from free-traders like *New York Times* writer Thomas Friedman, who hailed the prospects of a globalized economy in 2004's bestselling *The World Is Flat,* to angry protesters against the World Trade Organization on the streets of Seattle in 1999.[4]

The uproar over globalization at the turn of the 21st century capped years of consternation over changes to business and employment. As early as the 1980s, labor economists had pointed to the long-term decline in American manufacturing and the concomitant decline in the political and logistical power of organized labor. (Union membership as a percentage of the workforce peaked in 1955.)[5] Debates over NAFTA in the early 1990s revolved around the trade-off between the advantages of cheaper consumer goods and the "giant sucking sound" (in the famous phrase of presidential candidate and populist business leader Ross Perot) of American manufacturing jobs fleeing to Mexico.[6]

Yet the processes of "deindustrialization" that attracted so much public attention in the 1980s and 1990s had far deeper roots than many commentators seemed to recognize. Manufacturing firms had a long history of uprooting their operations to different areas in search of more favorable business conditions. Although such conditions could refer to regulations or access to raw materials, the most important was the cost of labor, far lower in poorer places with weaker unions. In the early decades of the 20th century, the first wave of "deindustrialization" swept the Northeast as the textile mills—the heart of the First Industrial Revolution along Massachusetts rivers a hundred years earlier—decamped to the South. Other labor-intensive industries, from furniture and steel to electronics and automotive, followed suit, taking advantage of a weaker labor movement and lower cost of living.[7]

The phenomena we associate with "deindustrialization"—shuttered factories, offshored production to low-wage countries, and the disappearance of well-paid working-class jobs for people with only modest educations—were part of a larger shift in the American economy that unfolded over the course of the 20th century. In the years after World War II, American firms expanded in size, scope, and productive capacity, fueling widespread prosperity and economic growth. Millions of Americans achieved the stability of a middle-class lifestyle, including homeownership and a steady paycheck, as well as the trappings of a consumption-based existence.

Integral to the mass consumption society was the steady rise of service-oriented business, which gradually supplanted manufacturing as the most important part of the national economy. Since the rise of industry in the 19th century, the American economy had been fundamentally driven by *producers*—firms that extracted and refined raw materials and assembled new products. Nonproducing companies, such as insurance, banking, or accounting, were peripheral to the early industrial economy, as were such *personal* service providers as health care or retail.

That situation changed in the 20th century. In 1900, according to the U.S. Census, American workers were employed roughly equally between manufacturing and service jobs, at about 25 percent each. The other half were farmers. By 1950, however, half of all Americans worked in the service economy, whereas farming jobs declined to 20 percent and manufacturing reached 30 percent. By the year 2000, the inversion was nearly complete: Fewer than 5 percent of Americans worked in agriculture, where machines proved far more efficient than human hands, while only 15 percent worked in manufacturing. The remaining 80 percent had service-sector jobs.[8]

But the story of the service economy goes beyond employment figures. By the last third of the 20th century, service-oriented businesses accounted for a far greater share of profits, growth, and social impact as well. In the mid-1950s, the leadership of the Fortune 500, a list of the biggest American firms by total revenue, was dominated by industrial heavy hitters such as General Motors, U.S. Steel, Standard Oil, and DuPont. By the 2000s, the most important companies in the country included Walmart, Citigroup, State Farm Insurance, and (before it went bankrupt and was taken over by the federal government) mortgage company Fannie Mae.[9]

The long rise of services created a highly diverse economy that included a wide range of winners and losers. Certain types of service work generated tremendous wealth and success, particularly in the knowledge-based industries, such as high technology, scientific research, and, especially by the latter decades of century, financial services. Other service-sector businesses proved lucrative for their owners and advantageous for their customers, but far less beneficial for their employees. Lower-skilled jobs in retail, food services, and hospitality came with far lower salaries than similarly low-skilled manufacturing work had provided to earlier generations.

The mass consumption economy of the 1940s, 1950s, and 1960s was built on a shared prosperity and a growing middle class. Yet critical developments in key business sectors, particularly related to the rising importance of services, laid the foundation for dramatic changes by the end of the century. From fast-food and retailing to information technology, the transition to a service economy had profound consequences for American public life.

Catering to Consumers

Perhaps no business typified the suburban consumer spirit of post–World War II America more than McDonald's. The iconic fast-food restaurant started life in 1940 as "McDonald's Bar-B-Que" in San Bernardino, California, where brothers Mac and Dick McDonald cooked up pork, chicken, and beef specialties. But as the brothers later explained, the quality, cost, and availability of their food varied day to day and throughout the year—sometimes the beef was too tough, sometimes the pork was too greasy. And customers took notice. Not satisfied with running a traditional restaurant, the McDonalds spent the 1940s searching for a way to simplify. They wanted a food item that they could perfect and sell at a constant, affordable, and profitable price. They settled on the hamburger.

In the fall of 1948, the McDonald brothers dropped the word "Bar-B-Que" and reorganized the entire restaurant. They limited the menu to hamburgers, cheeseburgers, shakes, and fries. They redesigned the kitchen to operate like an assembly line, and they eliminated curbside delivery to make the entire operation self-service. In essence, this shift to the now-familiar fast-food model represented a successful adoption of the business principles that had been remaking the world of large industrial corporations for a generation. The McDonald brothers took the efficiency and precision of Big Business and applied it to food preparation. Business soared.

In addition to streamlining their product and process, the McDonald brothers succeeded by meeting the new consumer demands of suburban culture in the 1950s. Fast food provided an out-of-home dining experience at a comparatively low price, and the restaurant catered to families with young children. Even before the company's mascot, the red-haired, white-faced clown Ronald, was born in the 1960s, McDonald's (as well as its imitators) worked to create a family-friendly environment, free of jukeboxes, cigarette vending machines, or arcade games. In the 1970s, drive-thru windows—bringing the ease of fast dining to families on the go—and Happy Meals with toys solidified the company's image.

Yet the most significant contribution that McDonald's—and the fast-food industry it spawned—made to American public life came as much from its business model as from its actual food. Convinced that they had found a winning formula for the hamburger business, Mack and Dick McDonald began a search for partners in the early 1950s. In 1953, a businessman in Phoenix, Arizona, opened the first McDonald's *franchise*, complete with the eye-catching "Golden Arches" design. The next year, a midwestern sales representative for malted-milk mixers named Ray Kroc visited the San Bernardino restaurant (which used eight of his mixers) and saw the enormous potential. As Kroc later recalled, "I thought, 'Well, jeepers, maybe the way for me to sell multimixers is to open up these surefire hamburger units all over the country myself.'" Within a few years, Kroc revolutionized the concept of the business franchise.[10]

The franchise model is an arrangement between a producer of a good or service—generally well-known and established—and a smaller and often more locally oriented retailer or seller of that product. The former, known as the *franchisor*, licenses a certain product, brand, and method to the latter, or the *franchisee*, who assumes the business risks of small proprietorship but has the advantage of selling a proven product. In the mid-20th century, franchises became a common alternative to the chain store model that dominated grocery and other retail fields, particularly in areas such as fast food and hospitality.

But the history of franchises began far earlier. As far back as the 1850s, Samuel Singer—who had invented a particularly effective and popular version of the sewing machine—pioneered the idea of providing a special license to certain salespeople for his machines. While textile factories tended to purchase sewing machines in bulk, Singer also targeted his product to individual consumers. Reaching such consumers, who were spread out geographically and required individual attention, proved time-consuming, particularly since many people were wary of buying a complicated machine if they did not have ready access to training or maintenance. So Singer sold special licenses to his franchisees, who had the unique authority to sell the machines and train customers in their use.[11]

Despite Singer's innovations, the franchise model remained uncommon throughout the late 19th and early 20th centuries. The automobile industry picked up on the concept by the 1910s and 1920s, as car manufacturers such as General Motors contracted with specially licensed sellers to both sell and service their products. Yet in the retail industry, the chain store model proved far more popular. Regional or even national corporate retailers like A&P and Sears kept a far tighter grip on their products, distribution channels, and pricing schemes.

Yet in the mid-1950s, Ray Kroc led the way in bringing the franchise model to the service sector, particularly through the highly specialized and streamlined world of fast food. In 1954, Kroc struck one of the most lucrative long-term business deals in history when he convinced the McDonald brothers to grant him the exclusive right to set up and manage McDonald's restaurant franchises around the country, in exchange for one-half of one percent of all gross sales. (Kroc bought the company outright for $2.7 million in 1961.) By 1967, more than 1,000 McDonald's franchises dotted the nation, and Kroc licensed his first franchisee abroad (in Canada). Today, the company boasts more than 12,000 U.S.-based franchises, more than 16,000 international franchises, and more than 6,500 company-owned establishments.[12]

The franchise model proved a winner both because it lowered Kroc's own capital expenses, which he pushed off onto his franchisees, and also because it allowed him to maintain scientific precision in the business. "We've worked out the precise formula for making a hamburger to the public's liking," he explained in 1968, "down to the exact size of the bun." The franchise model ensured that Kroc retained total control over strategy, brand advertising, and workforce training. His control extended not only to the menu but also to the details of restaurant operation. Early on, a drive-in theater operator in Minneapolis inquired about opening a franchise, which he thought he would open in April and close down in November. "No, no," Kroc told him, "This is based on a year-round operation." Only by operating on a precise model, all year long, could he guarantee the efficiencies of scale that kept his prices low.[13]

By the 1960s, the franchise model had become a mainstay of the expanding service sector in such fields as convenience stores and gas stations, motels, cafés, and particularly fast food. Franchises grew faster in the mid-20th century than any other type of business. By the 2010s, the United States was home to more than 750,000 franchise units, which employed more than 8.2 million people.[14] In addition to their economic effect, franchises—particularly the vast majority that cater to consumers in the service sector—have had a homogenizing effect on American culture. Consumers can enter a McDonald's, Days Inn, or Subway anywhere in the country (or indeed around the world) and have a clear sense of what to expect. As a business model, franchises met the demands of an increasingly consumer-focused culture—they provided the advantages of an organized and corporate structure and international branding with at least a nod toward local ownership and a hometown feel. In an economy geared toward serving consumers, the Big Mac was Big Business.

American fast-food restaurants achieved icon status for far more pernicious reasons as well. Low-cost food came with tremendous health consequences. Americans generally became more health conscious starting in the 1970s, as activities such as jogging gained popularity and tobacco smoking declined. At the same time, health professionals called out McDonald's for its high-fat menu. As Americans paid greater attention to the growing obesity epidemic in the early 21st century, many critics trained their fire on the fast-food industry, and studies linked obesity rates to overconsumption of cheap prepared food, particularly among poorer Americans.[15]

On a cultural level, critics charged that fast food's homogeneity and efficiency—so central to the franchise model—embodied the worst aspects of an impersonal and exploitative capitalist system. As such corporations as McDonald's established and expanded their global presence in the last three decades of the century, accusations soared of a renewed form of American cultural imperialism, at the expense of local food culture in places as far-flung as Paris, Tokyo, and Jerusalem.

The rise of fast food on the franchise model also recapitulated the social and economic anxieties that marked the long transition from a manufacturing to a service-oriented economy. As American manufacturers sought cheaper labor abroad by the 1980s and 1990s, factories shuttered and traditional blue-collar employment dried up across the country. Low-skilled, low-paid service sector work largely took the place of industrial jobs, and "flipping burgers" became synonymous with undesirable and devalued employment. Despite widespread beliefs that fast-food workers were largely teenagers or young people working their way up in the world, statistics tell a different story. Between 2010 and 2012, researchers found that the majority of fast-food employees had a high school degree, nearly a third had at least some college experience, and 40 percent were over the age of twenty-five. Seventy percent earned ten dollars an hour or less.[16]

A Revolution in Retail

Even as hamburger and doughnut franchises reshaped Americans' relationship with food, the modernization of the retailing industry changed how people acquired consumer goods. In 1955, the American automobile giant General Motors topped *Fortune* magazine's list of global companies ranked by annual revenue. For the remainder of the century, GM held that crown. Yet in 2002, it fell to second place, bested by a company that had barely been known outside of Arkansas in 1980 but exploded onto the international stage thereafter: Walmart. That upstart company, far more than just a store, succeeded by redefining retailing and, in the process, assumed an economic and political power that had previously been reserved for industrial manufacturers.

The son of a farmer-turned-debt-collector, a teenage Sam Walton spent the Great Depression with his father foreclosing on delinquent farms in Missouri. He witnessed the dramatic social consequences of the rapid decline of small-scale farming. Beginning in the 1920s, large agricultural corporations consolidated the market, buying up smaller family farms that lacked the resources to invest in labor-saving equipment or weather the fluctuations in the international prices of staples such as corn, wheat, and cotton. By the 1950s, the number of farm workers in such states as Oklahoma, Arkansas, and Texas had fallen by half. The future in this new economy, Sam Walton came to believe, lay not in growing but in selling.

Graduating from the University of Missouri with a business degree in 1940, Walton took a management trainee position with the national department store J.C. Penney, which he resigned a year and a half later to join the army. At the war's end, he launched his business career as owner of a Ben Franklin store, competing with other "five-and-dime" general-purpose retailers such as Woolworth's and S.S. Kresge (later Kmart). Over the next fifteen years, he opened and operated more than a dozen chain stores. In 1962, he pooled capital from his existing network of stores to create the first Walmart, in Rogers, Arkansas.

Walmart marked a key departure from the traditional variety store model. As the owner of Ben Franklin chain stores, Walton had been frustrated by the structural limitations of the business. Competition among small to midsized stores was fierce, driving down the prices he could charge. Walton's strategy was to locate wholesalers that would sell him popular products at a bulk discount and then lower his own sale price, undercutting his competition. But as a five-and-dime chain, he was at the mercy of suppliers and distributors to stock his shelves. As an independent retailer, however, Walton could overcome the distribution problem by setting up his own warehouse and distribution center, which he did in Bentonville, Arkansas, in the late 1960s.

With tight command over its supply and distribution networks, Walmart went public in 1970 and embarked on what one historian has called its "miracle decade," eventually achieving $1 billion in annual sales. The secret was Sam Walton's deep understanding of the importance of low-cost consumer goods and his willingness to focus on rural customers whom the traditional large chain and department stores overlooked. By 1980, he was opening fifty stores a year (and employing more than twenty thousand people), almost exclusively in towns with populations below ten thousand. By providing a wide range of daily household items, Walmart supplanted smaller stores in these sparsely populated areas. Walton kept prices low but profits high through what economists call *monopsony* power: As the primary *purchaser* from local suppliers, he could dictate lower prices, which he then "passed on" to Walmart shoppers.

In addition, Walton mastered the art of logistics, applying the logic of scientific management, which had reshaped industrial production, to the retailing trade. Operating his own warehousing and transportation fleet entailed costs, but Walton more than covered them by streamlining the movement of products, putting deliveries on a tight schedule, and ensuring that each store had the products it needed at the right time. Bar-code scanning technology and the Universal Product Code (UPC), first introduced in the mid-1970s but increasingly prominent in the 1980s, enhanced this efficiency, allowing Walmart store managers to track thousands of products in enormous stores.[17]

In the 1980s, Walmart expanded beyond the Ozarks and established itself as a national retailer. The company opened stores first in the Southeast and then in the Midwest. By 1991, the year before Sam Walton died, it had operations throughout the country and opened its first international location, in Mexico. Like McDonald's, Coca-Cola, and other prominent corporate brands, Walmart became a symbol of American capitalism around the world.

As the world's largest retailer and highest-revenue corporation, Walmart has taken on a profound cultural importance in the last thirty years. Its leaders have cultivated an image as a wholesome, traditional, and particularly moral enterprise. Its small-town origins and commitment to discount prices have helped protect the company from the populist charges of elitism or profiteering that so often haunt large commercial ventures.

Perhaps more important, the company's legacy is its corporate culture and devotion to the value of "service," which has come to dominate the rhetoric and strategy of retailers across the country. Walmart workers performed the tasks of the service economy—

stocking shelves, ringing up purchases, and tracking inventory. Yet the concept of "service" at Walmart extended beyond labor tasks to shape the company's overall ethic. Its leaders have self-consciously fostered a culture that prizes the Christian values of service and humility—in interactions both with customers and between workers and managers, or what Sam Walton called "Servant Leadership."

Rural America had traditionally been a hotbed of populist opposition to unfettered capitalism, from the anti-chain-store movement to opposition to the gold standard and eastern finance. Yet by the late 20th century, conservative politicians found greater success linking evangelical Christianity with free market economics. Ralph Reed, the conservative political activist who served as executive director of the Christian Coalition, declared in 1995: "If you want to reach the Christian population on Sunday, you do it from the church pulpit. If you want to reach them on Saturday, you do it at Walmart." As the historian Bethany Moreton has argued, the servant ethic at the heart of the service economy helped smooth that cultural and political transition.[18]

Yet such dominance has not come without controversy. As the embodiment of the service economy, Walmart for many people has come to epitomize the worst excesses of modern capitalism. In a deindustrialized economy marked by employment instability and stagnant wages, most especially for less-skilled workers, Walmart's labor practices have drawn attack. Emerging from the largely unionized rural South, the company joined the political fray as it expanded, pushing back against pro-union legislation. To head off unionization efforts within its ranks, the company turned to the classic strategy of *welfare capitalism*. In the 1970s, Sam Walton pioneered efforts to make employees feel a vested interest in the company through profit-sharing plans and stock ownership. More recently, the company has faced class action lawsuits alleging discrimination and unlawful termination of workers, as well as lawsuits alleging wrongful deaths.

In many ways, today's cultural and political conflicts over Walmart recast the chain store debates that raged in the 1920s and 1930s. Then as now, large discount retailers thrived by cutting costs and outcompeting other sellers. This dynamic inherently pits the interests of consumers, who benefit from low-cost goods, against other considerations, including higher wages for local workers, the viability of suppliers, and economic diversity. Yet the retailing world Walmart dominates today differs from the environment in which chain stores such as A&P and Woolworth's emerged a hundred years ago. Despite marginal successes by local communities in limiting the company's expansion, most of the anti-Walmart sentiment is rhetorical. Earlier activists formed a real political coalition to push significant regulations of chain stores, including price ceilings and legislation to break up monopolistic and monopsonistic sellers.[19] No similar legislation has shown much life today, a powerful testament to the power of a consumer (rather than producer or labor) economy and the dominance of the service sector.

The Internet Economy

The rise of services and the eclipse of manufacturing helped usher in a new economic order by the late 20th century. If the widespread prosperity of the postwar decades was built on the back of corporate triumph and industrial manufacturing, the shift to services had a bifurcating effect: While retail and fast food brought lower wages, knowledge-based and technical service industries created tremendous wealth and opportunity at the top.

While rapid advances in computing technology, including the invention of the silicon-based transistor and the microchip, allowed large corporations and government agencies to process, analyze, and store vast quantities of information, by the 1980s and 1990s the story of information technology (IT) intersected with the consumer economy, first through the personal computer and then through the spread of Internet technology. These developments ignited a new Information Age and brought new opportunities for consumers as well as businesses.

In the 1970s, the room-sized computers of old, such as IBM's System/360, gave way to smaller devices as engineers learned to compress multiple microprocessors onto chips, exponentially increasing computational power. By 1974, a small calculator company called MITS (for Micro Instrumentation and Telemetry Systems) announced the release of the first primitive version of what would later be called a personal computer. Small in comparison to its predecessors (it was roughly the size of a breadbox), the Altair 8800 microprocessing machine used a central processing unit (CPU) manufactured by Intel. It featured an eight-inch floppy drive, but lacked a keyboard or monitor. Although cutting-edge in its size and power, it had little practical use beyond the world of electronics hobbyists.

Just as the early automobile industry grew from hobbyists such as Henry Ford tinkering with engines and carriages in their spare time, so, too, did computer technology proceed. One such hobbyist was a nineteen-year-old student named Bill Gates, who invented a programming language (or software), known as BASIC, for the Altair machine. In 1975, Gates dropped out of Harvard University and moved to New Mexico, near MITS, and founded a company to design *soft*ware for *micro*processing computers—he called it Microsoft. By the early 1980s, Microsoft—which relocated and incorporated in Washington State in 1981—had emerged as the leading creator and producer of computer software, fast becoming one of the most profitable companies in the world. When Gates stepped down from Microsoft in 2014 (having reduced his role since 2000), he was the wealthiest person on Earth.

While Microsoft made its fortune in software development, another famous pair of innovators launched a company that played a vital role creating the mass market for personal computers. In 1976, two young friends from California—Steve Wozniak and Steve Jobs—founded the Apple Computer Company and released their version of a personal computer. Designed and hand-built by Wozniak, the Apple (later called the "Apple I" to distinguish it from subsequent versions) was a user-friendly and relatively cheap machine that featured a keyboard and an external disk drive. Seeing the potential wide use in a self-contained product that could connect to a monitor and other accessories, Jobs marketed the product and its 1977 successor, the Apple II, aggressively. Within four years, Apple had sold 120,000 machines, mostly to companies.

While upstart companies such as Microsoft and Apple pushed the boundaries of personal computing, the long-time leader in computer technology, IBM, largely stayed on the sidelines. Throughout the 1970s, IBM executives monitored the growing interest in small, personal-use computers, but decided to keep their focus on their corporate and government contracts. In 1981, however, IBM entered the PC game, using its substantial resources and market power to shoot to the lead. IBM sold eight hundred thousand units in its first year in the business, and more than 6 million by 1985, eclipsing Apple. By the end of the 1980s, personal computers—mostly running software written by Microsoft and using microprocessors produced by Intel—had become a fixture of upper-middle-class homes and white-collar workplaces.[20]

In addition to creating an important industry in its own right, computing had profound effects on the operation of all aspects of existing businesses. Giant retailers such as Walmart could process daily sales reports, using bar-code scanners to keep track of inventory in fine detail. Firms could complete orders, manage payroll, and track consumer trends and preferences with unprecedented accuracy. Streamlined communication meant smoother management and greater productivity—getting more done in less time—for workers.[21]

The boom in productivity accelerated in the late 1990s, with the beginning of yet another stage in the IT revolution: the spread of the Internet. The term "Internet" describes a *net*work of *inter*connected computers. The concept had its origins in the Department of Defense in the late 1960s, when government engineers designed an infrastructure to connect military computers across vast distances. Between 1983 and 1994, as the Cold War ended, the Pentagon gradually loosened its control of nonmilitary aspects of those networks. Entrepreneurial people who knew computer software quickly found ways to profit from this technology.[22]

In the early 1990s, computer scientists developed a platform for sharing hypertext documents across computer networks—eventually creating what became known as the World Wide Web. Because sharing information on the Internet became so much easier, the number of Internet users grew dramatically, from about ninety thousand in 1993 to 90 *million* by 2000.

A related technology, electronic mail, developed as Internet connectivity spread. In the 1990s, companies such as AOL and Compuserve provided email accounts and developed software programs that allowed people without technical computer knowledge to send and receive messages. Internet access and email use spread with blazing speed in the mid-1990s, taking information technology from the obscure province of engineers to something that touched the lives of millions in a few short years. IT revolutionized all aspects of business life, shaping corporate strategy, research, and marketing. Venerable brands and corporations added "dot-com" to their name, and new, online-only firms grew to prominence. Mass retailer Amazon disrupted traditional sales, first of books and eventually of nearly all types of consumer and household goods. Tech giant Google began as a particularly sophisticated search engine in 1999 and soon expanded to provide a wide range of Internet-based services and products, from document storage to software and equipment.

By the first decade of the 21st century, Internet technology had become integral to the consumer-oriented economy that had been growing for decades. In the early years of the new millennium, commentators invoked the term "Web 2.0" to describe a new phenomenon: the two-way exchange of information that erased the distinction between "producers" and "consumers" of Web content.[23] Video-sharing sites such as YouTube (bought by Google in 2006, a year after its founding) and "social media" companies such as Facebook and Twitter connected users around the world, redefining our sense of "Big Business" in the process.

The World Gets Flatter

In the second half of the 20th century, American business grew increasingly oriented toward mass consumption and shifted away from manufacturing and toward providing services. Those decades witnessed not only massive changes in technology, retail, and employment, but also the astronomical rise to dominance of the financial sector. Critically, all of these changes unfolded against the backdrop of pivotal global developments—specifically the trend toward increased global trade and production, generally called *globalization*—that recast the environment in which American business operated.

We often think of globalization as a product of the late 20th century—the modern world order defined by international brands, corporations that operate on a global scale, and the steady flow of low-skilled, low-paid jobs from more to less developed regions. In reality, many scholars note that we should think of our modern experience as a process of *re*globalization. On the eve of World War I, the global industrial powers presided over massive empires and engaged in extensive transnational trade with one another. Corporations operated and financial institutions invested across national and imperial boundaries at a rate, if we hold global economic output constant, not seen again until 2004. Yet the long conflict between 1914 and 1945 ripped apart the political institutions, alliances, and empires that had governed the world economy of the 19th century and destroyed that first moment of globalization. The history of global business in the 20th century is thus one of the gradual reconstruction of an interconnected world order.[24]

American manufacturing boomed at midcentury largely because the United States escaped World War II relatively unscathed, particularly with regard to other industrialized countries such as Germany, Japan, Britain, and the Soviet Union. American firms led most modern industries. The U.S. dollar, fixed to gold under an international accord negotiated in Bretton Woods, New Hampshire, in 1944, operated as the reserve currency for banks throughout the world, limiting international trade because countries could not exchange currency directly.

A combination of factors recast this postwar economic order by the 1970s, however. The gradual revival of foreign manufacturing, particularly (and ironically) by former foes Germany and Japan, strained American exporters. Despite their political and ideological commitment to free-market capitalism, many automobile industry executives joined with labor unions to champion protectionist trade policies, especially with Japan, whose government they accused (not without some evidence) of propping up its own car industry. At the same time, many industrialists argued that new government regulations, particularly concerning environmental pollution and product safety, exacerbated the competitive disadvantage they faced.

Increasing volumes of global trade also strained the supply of American dollars, which the Bretton Woods system ostensibly limited based on the amount of gold stored in American vaults. In practice, the United States printed more dollars than it could back up with gold, contributing to a panic over price inflation in the late 1960s. Faced with a shortage of gold and a desire to push the problem of inflation onto foreign trade partners, the Nixon administration suspended the convertibility of dollars to gold in 1971. The end of Bretton Woods created a system of floating exchange rates and reduced controls over the international transfer of capital, permitting firms to invest abroad more easily.

In addition, a series of international agreements reduced the barriers to international trade. A free trade agreement between France and Germany in 1957 evolved into the European Union, which expanded to twenty-eight member countries as of this writing (including the United Kingdom). Major world powers reduced barriers to international commerce with the first General Agreement on Tariffs and Trade (GATT) in 1947, an accord that they expanded through subsequent rounds of negotiations in the 1960s. It eventually transformed into the World Trade Organization in 1994. Also that year, the United States, Canada, and Mexico inaugurated NAFTA, the North American Free Trade Agreement, which created a free trade zone between those three countries. This arrangement made it easier for such American companies as RCA, as we saw at the beginning of this chapter, to manufacture electronics cheaply in Mexico and then import them for sale in the United States.

Lower barriers to trade and increased cross-border capital flows combined to spawn a new entity by the 1980s: the "multinational corporation" (MNC). MNCs, defined vaguely by their degree of operation and investment in multiple countries (despite being legally incorporated in a specific place), experienced a growth rate by the end of the 20th century that outpaced the rate of growth either for world exports or for total world output. International mergers increased, and "global brands" such as Coca-Cola and British Petroleum spread. The collapse of the Soviet Union, the economic liberalization of the former communist bloc, and the increased global integration of China in the 1990s and 2000s created even greater space for firms with international reach.[25]

By the year 2000, the new global economic order had become an inescapable part of American public life. Many decried the inequalities and depredations of globalization and the seemingly unstoppable trend toward "outsourcing," which increasingly relocated service jobs in addition to manufacturing. High-speed phone and Internet allowed companies to transfer certain service roles to cheaper labor markets overseas, such as customer service call centers in India.

The overall level of employment in the United States fluctuated with the business cycle in the late 20th century, declining during recessions and then recovering, despite the long-term change in business practices. What changed was the *type* of employment available to domestic workers. After expanding for thirty years, the average wage of American workers has stagnated since the 1970s. In many parts of the country, traditional manufacturing jobs have fled and left residents with few options. More educated and skilled Americans have found great success and opportunity in the "knowledge economy" and high-tech fields, while opportunities for social and economic advancement for others remain rare. Global outsourcing and the relocation of manufacturing outside the United States created the profound anxiety and uncertainty with which many Americans greeted the new century.

12

FINANCE TAKES FLIGHT

At the beginning of 2008, five venerable and highly respected investment banks—the descendants of the "House of Morgan"—sat atop American financial capitalism. By the fall of that year, none of them existed. Two, Bear Stearns and Merrill Lynch, avoided bankruptcy through emergency mergers (engineered to a significant degree by government officials and the Federal Reserve) with J.P. Morgan and Bank of America, respectively. The 150-year-old Lehman Brothers was not so lucky. After its leaders failed to convince government regulators to offer either a direct bailout or a "shotgun marriage" to another financial institution, Lehman entered the largest bankruptcy in history on September 15. The remaining two, Goldman Sachs and Morgan Stanley, surrendered their status as investment banks and transformed themselves legally into traditional bank holding companies, which faced far greater government regulation in exchange for easier access to government loans. As the former chairman of the Federal Deposit Insurance Corporation put it, it was "the end of Wall Street as we have known it."[1]

The Financial Crisis of 2008, triggered by a spectacular collapse of the housing market, launched the Great Recession that redefined political and social life in America and around the world. By far the worst economic downturn since the 1930s, the recession cost millions of people their jobs and homes, spawned a debt crisis that threatened to break up the European Union, and curtailed global industrial development, most notably in China. In the United States, the timing of the financial crisis helped guarantee Barack Obama's election. (Of course, after eight years of the increasingly unpopular Republican president George W. Bush, the Democratic candidate was in a favorable position even before the collapse in the fall of 2008.) Nonetheless, the politics of recession contributed to the paralysis of domestic policymaking during Obama's tenure.

The Financial Crisis of 2008 also led to unprecedented (and perhaps insufficient) government involvement in the intimate workings of financial capitalism. From the engineered merger of Bear Stearns with J.P. Morgan to the government takeover of mortgage corporations Fannie Mae and Freddie Mac (which were put into "receivership" as they faced bankruptcy in early September), to the unknowable billions of federal dollars injected into failing banks, automobile companies, and other corporations in the ensuing months, the crisis redefined the role of the federal government in the modern economy.[2]

Debates over the justice of federal bailouts hinged on a conflict between philosophical idealism and harsh economic pragmatism. Many Americans have long clung to a faith that private enterprise and a "free market" could regulate themselves if only external forces, especially government, stayed away. According to this logic, poorly performing firms would fail, punishing their investors and giving everyone an incentive to allocate resources wisely and fruitfully. Government bailouts would only encourage foolish or excessively risky behavior, creating a danger known as "moral hazard."

Yet by the early 2000s, the financial services profession had taken on such an outsized role in the national (and international) economy that, for many people, the old rules no longer applied. Massive financial institutions had constructed such intricate webs of loans and obligations to each other that if one failed, the companies it owed money to would also fail. Indeed, this exact scenario unfolded when Lehman Brothers collapsed, exposing the "systemic risk" inherent in the finance-driven economy and prompting massive new levels of federal government involvement—not just new regulations (which had been particularly lax), but also direct cash payments to save badly performing institutions.

The ultimate economic and political consequences of the Financial Crisis of 2008, the ensuing Great Recession, and the tepid recovery that followed beginning in 2009 have yet to play out. The story of how the crisis came about in the first place shows how changes in the nature of capitalism led to the defining moment of the early 21st century. While traditional business firms—large and small, industrial and service-oriented—still exist and often thrive, the center of gravity of American business shifted toward Wall Street starting in the 1970s.

An Era of Crisis: Finance in the 1970s

Americans often remember the 1960s as a period of upheaval. Images of political assassinations, civil rights and antiwar protests, the counterculture, and psychedelic rock music dominate our collective memory. The 1970s, by contrast, often seem like an afterthought. A cultural hangover after years of tumult, marked by cheesy clothes, hair, and music. A political wasteland, more defined by scandal (Nixon) or malaise (Carter) than high-minded ideas and debates.[3]

But dismissing the 1970s would be a mistake. From the perspective of business, work, and policies that shape our daily material lives, a growing number of historians now conclude the decade was as pivotal to shaping our national history as the 1930s. The very issues that made so many Americans want to forget the 1970s—inflation, the oil and energy crises, trade debates, urban decay—are what make the period so critical for understanding the rise of finance that would come to dominate American business in the decades to follow.

As we've seen, the tremendous economic growth that followed World War II in the United States as well as other industrialized countries slowed dramatically in the early 1970s. During the 107 months between John F. Kennedy's inauguration (January 1961) and Richard Nixon's first Christmas in the White House (December 1969), the American economy expanded without interruption. Yet in the years that followed, the country confronted a series of nasty recessions, each worse than the previous one, in 1970, 1974, 1978, and 1981.

At the same time, inflation was rising. From 1973 to 1983, the Consumer Price Index increased by an average of 8.2 percent per year; in several of those years, inflation topped 10 percent. Scholars, then and now, debate the exact mechanisms for the overall increase in the price level, but a number of important factors contributed. Beginning in 1965, increased government spending on both the Vietnam War and President Lyndon Johnson's Great Society initiatives exacerbated inflation. So, too, did monetary mismanagement by the Federal Reserve Board, which pursued economic growth by keeping interest rates low.[4]

International affairs mattered, too. In the fall of 1973, the Arab members of the Organization of Petroleum Exporting Countries (OPEC) launched an embargo against the United States and several Western European countries in retaliation for their support of Israel against Syria and Egypt in the Yom Kippur War. A second oil shock unfolded in 1979, this time as a result of the Iranian Revolution—in which religious fundamentalists overthrew the American-backed shah. By 1980, a barrel of oil cost about twelve times what it had cost in 1970. And because oil was such a vital resource, its price affected the costs of many different types of business—from transportation to agriculture to manufacturing, exacerbating inflation woes.[5]

The combination of rising unemployment, shrinking business profits, greater foreign competition for manufactured goods—particularly from Japan and Germany—and higher prices for everything from gas to beef created a miserable economic environment for much of the 1970s. Today, those who remember the decade frequently recall the specter of "stagflation," that unusual combination of price inflation and a stagnant economy, that packed a double wallop: Consumers had less money to spend even as the price of everything went up.

Stagflation had a profound effect on Americans' relationship with their money, affecting patterns of consumption, savings, investing, and retirement planning. In 1974, a group of legislative reformers passed the Employment Retirement Income Security Act (ERISA), which regulated the system of private retirement pensions, over the staunch objections of many large corporations—the country's largest employers. The law's supporters, who included liberal senator Jacob Javits (Republican from New York), saw the new regulations as a means to protect workers if corporations reneged on pension agreements. By making the system of employer-sponsored health and pension benefits more transparent, ERISA strengthened the retirement savings system. Yet it also created a massive new market for financial investment, as corporations sought third-party money managers to reap positive returns from the new flows of capital that workers contributed to their defined benefit plans.[6]

For their part, financial institutions worked to solve the problems created by stagflation. In a period of inflation, money loses value over time. Many people respond by either spending it quickly, with luck on something of durable value, or else finding a way to invest it at a rate of return that exceeds the inflation rate. Historians have noted that stagflation in the 1970s depressed the savings rate and boosted consumption, driving up the price of goods even higher in the process. Yet if consumers responded by changing their spending habits, savers had a harder time finding fruitful ways to store their money. New investment vehicles offered by enterprising financial institutions offered an attractive solution.

Under the banking regulation system enacted during the Great Depression (a time of pronounced *de*flation), the interest rates that commercial banks could offer were limited by law. However, these interest rate limitations only applied to commercial banks. The 1933 Glass-Steagall Act legally separated the functions, and regulations, of commercial and investment institutions, creating a different regulatory regime for investment banks. Traditionally, only investment banks like Goldman Sachs could bundle capital from wealthy corporate and individual clients to purchase securities. By the early 1970s, financial firms had altered this dynamic by increasingly offering money market mutual funds. Regulated like traditional securities investments, these accounts retained the look of commercial checking accounts, giving account holders the ability to withdraw from them at no cost. Yet by avoiding the regulations on commercial banks, they offered far higher rates of return. In the process, noncommercial banks were flooded with new capital to invest.[7]

Stagflation also reshaped traditional avenues for investment, most importantly in the bond market. Traditionally, investment banks such as Goldman Sachs, Lehman Brothers, and Morgan Stanley had restricted themselves to underwriting bonds for safe, well-established companies and governments that needed to raise capital. After vouching for the creditworthiness of the bond issuer, the investment banks would sell these conservative bonds to wealthy people and insurance companies. Corporate bonds in particular were generally safe and stereotypically boring. They didn't carry tremendous risk, and thus didn't pay particularly high rates of interest.

Yet the new economic climate meant that greater volumes of capital flowed to such investment vehicles as pensions and mutual funds, and investors had a greater appetite for higher risks if it meant beating inflation. Financial innovators developed different types of bonds—less safe and established, but offering higher yields. Such high-yield bonds, called "junk bonds," became mainstays of Wall Street investment by the 1980s.

Changing the Rules: The Politics of Deregulation

On a political level, the economic crises of the 1970s contributed to an important change in national political culture—growing skepticism of the government's ability to steer the economic ship. Declining public faith in economic planning stemmed from both the right and left sides of the political spectrum. On the left, it reflected disillusionment over the war in Vietnam, charges of collusion between private enterprise and the Department of Defense, and disgust over the levels of political and corporate corruption exposed through the Watergate scandal. On the right, it reflected the growing strength of the conservative movement's assault on the liberal principles that underlay the federal welfare state and the Johnson administration's domestic agenda, including the War on Poverty.

That political shift proved to be a guiding force behind the movement for widespread *deregulation*, which often garnered the support of groups that otherwise opposed each other politically. In 1978, President Jimmy Carter signed the Airline Deregulation Act, a law spearheaded by liberal politicians such as Ted Kennedy (D-MA) and consumer activist Ralph Nader, as well as free-market conservatives like the economist Milton Friedman. The opponents to airline regulation argued that a more market-driven airline industry would face greater competition to cut rates and, eventually, provide better service.[8]

Similar deregulatory legislation reshaped transportation and distribution. The Railroad Revitalization and Regulatory Reform Act (1976) and the Motor Carrier Act (1980) allowed railroad and trucking companies, respectively, to make their own decisions on pricing and routes. By the mid-1990s, having stripped away most of its functions, Congress finally dissolved the Interstate Commerce Commission—the nation's oldest federal regulatory agency.[9]

Deregulation also affected utilities. By the mid-1970s, many people worried that AT&T's monopoly over basic local and long-distance telephone service was making the company too large—that it was blocking out competition in other kinds of telecommunications, in new types of equipment, and in microwave and satellite technology. In 1974, the Department of Justice finally launched a massive antitrust suit against AT&T, and that suit led—eight years later—to the break-up of the company. It spun off its local telephone providers and concentrated on long-distance service, where it was in direct competition with newer companies such as MCI and Sprint.[10]

The deregulatory binge of the 1970s, which continued through the 1990s, largely reflected a false dichotomy between "more" and "less" government involvement in economic affairs. Yet scholars of regulation have shown that rather than create an objectively "freer" market, deregulation initiatives just changed the rules and structure of the regulatory system.[11] Often, these changes unfolded through conscious efforts to create and nurture markets—to create competition where none existed. By ending price controls on natural gas, for example, Congress forced companies that owned pipelines to offer the same rates and services to all customers, regardless of the market wisdom of doing so.

The deregulatory movement had dramatic effects on business. Airline fares fell sharply, allowing more people to take airplanes. The number of air passengers rose from 297 million in 1980 to 466 million in 1990 to 770 million in 2007. Long-distance telephone rates declined from around twenty-five cents a minute in the 1970s to five to ten cents a minute in the 1990s.

At the same time, many deregulated industries consolidated. Airlines in particular were able to take advantage of the economies of scale inherent in their industry to eliminate or take over rivals. By the 1990s, only a few airlines controlled most of the air traffic in the country. The reduction in the number of airline companies meant that deregulation, counter to its intentions, actually *decreased* competition in air travel.

The deregulatory spirit of the 1970s also led to dramatic changes to financial services. Since the 1930s, key financial services functions had been separated into distinct spheres. Commercial banking remained distinct from home mortgage lending, which was in turn distinct from investment banking. A financier like David Rockefeller, the grandson of the founder of Standard Oil and head of Chase Manhattan Bank, was prohibited by federal law from making loans to people who wanted to purchase a home. Moreover, regulations restricted *where* Rockefeller could conduct business—Chase Manhattan Bank could not establish branch offices outside its home state of New York. And even within New York, state regulators barred Chase from setting up shop in certain counties, in the interest of protecting smaller banks from competition. Moreover, the law limited investment banks to activities such as providing financing to corporations, funding mergers, and making bond issues. They couldn't sell mortgages to homeowners, or accounts to depositors.

In 1980, Congress began a long-term process of loosening those restrictions. The Depositary Institutions Deregulation and Monetary Control Act loosened regulatory requirements on banks and other types of financial services companies. Commercial banks expanded their service offerings by opening brokerage arms, helping customers buy and sell stocks. The new law also permitted banks to merge more easily, spawning a major merger wave. Interstate banking expanded under a regime of steadily looser restrictions, leading to the rise of first regional and then national commercial banking companies by the 1990s. Finally, in 1999, President Bill Clinton signed legislation passed largely at the behest of CitiGroup, which had merged with Travelers Insurance Company the previous year. The Gramm-Leach-Bliley Act (or the Financial Services Modernization Act) granted official sanction to a set of banking practices that had been developing for two decades, legally sending the last nail into the coffin of the New Deal's Glass-Steagall Act.[12]

Financial deregulation, launched under the soon-to-be-lame-duck Carter administration in 1980, changed the world of financial services and the role of Wall Street, both in business and in the cultural imagination. The saga of the savings and loan industry provides a striking illustration of the changes financial deregulation wrought.

Traditionally, savings and loan associations (S&Ls) had been conservative, small-town lenders that held deposits and made small, safe local loans, such as home mortgages. Before 1980, the interest rates they were allowed to pay to their depositors had been strictly limited. With 1970s inflation raging, however, depositors balked at depositing money where, even after earning interest, it lost value. The 1980 deregulation law freed S&Ls to raise interest rates to attract depositors, in hopes of making them more competitive.

A problem soon arose, however. Although S&Ls managed to attract more depositors by promising higher interest rates—say, 8, 9, or 10 percent—their *income* flows all came from older loans—long-term, stable, thirty-year mortgages *that had been fixed at low rates*. Across the country, S&Ls thus found themselves in the terrible business position of buying high and selling low, and many were on the path to bankruptcy. Just as commercial banks were backed up by the Federal Deposit Insurance Corporation (created as part of Glass-Steagall in 1933), so, too, were S&Ls eligible for government assistance. In the early 1980s, government officials estimated that a full-scale bailout of the savings and loan industry would cost $15 billion.

Many members of Congress, imbued with a faith in the free market and an antipathy to government involvement in the economy, concluded that such a price tag was too high. Greater deregulation, they argued, would solve the problem. In 1982, Congress again modified the regulatory requirements, permitting S&Ls to make higher-risk, higher-return investments with their deposits. One popular source of investment was real estate in Texas, where the high price of oil had driven up land valuations.

Yet by the mid-1980s, the global price of oil had declined markedly, due in part to an easing of global tensions as well as the success of more fuel-efficient cars (themselves a product of the high gas prices since the early 1970s). This great news for drivers, of course, spelled doom for investors in Texas real estate. Similar circumstances unfolded in other investments. Between 1986 and 1995, one in three of the nation's three thousand savings and loan associations had failed. In the mid-1990s, the General Accounting Office estimated the total cost of the savings and loan crisis at $160 billion, of which $130 billion came from the federal government's budget—through repossessing institutions, insuring depositors, and repaying loans.[13]

"Greed Is Good" and Other Clichés: Wall Street in the 1980s

The United States entered the 1980s with an economy every bit as depressed as it had been during the 1970s. In 1979, President Carter appointed a new Federal Reserve chairman, Paul Volcker, who took a hard line against inflation by implementing an extremely tight monetary policy. By dramatically restricting the growth of the money supply, Volcker's Fed essentially wrung price inflation out of the economy, but at the cost of a major downturn. The worst recession since the 1930s certainly did no favors for Carter's embattled presidency, and its lingering effects, until well into 1983, hamstrung his successor,

Ronald Reagan. By 1984, however, just as Reagan geared up for what would be a historic re-election campaign (he lost only Minnesota and the District of Columbia and won more electoral votes than anyone ever), the economy turned around.[14]

What distinguished the economic recovery of the 1980s was the new emphasis on finance. The face of "Corporate America" shifted from steel and oil executives to high-flying traders, brokers, and bankers. Popular culture captured and critiqued the overwrought glamour of high finance with movies such as Oliver Stone's *Wall Street*, whose famous antagonist, Gordon Gekko—played by Michael Douglas—famously announced that "Greed, for lack of a better word, is good." Audiences were supposed to find the sentiment repugnant, but Douglas himself reported that many young finance professionals approached him for years afterward proclaiming their admiration— not for his performance, but for the character himself![15]

In Stone's film, Gordon Gekko was a "corporate raider"—a new breed of wealthy investor who raised sufficient money to buy a controlling interest in a company, despite the wishes of the target firm's board of directors. Although the screenwriters denied that they modeled Gekko on any single individual, he resembled a number of financial tycoons who gained public notoriety, including "junk bond king" Michael Milken (who was indicted for securities fraud during an insider trading investigation in 1989). Moreover, the famous quote about greed echoed a sentiment by the famous trader Ivan Boesky, who called greed "all right" and "healthy" as a motivator for risk-takers.[16]

Corporate raiders were very much a reality, however, and "hostile takeovers" became increasingly common as the American business world entered yet another merger wave in the mid-1980s. The redirection of capital to financial pursuits—the hallmark of the process of financialization—led to growing number of deals known as "leveraged buy-outs" (LBOs)—mergers that depended on tremendous amounts of borrowed money. LBOs marked a significant innovation in finance because they allowed one company to purchase another without putting great amounts of its own resources into the deal. In other words, acquiring firms could keep their own capital working more efficiently (generally invested in high-yield areas), rather than tie it up in a costly corporate merger process. Instead, investment banks took on the risk of the deal (and charged substantial fees for their efforts) by raising money for the acquisition. And in making loan decisions, those investment banks generally considered the assets of the company being acquired as collateral in addition to the assets of the company doing the acquiring.[17]

The rise of Wall Street culture in the 1980s shined a spotlight on the massive transition to a financialized business world. But as the banking world prospered, other segments of the business community felt left behind. Industrialists in particular greeted the new big-money landscape of the 1980s with alarm, particularly when they became the targets of hostile takeovers.

"Hostile takeovers," declared Andrew Sigler, CEO of Champion International Paper, in 1984, "threaten the well-being of the country by causing corporations to react to intense pressures for short-term results." This new financial culture, he worried, brought "dramatic change in corporate ownership" and threatened long-standing corporate values. Instead of focusing on the stability and long-term profitability of a company, corporate raiders were only "looking for quick gains."

Other business leaders disagreed. Oil tycoon T. Boone Pickens, who gained national renown through several highly publicized hostile takeover efforts in the mid-1980s, accused industrialists like Sigler of being dinosaurs, relics of a staid old system. Since they could not keep up with the fast-moving and aggressive new capitalism, he charged, they favored "regimentation, stifling of the entrepreneurial spirit, disregard for stockholders, and obsessions with perquisites and power."[18]

The central debate between new and old capitalists revolved around what scholars describe as the rise of "shareholder capitalism." Although American corporations had successfully raised capital by issuing stock since the 18th century and encouraged broad-based stock ownership as early as the 1920s, the rhetoric of corporate managers and other observers—including business school professors and consultants—increasingly equated stock prices with the company's inherent worth in the 1980s. Firms defined their fundamental missions less in terms of the product they sold or the need they filled, and more in terms of "creating shareholder value." The overwhelming trend by the end of the decade was to break up large conglomerates, which frequently provided long-term employee benefits, including pensions, and to replace them with leaner, more streamlined organizations favored by financial markets.

Industrialists such as Andrew Sigler worried that the growing focus on financial valuation was shortsighted, since shareholders by their nature favored decisions that raised share prices in the short term, allowing them to sell and make a profit. For Wall Street heroes like Pickens, this was precisely the point. The collective wisdom of the masses of shareholders, mitigated through the free market, would undoubtedly yield better results than the limited, potentially corrupt or stuck-in-the-mud policies of bureaucratic managers. "Shareholder activism" thus emerged as a rallying cry in an increasingly financialized corporate universe.

Dot-Coms and Dot Bombs

Financialization shook up not only traditional business sectors such as industrial manufacturing and banking, but also the new world of high tech. In the 1990s, the rapid adoption of Internet technology created tremendous new business opportunities. Early adopters, especially tech icons such as Bill Gates and Steve Jobs, had reaped fortunes. The early architects of user-friendly Internet access, such as the Web platform Netscape and email provider America Online, had also rocketed to the top of the corporate world. In a near-frantic search for the next big win, investors in the latter half of the decade poured vast sums of capital into new technological ventures, creating a speculative bubble in the stock market. Since new Internet-based businesses were based online, many became known by their Web domain names, which, in the United States, typically ended in ".com" (designating the venture as commercial). The resulting boom in investment in technological start-ups thus became the "Dot-Com Bubble."

The Dot-Com Bubble inflated in the mid-to-late 1990s as enterprising and technologically sophisticated people, frequently young and often with little to no real business experience, announced new projects to fill particular business niches. For example, start-ups emerged to target clothing for teenage girls, or to sell pet supplies. Armed with an idea about how to use the new power of instant communication over the Internet, they sought funding from venture capitalists, early backers hoping for a clear and, generally, quick return on their investment when the new company was either sold in a merger (a common hope) or became publicly traded. In the latter case, the start-up's owners would work with investment banks to arrange an initial public offering (or IPO). In the short term, stock prices generally rose, allowing the company to pay back early investors (with interest) and, if the founders sold their shares, pocket a tidy sum. In the late 1990s, IPO activity among tech companies spiked dramatically.[19]

The fixation on stock valuation became a hallmark of business culture as the new millennium approached, a testament to the growing power of financial institutions. The stock mania was propelled by the dot-com frenzy, but it was not limited to new Internet-based companies. Corporate managers across all business sectors defined their success by the market price of their stocks, rather than by more traditional metrics such as production or even profit margins. Perhaps most famously, the executives at Texas-based energy company Enron grew so focused on their stock price, which they found they could manipulate through complex—and, it turned out, illegal—accounting practices, that they drove the giant company into insolvency. Enron's bankruptcy in 2001, the largest in history to that point (eclipsed by Lehman Brothers in 2008), reflected the darkest side of financialization.[20]

By the year 2000, American business culture had developed a single-minded obsession with stocks. Nowhere was this trend more visible than in the extraordinary attention paid to the NASDAQ stock index. Unlike the Dow Jones Industrial Average or the Standard & Poor's (S&P) 500 indices, which tracked the aggregate performance of publicly traded corporations from a variety of sectors, the NASDAQ index included only high-technology firms. Launched in 1971, the index grew slowly from its baseline of 100 to reach about 500 twenty years later. Thereafter, however, its rapid ascent tells a remarkable tale. The index doubled again by 1995, hitting 1,000, and continued its meteoric rise. In five more years, the NASDAQ topped out at more than 4,500.

Yet like the massive stock market inflation of the 1920s (and countless other speculative bubbles throughout history), this tech mania did not last. While determining the exact reason that such bubbles burst is often quite difficult or impossible, scholars note that stock traders grew increasingly worried that tech shares were overvalued, particularly as many new tech companies failed to demonstrate an ability to reap real profits. Moreover, the infrastructure that underlay the Internet boom created misaligned priorities—private companies had laid more miles of fiber-optic cables and created more bandwidth than people could use, given processing speeds at the time, and that meant their value decreased. Several spectacular failures of highly overvalued dot-com companies augured poorly for the tech sector as a whole, and a critical mass of investors moved to sell their shares. In March 2000, the NASDAQ index entered free fall, losing two-thirds of its value (from 4,500 to 1,500) in the next two years. And in early 2001, the U.S. economy dipped once again into recession, marking a statistical end to the boom period of the 1990s.[21]

The Housing Bubble and the Financial Crisis

The recession that began in 2001, made worse by international supply shocks and a decline in business activity following the 9/11 terrorist attacks on New York and Washington, D.C., quelled some of the "irrational exuberance"—described by Federal Reserve chairman Alan Greenspan—that had defined the previous decade.[22] Overspeculation in upstart companies subsided and a handful of large technology companies, led by newcomers such as Google and Amazon as well as such stalwarts as Apple and IBM, oversaw a more stable expansion. Yet in the larger sense, the sobering experiences of economic decline and new foreign policy crises, including the threat of terrorism and the wars in Afghanistan and Iraq, did nothing to stop the push toward financialization. By the early years of the 2000s, speculation in a different type of asset had the replaced dot-com stock bubble. Financialization—and its partner, deregulation—created a new threat: the housing bubble.[23]

Before the mid-20th century, just under 50 percent of American households owned their own home. Excluding farmers, who owned land at disproportionate rates, the rate of homeownership was below 40 percent. Between 1940 and 1970, American homeownership rose steadily to about 65 percent, due to a variety of factors, including government mortgage loan assistance programs created through the New Deal, the G.I. Bill (which provided preferential mortgage rates to veterans), and the overall expansion of the middle class. Indeed, homeownership in those middle years of the century became a widely acknowledged symbol of middle-class social status.

After hovering around 65 percent for several decades, homeownership rates rose quickly between the late 1990s and 2007, reaching 69 percent. As the world learned in dramatic fashion that year, the rapid uptick in homeownership reflected neither greater economic prosperity nor more affordable housing. (In fact, neither was the case—houses grew more expensive, and the difference between the 65 percent homeownership rate in 1997 and the 69 percent rate in 2007 came from the lower end of the earning scale, where real wages had stagnated since the 1970s.) Instead, the increase in homeownership created a perilous speculative bubble whose bursting launched the Financial Crisis and Great Recession.[24]

How did this bubble emerge?

Part of the story concerns low interest rates. After the recession of 2001, the Federal Reserve, chaired by the conservative Greenspan, held interest rates extremely low in an effort to encourage borrowing and boost spending, to allow the economy to grow. This low-rate environment made buying a home less expensive, but rather than pay less, many Americans opted instead to purchase more expensive houses. Fed policy had its intended effect of spurring demand, but greater demand for homes only inflated their prices.

Far more important, the deregulatory and financialized economy of the 2000s created an environment in which lenders were more willing to extend credit and mortgages to a greater number of people. More and more Americans, who weren't any richer than they had been before, became eligible to buy homes. The widespread belief that home values only ever rose, and thus that one could buy a home at the limits of one's budget and either renegotiate the loan or resell the home later at a profit, convinced many people that homeownership was a foolproof investment. "They're not making any more land," went a common refrain.[25]

This unfounded faith in the never-falling value of houses was perpetuated by mortgage lenders and the real estate business, which profited from every loan made and every home purchased. (Economic historians showed that the misunderstanding of historical home price values came from the simplest of oversights: Once you account for the overall increase in prices over time, the real—noninflationary—price of homes remained remarkably stable throughout the entire 20th century.)

Home sales accelerated in the 2000s primarily due to this new type of buyer, and a new term entered the national business lexicon: "subprime borrower." A subprime borrower was someone whose income and credit history would, under traditional circumstances, have prevented her or him from obtaining a certain loan. Yet such subprime loans proliferated, often based upon complex repayment plans. For example, an underqualified borrower might get a home loan with no money down and a low interest rate (which translated into low monthly payments) for a short period of time, after which the interest rate would rise. But since market professionals insisted that home values would increase, most subprime borrowers believed that they would be able to either sell or refinance a more valuable home before having to make higher monthly payments.

But why would banking institutions, which loaned money to home buyers and were ultimately on the hook if those borrowers became unwilling to pay, participate in this precarious system? Part of their willingness to take these risks came from the widespread belief that home prices would in fact rise indefinitely. Yet far more important were the structural changes wrought by a deregulated financial services industry, which diffused responsibility and accountability for bad loans while rewarding their purveyors.

In the aftermath of the financial deregulation that culminated in the late 1990s, new kinds of financial services institutions marked the business landscape. Mortgage lenders like New Century Financial and Countrywide Financial did not operate like traditional banks. Rather, they made far riskier loans, reducing down payments often to zero, offering attractive introductory rates and in many cases not requiring borrowers to document their income or employment. Lenders took such risks because, unlike traditional banks that retained a relationship with a mortgage borrower for the decades it took to repay the loan, these new institutions never intended to keep the mortgage. Rather than making money by collecting interest payments over time, their business model depended on taking sales commissions and fees on completed transactions and then *selling* the right to collect on that loan to a third party.

Mortgage lenders could sell away the rights to individual home mortgages because of the widespread practice of *securitization*, which, despite having been developed decades earlier, became endemic in the financial world in the 2000s. Securitization allowed a financial institution that acquired hundreds or thousands of mortgages, all of which came with the promise of a certain flow of interest income, to use that expected income as the basis to issue a bond—known as a mortgage-backed security (MBS). Investment banks then sold these MBSs, whose value depended on a complicated formula based on thousands of mortgages and which were notoriously hard to determine. This process of securitization linked the housing bubble to widespread overspeculation within the financial services industry and ultimately led to the crisis itself.

When the housing bubble peaked in 2006, growing numbers of people who had taken on mortgages with a three-year introductory interest rate (known as an ARM, for adjustable rate mortgage) found themselves unable to either refinance their mortgages (because banks grew suspicious that homes were really worth as much as they were sold for) or make their suddenly much higher monthly payments. An increase in foreclosures poured cold water on the home-buying frenzy, and home prices began to decline. With fewer homeowners making monthly payments, the income stream into the mortgage-backed securities declined. But because of the complexity of the securitization process, financial institutions that held those MBS bonds had difficulty determining their real value.[26]

By early 2008, a situation first described as the "subprime crisis" had spread to every corner of the financialized economy. Investment banks such as Bear Stearns and Lehman Brothers held vast quantities of securities whose value was both unknowable and rapidly declining, and they used these "toxic assets" as collateral to take on additional debt. This "contagion" spread throughout the financial system, in such a way that the failure of any large institution threatened to bring down everyone else.

The result was the Financial Crisis of 2008, the most cataclysmic economic event since the Great Depression. Analysts for the United States Government Accountability Office estimated that the total economic cost of the crisis "could range from a few trillion dollars to over $10 trillion," or more than half of the entire annual production of the American economy.[27] Yet the full costs in lost opportunities, life savings, and potential growth can never be completely known. The political and economic repercussions of the crisis continue to shape global affairs, from the political and monetary instability of the European Union and underdevelopment in Latin America to the slowing Chinese economy, as well as the debates about budgets and spending that dominated the Obama administration. What remains clear is that the Financial Crisis of 2008 marked the culmination of decades of increased financialization, abetted by a deregulatory political attitude that overtook not only American business but global capitalism as well.

Whether we rise and make progress from the ashes of the crisis depends on our ability to learn the lessons of business history.

CONCLUSION

AFTER THE CRISIS

The Financial Crisis of 2008 and the traumatic Great Recession that followed brought home for many Americans the profound importance of business—and its history—to our daily lives. The near-collapse of the world's financial system brought down such giants as Lehman Brothers, spawned the greatest loss of value in the stock market, and pushed the American unemployment rate above 10 percent—by far the worst jobs crisis since the 1930s.

Yet the catastrophe would have been far worse without forceful action by the federal government. Overcoming powerful resistance from anti-interventionists in the political sphere, who drew on the long-standing American fear of an aggressive government as well as a populist dislike for the concentration of power that Wall Street represented, the presidential administrations of George W. Bush and, later, Barack Obama took unprecedented steps to overcome the systemic damage the Financial Crisis caused. Beginning in the fall of 2008, the Treasury Department, working with the Federal Reserve, injected billions of dollars into failing banks through a program known as the Troubled Asset Relief Program (TARP), sparing large segments of the industry from insolvency. In February 2009, Congress passed and Obama signed the American Recovery and Reinvestment Act, extending federal aid to other segments of the business community that suffered in the wake of the financial meltdown, including the long-suffering automobile manufacturing industry. By 2010, the economic skid reached its low point, and both employment figures and business activity began a slow recovery.

Persistent economic fragility defined key debates in American public life in the years that followed. The previously unfathomable outlays of federal government money required to save the nation from financial cataclysm left a deep and troubling hole in the government's balance sheet. Throughout most of the Obama presidency, vicious partisan battles raged over the politics of taxes, spending, and the space between them: the budget deficit. Republican lawmakers urged substantial cuts in government spending, especially on social welfare programs, while Democrats proposed higher taxes on wealthier citizens to fill the gap. In the fall of 2013, the budget impasse caused Congress to permit a lapse in the Treasury Department's legal ability to issue bonds to cover debts, shutting down the federal government. Long a source of tension, the imbalanced budget became an all-encompassing political battleground in the wake of the Great Recession.

The Financial Crisis and Great Recession reshaped American politics in other ways as well. In February 2009, a pundit in the televised business press named Rick Santelli launched a widely viewed political rant against homeowners who sought government aid because their mortgages had gone "underwater"—that is, they owed more than the home was worth. Santelli amplified a critique, prominent among conservatives, that government bailouts for either individuals or corporations were "promoting bad behavior" by encouraging the type of risky behavior that had spawned the crisis in the first place. He called for a "Chicago Tea Party" where all "capitalists that want to show up" could join him in "dumping securities derivatives" into Lake Michigan.[1]

In a media age characterized by rapid information sharing, Santelli's diatribe quickly "went viral" and attracted a widespread viewership. Within a few months, groups calling themselves "Tea Party Patriots" emerged across the country, organizing antigovernment and promarket political constituencies. The Tea Party movement, as it quickly became known, represented a modern incarnation of a long-standing theme in America's political and economic history. Its members opposed President Obama's universal health care law (the Patient Protection and Affordable Care Act, or Obamacare) and a package of reforms to more strictly regulate the financial services industry (the Dodd-Frank Wall Street Reform and Consumer Protection Act), both of which only narrowly passed Congress in 2010. Giving voice to the anxieties of many of the people whom the modern economy had left behind and redirecting their angst about the federal government, the Tea Party came to play a major role in national politics during the Obama administration.

At the same time, the politics of recession also animated activists on the political left. In the fall of 2011, a group of protesters staged a protest in Zuccotti Park in lower Manhattan to protest the continued wealth, power, and influence of Wall Street. Soon dubbed the "Occupy Wall Street" movement, these protesters channeled widespread anger over stagnating middle-class wages and broadening income inequality, both hallmarks of the changes in American business since the 1970s.

The Occupy and Tea Party movements seemed like polar opposites—the former deeply critical of unfettered capitalism, the latter opposed to government intervention in the economy. Yet even if they defined their enemies differently, they both emerged, nearly simultaneously, in response to the same problems: economic instability and insecurity in the face of a new business climate that seemed increasingly out of reach to everyday Americans. Both tapped into deep veins of populist opposition to the global financial elite and longed for a return to a more egalitarian past. Both movements likewise found echoes in the outsider-populist political campaigns of Vermont senator Bernie Sanders and celebrity businessperson Donald Trump in 2016.

In both its trajectory and its political and cultural consequences, the Financial Crisis recapitulated several of the major themes in the history of business in the United States. The recent history of business had forced Americans to wrestle with the question of the government's role in the national economy. When private actors conflict, how should the state choose sides? When should private businesses suffer the travails of a dangerous market, and when is the public interest better served by helping them out? As it has been throughout the history of capitalism in America, the central question is not "*Should* the government play a role in the market?" but "In whose interest?"

These questions have recurred throughout the history of private affairs and public life in America, but the story of business in the United States shows that they manifest in different ways. The early market revolution and commercialization of slavery and cotton production represented one such moment of crisis early in our national history, as did the turmoil of heavy industry and the rise of the corporate form that confronted the country a hundred years later.

Globalization and financialization, which have redefined both employment opportunities and the balance of power during the last generation, are the chief destabilizing forces of our time. The business firm itself looks far different today than it did even in the relatively recent past. The apparent triumph of the "shareholder activism" movement in the late 20th century, combined with powerful new technologies that permit unprecedented atomization and outsourcing of nearly all corporate functions, have made today's major firms less concentrated, less hierarchical, and less permanent. How our society organizes the vital tasks of providing goods and services to its citizens—how we navigate the complexities of mass distribution or manage the bounty of mass production—will unfold in a business climate different from any we have ever known. The current path is unstable, unequal, and troubling. Yet it also brings the promise of new advances to improve the quality of life for greater numbers of people, new tools to create and allocate resources more equitably, and new value systems rooted in shared prosperity.

What does the future hold for business? Historians resist the temptation to make bold predictions, since, if nothing else, history teaches us that the future is always in flux. Nonetheless, we historians hold this truth to be self-evident: We study the past so we can understand the present, and perhaps, with luck, help craft a better future. And as this book has attempted to show, the history of business has a great deal to tell us about where we are today. What's clear is that future challenges and advances will inevitably be built on centuries of business history.

NOTES

INTRODUCTION:
HOW BUSINESS EXPLAINS AMERICA

1 Carmen Reinhart and Kenneth Rogoff, *This Time Is Different: Eight Centuries of Financial Folly* (Princeton, 2009); Thomas Piketty, *Capital in the Twenty-First Century* (Cambridge, MA: 2014).

I : CONQUEST, COLONIES, AND CAPITALISM

1 Kevin O'Rourke and Jeffrey Williamson, "After Columbus: Explaining Europe's Overseas Trade Boom, 1500–1800," *Journal of Economic History* 62 (2), June 2002, 417–56.

2 David Eltis, *The Rise of African Slavery in the Americas* (Cambridge, UK: 2000).

3 Alison Games, "Migration," in *The British Atlantic World*, David Armitage and Michael Braddick, eds. (New York, 2002); Anthony McFarlane, *The British in the Americas 1480–1815* (London, 1992).

4 See, for example, C. A. Bayly, *Birth of the Modern World, 1780–1914, Global Connections and Comparisons* (Oxford, UK: 2004).

5 On the origins and development of world trade, see Kenneth Pomeranz and Steven Topik, *The World That Trade Created: Society, Culture, and the World Economy, 1400 to the Present* (3rd ed.) (New York, 2013).

6 Carl Degler, *Out of Our Past: The Forces That Shaped Modern America* (New York, 1970).

7 J. H. Elliott, *Empires of the Atlantic World: Britain and Spain in America, 1492–1830* (New Haven, CT: 2006).

8 Elvira Vilches, *New World Gold: Cultural Anxiety and Monetary Disorder in Early Modern Spain* (Chicago, 2010).

9 Eric Jay Dolan, *Fur, Fortune, and Empire: The Epic History of the Fur Trade in America* (New York, 2010).

10 Nicholas P. Canny, "The Ideology of English Colonization: From Ireland to America," *The William and Mary Quarterly* 30(4), October 1973, 575–98.

11 Nuala Zahedieh, "Economy," in *The British Atlantic World, 1500–1800*, David Armitage and Michael Braddick, eds. (New York, 2002). See also Kenneth R. Andrews, *Trade, Plunder, and Settlement: Maritime Enterprise and the Genesis of the British Empire, 1480–1630* (Cambridge, UK: 1984).

12 McFarlane, *The British in the Americas.*

13 Matthew Dowd Mitchell, "The Royal African Company of England, 1672–1752: Joint-stock capitalism in the early modern Atlantic" (Ph.D. diss., University of Pennsylvania, 2012).

14 "The First Charter of Virginia, April 10, 1606," available at avalon.law.yale.edu/17th_century/va01.asp.

15 Ronald Heinemann et al., *Old Dominion, New Commonwealth: A History of Virginia, 1607–2007* (Charlottesville, VA: 2007).

16 Edwin Perkins, "The Entrepreneurial Spirit in Colonial America: The Foundation of Modern Business History," *Business History Review 63,* Spring 1989, 169–86.

17 Benjamin Franklin, "Advice to a Young Tradesman," in Albert H. Smyth, ed., *The Writings of Benjamin Franklin*, vol. 2 (New York, 1905).

18 Cited in Thomas Breen, "'Baubles of Britain': The American and Consumer Revolutions of the Eighteenth Century," *Past and Present* 119, May 1988, 73–104.

19 Zahedieh, "Economy."

20 Thomas Doerflinger, *A Vigorous Spirit of Enterprise: Merchants and Economic Development in Revolutionary Philadelphia* (Chapel Hill, NC: 1985).

21 Richard Bushman, "Markets and Composite Farms in Early America," *William and Mary Quarterly*, 3rd ser., 55, 1998, 351–74.

22 John J. McCusker and Russell R. Menard, *The Economy of British America, 1607–1789* (Chapel Hill, NC: 1991).

23 Kathleen DuVal, *Independence Lost: Lives on the Edge of the American Revolution* (New York, 2015); Eltis, *The Rise of African Slavery in the Americas.*

24 Charles Beard, *An Economic Interpretation of the Constitution of the United States* (New York, 1913).

25 Alexander Hamilton (as Publius), "The Utility of the Union in Respect to Revenue," *Federalist No. 12*, 1787.

2: THE BUSINESS OF BONDAGE

1 Solomon Northup, *Twelve Years a Slave* (New York: 1853).

2 Stephanie E. Smallwood, *Saltwater Slavery: A Middle Passage from Africa to American Diaspora* (Cambridge, MA: 2007).

3 Engle Sluiter, "New Light on the '20. and Odd Negroes' Arriving in Virginia, August 1619," *The William and Mary Quarterly*, Vol. 54, No. 2, April 1997, pp. 395–98; John Thornton, "The African Experience of the '20. and Odd Negroes' Arriving in Virginia in 1619," *The William and Mary Quarterly*, 3rd. ser., Vol. 55, No. 3, July 1998, pp. 421–34.

4 Peter Kolchin, *American Slavery, 1619–1877* (New York, 1993); *The Trans-Atlantic Slave Trade Database: Voyages*, www.slavevoyages.org.

5 Walter Johnson, *Soul by Soul: Life Inside the Antebellum Slave Market* (Cambridge, MA, 1999). For the classical assessment of the triangle trade, see Eric Williams, *Capitalism and Slavery* (Chapel Hill, NC: 1944).

6 Mark M. Smith, *Debating Slavery: Economy and Society in the Antebellum American South* (Cambridge, UK: 1998).

7   Charles B. Dew, *Bond of Iron: Master and Slave at Buffalo Forge* (New York, 1994); James C. Davis to William W. Davis, January 5, 1956, in Willie Lee Rose, ed., *A Documentary History of Slavery in North America* (New York, 1976).

8   Seth Rockman, *Scraping By: Wage Labor, Slavery, and Survival in Early Baltimore* (Baltimore, 2009).

9   Northup, *Twelve Years a Slave*; 4; David Brion Davis, "The Impact of British Abolitionism on American Sectionalism," in *In the Shadow of Freedom: The Politics of Slavery in the National Capital*, Paul Finkelman and Donald R. Kennon, eds. (Athens, OH, 2011).

10 Adam Rothman, *Slave Country: American Expansion and the Origins of the Deep South* (Cambridge, MA, 2005).

11 Kolchin, *American Slavery*.

12 Sven Beckert, *Empire of Cotton: A Global History* (New York, 2014); Giorgio Riello, *Cotton: The Fabric That Made the Modern World* (Cambridge, UK: 2013).

13 Angela Lakwete, *Inventing the Cotton Gin: Machine and Myth in Antebellum America* (Baltimore, 2003).

14 William Fogel and Stanley Engerman, *Time on the Cross: The Economics of American Negro Slavery* (New York, 1974).

15 Rothman, *Slave Country*.

16 James Henry Hammond, U.S. Senate, March 4, 1858. See also Drew Gilpin Faust, *James Henry Hammond and the Old South: A Design for Mastery* (Baton Rouge, 1982).

17 See Karl Marx, *Grundrisse* (1857).

18 Caitlin Rosenthal, "Slavery's Scientific Management: Masters and Managers," in Sven Beckert and Seth Rockman, eds., *Slavery's Capitalism: A New History of American Economic Development* (Philadelphia, 2016).

19 Edward Baptist, *The Half Has Never Been Told: Slavery and the Making of American Capitalism* (New York, 2014).

3: FACTORIES COME TO AMERICA

1   Alexander Hamilton, *Report on Manufactures* (1791).

2   See, for example, Charles Sellers, *The Market Revolution: Jacksonian America, 1815–1816* (Oxford, UK: 1991); Melvyn Stokes and Stephen Conway, eds., *The Market Revolution in America: Social, Political, and Religious Expressions, 1800–1880* (Charlottesville, VA: 1996).

3   Beckert, *Empire of Cotton*.

4   Alfred Chandler, *The Visible Hand: The Managerial Revolution in American Business* (Cambridge, MA: 1977).

5   Robert Dalzell, *Enterprising Elite: The Boston Associates and the World They Made* (New York, 1993).

6   Josephine L. Baker, "A Second Peep at Factory Life," *The Lowell Offering* 5 (1845), in Benita Eisler, ed., *The Lowell Offering: Writing by New England Mill Women, 1840–1845* (New York, 1977).

7   U.S. Census, "Table 4. Population: 1790 to 1990," www.census.gov/population /censusdata/table-4.pdf.

8   Lawrence Friedman, *A History of American Law*, 2nd ed. (New York, 1985).

9   Mansel Blackford and Austin Kerr, *Business Enterprise in American History*, 3rd ed. (Boston, 1994).

10 For a classic but informative survey of changes to transportation practice and technology, see George Taylor, *The Transportation Revolution: 1815–1860* (New York, 1951).

11 Gerard Koeppel, *Bond of Union: Building the Erie Canal and the American Empire* (Cambridge, MA: 2009).

12 Taylor, *The Transportation Revolution*.

13 Chandler, *The Visible Hand*; Douglas North, *The Economic Growth of the United States: 1790–1860* (New York, 1961).

14 Richard John, *Spreading the News: The American Postal System from Franklin to Morse* (Cambridge, MA: 1995).

15 Richard John, *Network Nation: Inventing American Telecommunications* (Cambridge, MA: 2010); Daniel Walker Howe, *What Hath God Wrought: The Transformation of America, 1815–1848* (Oxford, UK: 2007).

16 Chandler, *The Visible Hand*.

17 Friedman, *A History of American Law*; Robert Wright, *Corporation Nation* (Philadelphia, 2014).

4: THE POLITICS OF BUSINESS IN THE EARLY REPUBLIC

1   Hamilton, *Report on Manufactures*.

2   Thomas Jefferson, *Notes on the State of Virginia* (1787).

3   For recent scholarly work on the politics of the turn of the 19th century, see Jeff Pasley, Andrew Robertson, and David Waldstreicher, eds., *Beyond the Founders: New Approaches to the Political History of the Early American Republic* (Chapel Hill, NC: 2004).

4   Thomas McCraw, *The Founders and Finance: How Hamilton, Gallatin, and Other Immigrants Forged a New Economy* (Cambridge, MA: 2012).

5   Rothman, *Slave Country*.

6   Harry Watson, *Liberty and Power: The Politics of Jacksonian America* (New York, 1990).

7   Scott Nelson, *Nation of Deadbeats: An Uncommon History of America's Financial Disasters* (New York, 2012).

8   Watson, *Liberty and Power*. See also Arthur Schlesinger, Jr., *The Age of Jackson* (Boston, 1945).

9   Stephen Mihm, *A Nation of Counterfeiters: Capitalists, Con Men, and the Making of the United States* (Cambridge, MA: 2007).

10 Sean Wilentz, *Chants Democratic: New York City and the Rise of the American Working Class, 1788–1850* (Oxford, UK: 1984).

11 See Watson, *Liberty and Power*; Wright, *Corporation Nation*; Nelson, *Nation of Deadbeats*; and Mihm, *Nation of Counterfeiters*.

12 Mihm, *Nation of Counterfeiters*.

13 Andrew Jackson, "Veto Message [Of The Reauthorization of Bank of the United States]," July 10, 1832. Online by Gerhard Peters and John T. Woolley, *The American Presidency Project*, http: www.presidency.ucsb.edu/ws/?pid =67043.

14 Jessica Lepler, *The Many Panics of 1837: People, Politics, and the Creation of a Transatlantic Financial Crisis* (New York, 2013).

15 Schlesinger, *The Age of Jackson*.

16 On the South's economic fortunes after the war, see Gavin Wright, *Old South, New South: Revolutions in the Southern Economy since the Civil War* (New York, 1986).

17 Sven Beckert, *The Monied Metropolis: New York City and the Consolidation of the American Bourgeoisie, 1850–1896* (Cambridge, UK: 2001).

18 Eric Foner, *Reconstruction: America's Unfinished Revolution, 1863–1877* (New York, 1988).

5: BUSINESS GETS BIG

1 On the politics of Big Business Day, see Benjamin Waterhouse, "The Corporate Mobilization against Liberal Reform: Big Business Day, 1980," in Kim Phillips-Fein and Julian Zelizer, eds., *What's Good for Business: Business and American Politics Since World War II* (Oxford, UK: 2012).

2 John Steele Gordon, "The Public Be Damned," *American Heritage*, Vol. 40, Issue 6, September/October 1989.

3 Richard John, "Robber Barons Redux: Antimonopoly Reconsidered," *Enterprise and Society*, 13:1, March 2012.

4 Kenneth Warren, *Big Steel: The First Century of the United States Steel Corporation, 1901–2001* (Pittsburgh, 2001).

5 Chandler, *The Visible Hand*.

6 Chandler, *The Visible Hand;* Taylor, *The Transportation Revolution*.

7 Friedman, *A History of American Law*.

8 On the continental expansion of the railroads, see especially Richard White, *Railroaded: The Transcontinentals and the Making of Modern America* (New York, 2011).

9 Glenn Porter, *The Rise of Big Business, 1860–1920*, 3rd ed. (Wheeling, IL: 2006).

10 Daniel C. McCallum, "Superintendent's Report," March 25, 1856, in *Annual Report of the New York and Erie Railroad Company for 1855* (New York, 1856), pp. 33–37, cited in Alfred Chandler, "The Railroads and the Beginnings of Modern Management," Harvard Business School Case 377-231 (Boston, 1977; revised May 9, 1995).

11 On Carnegie, see Harold C. Livesay, *Andrew Carnegie and the Rise of Big Business* (Boston, 1975); David Nasaw, *Andrew Carnegie* (New York, 2007).

12 Andrew Carnegie, *Autobiography of Andrew Carnegie* (Garden City, NY: 1933).

13 On the Homestead strike, see David Brody, *Steelworkers in America: The Nonunion Era* (New York, 1960).

14 On the role of personal connections and networking, particularly along racial and class lines, in the history of American business, see Pamela Laird, *Pull: Networking and Success since Benjamin Franklin* (Cambridge, MA: 2006).

15 On Rockefeller, see Ron Chernow, *Titan: The Life of John D. Rockefeller* (New York, 1998).

16 Allan Nevins, *John D. Rockefeller* (New York, 1959).

17 Porter, *The Rise of Big Business.*

18 Louis Galambos and Joseph Pratt, *The Rise of the Corporate Commonwealth: U.S. Business and Public Policy in the Twentieth Century* (New York, 1988). Dollar conversion from *Economic History Association*, eh.net.

19 Thomas McCraw, "American Capitalism," in Thomas McCraw, ed., *Creating Modern Capitalism: How Entrepreneurs, Companies, and Countries Triumphed in Three Industrial Revolutions* (Cambridge, MA: 1997).

20 Mihm, *Nation of Counterfeiters.* On history of monetary policy in the late 19th century, the classic treatment remains Milton Friedman and Anna Schwartz, *A Monetary History of the United States, 1867–1960* (Princeton, NJ: 1963). For a recent analysis of the creation of the Federal Reserve system, see Peter Conti-Brown, *The Power and Independence of the Federal Reserve* (Princeton, NJ: 2016).

21 Chandler, *The Visible Hand.*

22 Ron Chernow, *The House of Morgan: An American Dynasty and the Rise of Modern Finance* (New York, 1991).

23 Naomi Lamoreaux, *The Great Merger Movement in American Business, 1895–1904* (Cambridge, UK: 1985).

6: WARRING WITH THE OCTOPUS—WORKERS, FARMERS, AND TRUSTBUSTERS

1 The story of the Great Railroad Strike is told in vivid detail in Jeremy Brecher's classic *Strike!* (San Francisco, 1972). For a scholarly assessment by a preeminent historian of American labor, see Nick Salvatore, "Railroad Workers and the Great Strike of 1877: The View from a Small Midwest City," *Labor History*, Vol. 21, Issue 4, 1980, pp. 522–45.

2 Richard Bensel, *Passion and Preferences: William Jennings Bryan and the 1896 Democratic National Convention* (New York: 2008). Speech available as text and audio at www.americanrhetoric.com/speeches/williamjennings bryan1896dnc.htm.

3 Ida Tarbell, *The History of the Standard Oil Company* (New York, 1904). See also Steve Weinberg, *Taking on the Trust: The Epic Battle of Ida Tarbell and John D. Rockefeller* (New York, 2008).

4 Preamble to the Constitution of the Knights of Labor, 1878, in Timothy Patrick McCarthy and John McMillan, eds., *The Radical Reader: A Documentary History of the American Radical Tradition* (New York, 2003).

5 Stanley Lebergott, "Labor Force and Employment, 1800–1860," in Dorothy S. Brady, ed., *Output, Employment, and Productivity in the United States after 1800* (NBER, 1966).

6   On the increase in the labor force, see Robert A. Margo, "The Labor Force in the Nineteenth Century," NBER Working Paper Series on Historical Factors in Long Run Growth (Cambridge, MA: 1992).

7   Melvyn Dubofksy, *Labor in America: A History*, 7th ed. (Wheeling, IL: 2004).

8   Leon Fink, *Workingmen's Democracy: The Knights of Labor and American Politics* (Urbana, IL: 1983).

9   Elliot Cowdin, "Capital and Labor. An address delivered before the American institute of the city of New York, in celebration of its semi-centennial anniversary, on Thursday evening, October 11, 1877," quoted in Beckert, *Monied Metropolis*, 282.

10 Fink, *Workingmen's Democracy*.

11 For a helpful overview of recent studies of organized labor, see Nelson Lichtenstein, *State of the Union: A Century of American Labor* (Princeton, NJ: 2002).

12 Brody, *Steelworkers in America*.

13 Mark Summers, *Rum, Romanism, and Rebellion: The Making of a President, 1884* (Chapel Hill, NC: 2000). On the politics of the 1880s and 1890s, see also Richard Hofstadter, *The Age of Reform: From Bryan to FDR* (New York, 1955).

14 David Papke, *The Pullman Case: The Clash of Labor and Capital in Industrial America* (Lawrence, KS: 1999).

15 Nick Salvatore, *Eugene V. Debs: Citizen and Socialist* (Urbana, IL: 1984).

16 "President Pullman's Statement at the Stockholders' Annual Meeting, October 18, 1894," in *The Strike at Pullman* (Pullman, IL: 1894).

17 Olivier Zunz, *Philanthropy in America: A History* (Princeton, NJ: 2012).

18 On welfare capitalism, see Sanford Jacoby, ed., *Masters to Managers: Historical and Comparative Perspectives on American Employers* (New York: 1991), and Lizabeth Cohen, *Making a New Deal: Industrial Workers in Chicago, 1919–1939* (Cambridge, UK: 1990).

19 Michael Kazin, *A Godly Hero: The Life of William Jennings Bryan* (New York: 2007); Charles Postel, *The Populist Vision* (Oxford, UK: 2007); Lawrence Goodwyn, *The Populist Moment: A Short History of the Agrarian Revolt in America* (New York, 1978).

20 Wyatt Wells, "Rhetoric of the Standards: The Debate over Gold and Silver in the 1890s," *Journal of the Gilded Age and Progressive Era* 14(1), January 2015, 49–68.

21 Robert Mutch, *Buying the Vote: A History of Campaign Finance Reform* (Oxford, UK: 2014).

22 On the political consequences of the free silver movement, see Elizabeth Sanders, *Roots of Reform: Farmers, Workers, and the American State, 1877–1917* (Chicago, 1999).

23 Thomas McCraw, *Prophets of Regulation: Charles Francis Adams, Louis D. Brandeis, James M. Landis, Alfred E. Kahn* (Cambridge, MA: 1984).

24 Samuel Huntington, "The Marasmus of the ICC: The Commission, the Railroads, and the Public Interest," *Yale Law Journal* 4(61), April 1952: 467–509.

25 26 Stat. 209, 15 U.S.C. §§ 1–7 (1890).

26 Tony Freyer, *Regulating Big Business: Antitrust in Great Britain and America 1880–1990* (Cambridge, UK: 1992).

27 *Standard Oil Co. of New Jersey* v. *United States,* 221 U.S. 1 (1911).
28 Louis Galambos, "The Monopoly Enigma, the Reagan Administration's Antitrust Experiment, and the Global Economy," in Kenneth Lipartito and David Sicilia, eds., *Constructing Corporate America: History, Politics, Culture* (Oxford, UK: 2004).
29 United States v. United States Steel Corp., 251 U.S. 417 (1920).
30 Brett Christophers, *The Great Leveler: Capitalism and Competition in the Court of Law* (Cambridge, MA: 2016).
31 Michael McGerr, *A Fierce Discontent: The Rise and Fall of the Progressive Movement in America* (Oxford, UK: 2003).
32 Robert Wiebe, *Businessmen and Reform: A Study of the Progressive Movement* (Chicago, 1962); Gabriel Kolko, *The Triumph of Conservatism: A Reinterpretation of American History, 1900–1916* (New York, 1963).

7: THE DAWN OF MODERN LIFE

1 For these statistics, see Thomas McCraw and Richard Tedlow, "Henry Ford, Alfred Sloan, and the Three Phases of Marketing," in Thomas McCraw, ed., *Creating Modern Capitalism: How Entrepreneurs, Companies, and Countries Triumphed in Three Industrial Revolutions* (Cambridge, MA: 1997), 266–302; and Harold Livesay, *American Made: Men Who Shaped the American Economy* (Boston, 1979).
2 Samuel Strauss, "Things Are in the Saddle," *The Atlantic Monthly* (November 1924).
3 Frederick W. Taylor, *The Principles of Scientific Management* (1911). On the rise and spread of scientific management, see Chandler, *The Visible Hand*.
4 Daniel Nelson, *Frederick W. Taylor and the Rise of Scientific Management* (Madison, WI: 1980).
5 David Hounshell, *From the American System to Mass Production, 1800–1932* (Baltimore, 1984).
6 Quoted in McCraw and Tedlow, "Henry Ford, Alfred Sloan, and the Three Phases of Marketing."
7 Henry Ford, *My Life and Work* (New York, 1922).
8 Stephen Mihm, *Mastering Modernity: Weights, Measures, and the Standardization of American Life* (Cambridge, MA: forthcoming).
9 Albert Rees and Donald Jacobs, *Real Wages in Manufacturing, 1890–1914* (Princeton, NJ: 1961).
10 Harold Livesay, *American Made: Shapers of the American Economy* (Boston, 1979).
11 Leo Ribuffo, "Henry Ford and 'The International Jew,'" *American Jewish History* 69(4): 437–77; Neil Baldwin, *Henry Ford and the Jews: The Mass Production of Hate* (New York, 2001).
12 Stefan J. Link, "Transnational Fordism: Ford Motor Company, Nazi Germany, and the Soviet Union in the Interwar Years" (Ph.D. diss., Harvard University, 2012).
13 Historians have long relied on research conducted by business historians in the 1960s and 1970s for our understanding of the expansion of retail. See, for example, Chandler, *The Visible Hand*, and Glenn Porter and Harold Livesay,

Merchants and Manufacturers: Studies in the Changing Structure of Nineteenth Century Marketing (Baltimore, 1971).

14 Marc Levinson, *The Great A&P and the Struggle for Small Business in America* (New York, 2011).

15 Jonathan Bean, *Beyond the Broker State: Federal Policies toward Small Business, 1936–1961* (Chapel Hill, NC: 1996); Mansel Blackford, *A History of Small Business in America*, 2nd ed. (Chapel Hill, NC: 2003).

16 "Does the Chain Store System Threaten the Nation's Welfare," *Congressional Digest*, August–September 1930.

17 Daniel Pope, *The Making of Modern Advertising* (New York, 1983).

18 Roland Marchand, *Advertising the American Dream* (Berkeley, CA: 1985).

19 Harris Corporation, "Founding Dates of the 1994 *Fortune 500* U.S. Companies," *Business History Review*, 70 (Spring 1996), pp. 69–90, cited in McCraw, "American Capitalism."

20 J. George Frederick, "The Great Automobile Duel of 1927: Mr. Ford and General Motors Choose Their Weapons," *The Independent*, Vol. 118, No. 4012, April 23, 1927.

21 Alfred Chandler, *Giant Enterprise: Ford, General Motors, and the Automobile Industry* (New York, 1964); Robert Sobel, *Car Wars: The Untold Story* (New York: 1984).

22 McCraw and Tedlow, "Henry Ford, Alfred Sloan, and the Three Phases of Marketing."

23 The classic study of decentralized management and the histories of DuPont and General Motors remains Alfred Chandler's *Strategy and Structure: Chapters in the History of Industrial Enterprise* (Cambridge, MA: 1962). On mass marketing, see Richard S. Tedlow, *New and Improved: The Story of Mass Marketing in America* (New York, 1990).

8: FROM ROOSEVELT TO ROOSEVELT: BUSINESS AND THE MODERN STATE

1 Theodore Roosevelt, "Address of President Roosevelt on the Occasion of the Laying of the Cornerstone of the Pilgrim Memorial Monument," Provincetown, MA, August 20, 1907.

2 Franklin D. Roosevelt, "Address at Madison Square Garden, New York City," October 31, 1936. Online by Gerhard Peters and John T. Woolley, *American Presidency Project*, http://www.presidency.ucsb.edu/ws/?pid=15219.

3 Quoted in Kim Phillips-Fein, *Invisible Hands: The Making of the Conservative Movement from the New Deal to Reagan* (New York, 2009).

4 Brian Balogh, *The Associational State: American Governance in the Twentieth Century* (Philadelphia, 2015).

5 Robert Wiebe, *The Search for Order, 1877–1920* (New York, 1967).

6 Modern data on campaign contributions can be found at *Center for Responsive Politics*, www.opensecrets.org.

7 On the origins of NAM and the Chamber of Commerce, see Benjamin C. Waterhouse, *Lobbying America: The Politics of Business from Nixon to NAFTA*

(Princeton, NJ: 2014). See also Jennifer Delton, *Racial Integration in Corporate America, 1940–1990* (Cambridge, UK: 2009), and Cathie J. Martin, "Sectional Parties, Divided Business," *Studies in American Political Development* 20:2 (October 2006): 160–84.

8   Both cited in Walter Friedman, *Fortune Tellers: The Story of America's First Economic Forecasters* (Princeton, NJ: 2014).

9   Ellis Hawley, "Herbert Hoover, the Commerce Secretariat, and the Vision of an 'Associative State,' 1921–1928," *The Journal of American History* 61(1), June 1974: 116–40.

10 John Ihlder, "The Business Man's Responsibility," *Nation's Business*, November 1925, cited in Arthur Schlesinger, Jr., *The Age of Roosevelt: The Crisis of the Old Order, 1919–1933* (Boston, 1957).

11 Beverly Gage, *The Day Wall Street Exploded: A Story of America in Its First Age of Terror* (Oxford, UK: 2009).

12 Brody, *Steelworkers in America*. On working-class culture and labor activism in the 1920s, see Cohen, *Making a New Deal*.

13 Douglas Craig, *After Wilson: The Struggle for the Democratic Party, 1920–1934* (Chapel Hill, NC: 1992).

14 W. Elliott Brownlee, *Federal Taxation in America: A Short History*, 2nd ed. (Cambridge, UK: 2004).

15 Lisa McGirr, *The War on Alcohol: Prohibition and the Rise of the American State* (New York, 2016).

16 John Kenneth Galbraith, *The Great Crash, 1929* (Boston, 1954).

17 Charles Kindleberger, *The World in Depression, 1929–1939* (Berkeley, CA: 1986).

18 Galbraith, *The Great Crash, 1929*; Kindleberger, *The World in Depression*.

19 *New York Times*, September 6, 1929; *New York Times*, October 16, 1929. See also Friedman, *Fortune Tellers*.

20 The best narrative description of the Crash remains Galbraith, *The Great Crash, 1929*.

21 Jason Scott Smith, *A Concise History of the New Deal* (New York, 2014).

22 Herbert Hoover, *The Memoirs of Herbert Hoover: The Great Depression, 1929–1941* (New York, 1952).

23 David Kennedy, *Freedom from Fear: The American People in Depression and War, 1929–1945* (New York, 1999).

24 William Leuchtenburg, *Franklin D. Roosevelt and the New Deal, 1932–1940* (New York, 1963).

25 On Roosevelt and the New Deal, see Kennedy, *Freedom from Fear*; Leuchtenburg, *Franklin D. Roosevelt and the New Deal*; Arthur Schlesinger, Jr., *The Age of Roosevelt: The Coming of the New Deal, 1933–1935* (New York, 1958); H. W. Brands, *A Traitor to His Class: The Privileged Life and Radical Presidency of Franklin Delano Roosevelt* (New York, 2008).

26 Kim McQuaid, *Big Business and Presidential Power: From FDR to Reagan* (New York, 1982).

27 *A.L.A. Schechter Poultry Corp.* v. *United States*, 295 U.S. 495 (1935).

28 *Washington Post*, June 17, 1935.

29 See Leuchtenburg, *Franklin D. Roosevelt and the New Deal*.

30 Sally Sherman, "Public Attitudes toward Social Security," *Social Security Bulletin* 52(12), December 1989.

31 McCraw, *Prophets of Regulation*.

32 Phillips-Fein, *Invisible Hands*.

9: IN LOVE WITH BIGNESS: THE POSTWAR CORPORATION

1 William Whyte, *The Organization Man* (New York, 1956); Joseph Nocera, "Foreword" to University of Pennsylvania reprint of *The Organization Man* (2002). C. Wright Mills, *White Collar: The American Middle Classes* (New York, 1956).

2 Olivier Zunz, *Making America Corporate, 1870–1920* (Chicago, 1990).

3 Blackford, *A History of Small Business in America*.

4 John Kenneth Galbraith, *The Affluent Society* (Boston, 1958).

5 Mark Wilson, *Destructive Creation: American Business and the Winning of World War II* (Philadelphia, 2016); Alan Milward, *War, Economy, and Society: 1939–1945* (Berkeley, CA: 1979).

6 Joel Davidson, "Building for War, Preparing for Peace: World War II and the Military-Industrial Complex," in Donald Albrecht, ed., *World War II and the American Dream: How Wartime Building Changed a Nation* (Cambridge, MA: 1995).

7 John Maynard Keynes, *The General Theory of Employment, Interest, and Money* (London, 1936).

8 Lizabeth Cohen, *A Consumers' Republic: The Politics of Mass Consumption in Postwar America* (New York, 2003); Meg Jacobs, *Pocketbook Politics: Economic Citizenship in Twentieth Century America* (Princeton, NJ: 2005).

9 Paddy Riley, "Clark Kerr: From the Industrial to the Knowledge Economy," in Nelson Lichtenstein, ed., *American Capitalism: Social Thought and Political Economy in the Twentieth Century* (Philadelphia, 2006).

10 David Mowery and Nathan Rosenberg, *Technology and the Pursuit of Economic Growth* (Cambridge, UK: 1989).

11 Alfred Chandler, *Scale and Scope: The Dynamics of Industrial Capitalism* (Cambridge, MA: 1990).

12 Dominique Tobbell, *Pills, Power, and Policy: The Struggle for Drug Reform in Cold War America and Its Consequences* (Berkeley, CA: 2012).

13 Jefferson Cowie, *Capital Moves: RCA's Seventy-Year Quest for Cheap Labor* (Ithaca, NY: 1999).

14 David Mowery and Nathan Rosenberg, *Paths of Innovation: Technological Change in 20th-Century America* (Cambridge, UK: 1998).

15 Thomas McCraw, *American Business, 1920–2000: How It Worked* (Wheeling, WV: 2000).

16 Margaret Pugh O'Mara, *Cities of Knowledge: Cold War Science and the Search for the Next Silicon Valley* (Princeton, NJ: 2005).

17 Patrick Gaughan, *Mergers, Acquisitions, and Corporate Restructurings* (Hoboken, NJ: 2011).

18 Robert Sobel, *The Age of Giant Corporations: A Microeconomic History of American Business, 1914–1992*, 3rd ed. (Westport, CT: 1993).

19 Timothy M. Hurley, "The Urge to Merge: Contemporary Theories on the Rise of Conglomerate Mergers in the 1960s," *Journal of Business and Technology Law*, Vol. 1., Issue 1 (2006), 185–205.

20 Louis Hyman, "Rethinking the Postwar Corporation: Management, Monopolies, and Markets," in Phillips-Fein and Zelizer, eds., *What's Good for Business*.

21 Robert Sobel, *The Rise and Fall of the Conglomerate Kings* (New York: 1984); William G. Blair, "Charles G. Bluhdorn, the Head of Gulf and Western, Dies at 56," *New York Times*, February 20, 1983.

22 David E. Lilienthal, *Big Business: A New Era* (New York, 1953); John Kenneth Galbraith, *American Capitalism: The Concept of Countervailing Power* (Boston, 1956); Jason Scott Smith, "The Liberal Invention of the Multinational Corporation: David Lilienthal and Postwar Capitalism," in Phillips-Fein and Zelizer, eds., *What's Good for Business*.

23 Dwight D. Eisenhower, "Farewell Radio and Television Address to the American People," January 17, 1961. Online by Gerhard Peters and John T. Woolley, *The American Presidency Project*. http://www.presidency.ucsb.edu/ws/?pid=12086.

1 0: THE PERSONAL, THE POLITICAL, AND THE PROFITABLE

1 Michelle Reeves, "'Obey the Rules or Get Out': Ronald Reagan's 1966 Gubernatorial Campaign and the 'Trouble at Berkeley,'" *Southern California Quarterly 92*(3), Fall 2010, 275–305.

2 Mario Savio, "Sit-In Address on the Steps of Sproul Hall," December 2, 1964, University of California at Berkeley. Speech video and text available at: www.americanrhetoric.com/speeches/mariosavioproulhallsitin.htm. Robert Cohen, *Freedom's Orator: Mario Savio and the Radical Legacy of the 1960s* (New York, 2009).

3 On "anti-establishment" politics among the New Left, see, for example, Rebecca Klatch, *A Generation Divided: The New Left, the New Right, and the 1960s* (Berkeley, CA: 1999).

4 Quoted in David Vogel, *Fluctuating Fortunes: The Political Power of Business in America* (New York, 1989).

5 Phillips-Fein, *Invisible Hands*.

6 Leonard Silk and David Vogel, *Ethics and Profits: The Crisis of Confidence in American Business* (New York, 1976).

7 Bethany Moreton, "Make Payroll, Not War: Business Culture as Youth Culture," in Bruce Schulman and Julian Zelizer, eds., *Rightward Bound: Making America Conservative in the 1970s* (Cambridge, MA: 2008).

8 Rachel Carson, *Silent Spring* (New York, 1962).

9 Mark Lytle, *The Gentle Subversive: Rachel Carson, Silent Spring, and the Rise of the Environmental Movement* (New York, 2007).

10 Judith Layzer, *Open for Business: Conservatives' Opposition to Environmental Regulation* (Cambridge, MA: 2012).

11 *Mount Pleasant (Michigan) Morning Sun*, March 15, 1980.

12 Ralph Nader, *Unsafe at Any Speed: The Designed-In Dangers of the American Automobile* (New York, 1965).

13 Thomas Whiteside, *The Investigation of Ralph Nader: General Motors vs. One Determined Man* (New York, 1972); Justin Martin, *Nader: Crusader, Spoiler, Icon* (New York, 2002).

14 Cohen, *A Consumers' Republic*.

15 "Welcoming Remarks of John D. Harper, Chairman, the Business Roundtable at the Annual Meeting of the Roundtable, New York City, June 16, 1976," cited in Waterhouse, *Lobbying America*.

16 Richard Lesher, "Can Capitalism Survive?" cited in Waterhouse, *Lobbying America*.

17 Silk and Vogel, *Ethics and Profits*.

18 Lewis Powell, "Confidential Memo: Attack on American Free Enterprise System." Document available online at law2.wlu.edu/deptimages/Powell%20 Archives/PowellMemorandumTypescript.pdf. See also Waterhouse, *Lobbying America*; Phillips-Fein, *Invisible Hands*.

19 Mutch, *Buying the Vote*.

20 Julian Zelizer, *On Capitol Hill: The Struggle to Reform Congress and Its Consequences* (Cambridge, UK: 2004).

21 Federal Election Commission, "PAC Count–1974 to Present." Available online at www.fec.gov/press/resources/paccount.shtml.

22 Lee Drutman, *The Business of America Is Lobbying: How Corporations Became Politicized and Politics Became More Corporate* (Oxford, UK: 2015).

23 Carrington Shields, "Associations and the Law: Lobbying and the Antitrust Laws," *Association Letter*, U.S. Chamber of Commerce, March 1971.

24 Waterhouse, *Lobbying America*.

I I : AFTER THE INDUSTRIAL ECONOMY

1 Cowie, *Capital Moves*.

2 Beth Macy, *Factory Man: How One Furniture Maker Battled Offshoring, Stayed Local—and Helped Save an American Town* (New York, 2014).

3 Richard McCormack, ed., *ReMaking America* (Washington, DC, 2013).

4 Thomas Friedman, *The World Is Flat: A Brief History of the Twenty-First Century* (New York, 2005).

5 Bennett Harrison and Barry Bluestone, *The Great U-Turn: Corporate Restructuring and the Polarizing of America* (New York, 1988).

6 H. Ross Perot, with Pat Choate, *Save Your Job, Save Our Country: Why NAFTA Must Be Stopped—Now!* (New York, 1993).

7 David Koistinen, *Confronting Decline: The Political Economy of Deindustrialization in Twentieth Century New England* (Gainesville, FL: 2013).

8 U.S. Department of Commerce, Bureau of the Census, 2003.

9 *Fortune* magazine keeps an archived list of its five hundred largest companies

on its website. See archive.fortune.com/magazines/fortune/fortune500_archive
/full/1955.

10   Ray Kroc, "Lessons of Leadership, Part 38: Appealing to a Mass Market,"
     Nation's Business 56 (July 1968), U.S. Chamber of Commerce.

11   Ruth Brandon, *Singer and the Sewing Machine: A Capitalist Romance* (Phila-
     delphia, 1977); Thomas Dicke, *Franchising in America: The Development of a
     Business Method, 1840–1980* (Chapel Hill, NC: 1992).

12   *Entrepreneur* magazine hosts a compendium of statistics on franchises on its web-
     site. See http://www.entrepreneur.com/franchises/mcdonalds/282570-0.html.

13   Kroc, "Lessons of Leadership."

14   The International Franchising Association maintains these statistics on its
     website. See http://www.franchise.org/slow-steady-growth-to-continue-for
     -franchise-businesses-in-2013.

15   For a representative critique, see Eric Schlosser, *Fast Food Nation: The Dark
     Side of the All-American Meal* (New York: 2001).

16   Jordan Weissmann, "More Than a Quarter of Fast-Food Workers are Raising
     a Child," *The Atlantic*, August 5, 2013.

17   Nelson Lichtenstein, *The Retail Revolution: How Wal-Mart Created a Brave
     New World of Business* (New York, 2009).

18   Bethany Moreton, *To Serve God and Wal-Mart: The Making of Christian Free
     Enterprise* (Cambridge, MA: 2009).

19   Bean, *Beyond the Broker State.*

20   Mowery and Rosenberg, *Paths of Innovation*; Michael Swaine and Paul
     Freiberger, *Fire in the Valley: The Birth and Death of the Personal Computer,*
     3rd ed. (New York: 2014).

21   On labor productivity in the 1990s, see Richard Anderson and Kevin Kliesen,
     "The 1990s Acceleration in Labor Productivity: Causes and Measurement,"
     Federal Reserve Bank of St. Louis Review (May/June 2006).

22   For a historical assessment of the development of the Internet in the context of
     a century of debates about technological standards and public use, see Andrew
     Russell, *Open Standards and the Digital Age: History, Ideology, and Networks*
     (New York: 2014).

23   To mark the significance of Web 2.0, *Time* magazine chose "You" as the "Per-
     son of the Year" for 2006. Lev Grossman, "You—Yes, You—Are TIME's
     Person of the Year," *Time*, December 25, 2006.

24   Jeffrey Frieden, *Global Capitalism: Its Fall and Rise in the Twentieth Century*
     (New York, 2006).

25   Geoffrey Jones, *Multinationals and Global Capitalism: From the Nineteenth to
     the Twenty-first Century* (Oxford, UK: 2005).

12: FINANCE TAKES FLIGHT

1   "End of an Era on Wall Street," *Bloomberg*, September 23, 2008.

2   Nouriel Roubini and Stephen Mihm, *Crisis Economics: A Crash Course in the
    Future of Finance* (New York, 2010).

3   Bruce Schulman, *The Seventies: The Great Shift in American Culture, Society,*

and Politics (New York, 2001); Edward Berkowitz, *Something Happened: A Political and Cultural Overview of the Seventies* (New York, 2006).

4 Wyatt Wells, *Economist in an Uncertain World: Arthur F. Burns and the Federal Reserve, 1970–1975* (New York, 1994).

5 Meg Jacobs, *Panic at the Pump: The Energy Crisis and the Transformation of American Politics in the 1970s* (New York, 2016).

6 Steven Sass, *The Promise of Private Pensions: The First Hundred Years* (Cambridge, MA: 1997).

7 Joe Nocera, *A Piece of the Action: How the Middle Class Joined the Money Class* (New York, 1994); Louis Hyman, *Borrow: The American Way of Debt* (New York, 2012).

8 McCraw, *Prophets of Regulation.*

9 Richard Harris and Sidney Milkis, *The Politics of Regulatory Change: A Tale of Two Agencies* (New York, 1996); Richard Vietor, *Contrived Competition: Regulation and Deregulation in America* (Cambridge, MA: 1994).

10 Robert Horwitz, *The Irony of Regulatory Reform: The Deregulation of American Telecommunications* (New York, 1989).

11 Steven Vogel, *Freer Markets, More Rules: Regulatory Reform in Advanced Industrial Countries* (Ithaca, NY: 1996).

12 Matthew Sherman, "A Short History of Financial Deregulation in the United States," *Center for Economic and Policy Research*, July 2009; Greta Krippner, *Capitalizing on Crisis: The Political Origins of the Rise of Finance* (Cambridge, MA: 2009).

13 Nocera, *A Piece of the Action*; Hyman, *Borrow*; Paul Krugman, *Peddling Prosperity: Economic Sense and Nonsense in an Age of Diminished Expectations* (New York, 1994).

14 Benjamin Friedman, *Day of Reckoning: The Consequences of American Economic Policy Under Reagan* (New York, 1988).

15 Joe McGovern, "A life in film: Michael Douglas on 8 of his greatest roles," *Entertainment Weekly*, April 16, 2015.

16 Bob Greene, "A $100 Million Idea: Use Greed for Good," *Chicago Tribune*, December 15, 1986.

17 Sanjai Bhagat, Andrei Shleifer, and Robert Vishny, "Hostile Takeovers in the 1980s: The Return to Corporate Specialization," *Brookings Papers on Economic Activity. Microeconomics* (1990):1–84.

18 T. Boone Pickens, "How Big Business Stacks the Deck," and Andrew Sigler, "Looking Beyond the 'Aw-Shucks' Act," *New York Times*, March 1, 1987.

19 Charles Kindleberger and Robert Aliber, *Manias, Panics, and Crashes: A History of Financial Crises*, 5th ed. (Hoboken, NJ: 2005).

20 Bethany McLean and Peter Elkind, *The Smartest Guys in the Room: The Amazing Rise and Scandalous Fall of Enron* (New York, 2003).

21 Roger Lowenstein, *Origins of the Crash: The Great Bubble and Its Undoing* (New York, 2004).

22 Alan Greenspan, "The Challenge of Central Banking in a Democratic Society," delivered before the American Enterprise Institute at the Washington Hilton Hotel, December 5, 1996.

23 Gerald Davis, "Not Just a Mortgage Crisis: How Finance Maimed Society," *Strategic Organization* 8(1): 75–82.

24 Robert Shiller, "Understanding Recent Trends in House Prices and Home Ownership," *NBER Working Paper* No. 13553, October 2007.

25 Gary Gorton, *Slapped by the Invisible Hand: The Panic of 2007* (Oxford, UK: 2010).

26 Roubini and Mihm, *Crisis Economics*.

27 United States Government Accountability Office, "Financial Regulatory Reform: Financial Crisis Losses and Potential Impacts of the Dodd-Frank Act," January 2013.

CONCLUSION: AFTER THE CRISIS

1 Theda Skocpol and Vanessa Williamson, *The Tea Party and the Remaking of Republican Conservatism* (Oxford, UK: 2012).

INDEX

A&P Supermarket, 126, 201, 208
activism, 99, 180–82, 230, 242. *See also
    specific person, movement, or
    organization*
Adams, Charles Francis Jr., 111
Adams, John, 63
Adams, John Quincy, 67, 73–74
advertising, 124, 127–28, 187, 202
Affordable Care Act (Obamacare), 241
Africa, 8–9, 10, 12, 27, 76
African Americans. *See* blacks
"Age of Exploration," 10
agrarian democracy, 61–62
agriculture
    American colonies and, 8, 18
    bank wars and, 70, 71
    and Civil War, 76
    conquest and, 16
    and debate about economy, 8
    on eve of American Revolution, 19
    and financial services in 1970s, 221
    Great Depression and, 148
    jobs in, 198
    and modern corporate organization,
        129
    politics of business in early republic
        and, 62, 63, 66, 70, 71, 76
    railroads and, 83, 84
    and rise of big business, 83, 84
    slavery and, 28, 33, 34–39
    and transportation and communication
        revolutions, 51
    and world economy between 1500 and
        1750, 10–11
    See also farms/farmers
Airline Deregulation Act (1978), 223

Alcoa, 187
Amalgamated Association of Iron, Steel,
    and Tin Workers, 103, 143
Amazon, 211, 233
America Online, 231
American Express, 54
American Federation of Labor (AFL),
    103, 105, 143
American Liberty League, 156
American Railway Union (ARU), 104–5
American Recovery and Reinvestment Act
    (2009), 240
American Revolution, 7, 17–20. *See also*
    colonies, American
"American System," 66–67
American Tobacco Company, 91
American Tobacco Trust, 115
Anderson, Jack, 190
anti-Semitism, 107, 122
antibusiness movement
    and antiwar movement, 177, 179,
        180–81
    and conservatives, 194
    and consumer movement, 183, 185–87,
        194
    countermobilization by business of,
        189–94
    and environmental movement, 183–85,
        187, 194
    and Free Speech movement, 177–79,
        180–81
antitrust movement, 99, 110–15, 116, 187
antiwar movement, 175, 177, 179, 180–81
AOL, 211
Apollo mission, 160
Apple Computer Company, 210, 233